THE MUMSNET RULES

Natasha Joffe and Justine Roberts

BLOOMSBURY
LONDON · BERLIN · NEW YORK · SYDNEY

First published in Great Britain 2011

Copyright © 2011 by Mumsnet Limited

The moral right of the authors has been asserted

The extract from 'Babel' is copyright © Louis MacNeice, from *Collected Poems*, 2007, Faber & Faber.
Reprinted with kind permission of David Higham Associates.

The extract from 'Afternoons' is taken from *Collected Poems* by Philip Larkin © The Estate of Philip Larkin.
Reproduced by permission of Faber & Faber Ltd.

Bloomsbury Publishing, London, Berlin, New York and Sydney

36 Soho Square, London W1D 3QY

A CIP catalogue record for this book is available from the British Library

ISBN 978 1 4088 0848 1
10 9 8 7 6 5 4 3 2 1

Typeset by Hewer Text UK Ltd, Edinburgh
Printed in Great Britain by Clays Limited, St Ives plc

MIX
Paper from
responsible sources
FSC® C018072
FSC
www.fsc.org

www.bloomsbury.com/mumsnet

For our children

CONTENTS

Dos and Don'ts

You're the Boss

Health and Safety

Fun and Games

Nearest and Dearest

School Gates

Introduction

SO WHAT ARE THESE RULES ANYWAY?

Speak roughly to your little boy,
And beat him when he sneezes:
He only does it to annoy,
Because he knows it teases.

Chorus: Wow! wow! wow!

Lewis Carroll, 'The Duchess's Lullaby'
from *Alice in Wonderland*

When my first baby was about six weeks old, I panicked about the fact that we seemed to be oozing along formlessly in our life together. He was mostly feeding or sleeping in my lap, the feeding being almost constant and the sleeping occurring in frequent but very short bursts. Neither of us had any sense of night and day. I panicked in particular because I had just purchased a book that looked friendly but which seemed to be telling me I had already messed it all up, that my baby should be eating and sleeping in a certain way and in certain places, and the fact that he was not doing so was a very bad thing – it was hindering his development and my happiness. I am not even sure that the book actually said any of this or at least said it with anything like the firmness I thought it did. I make no claims at all for my intellectual faculties at that time.

So I found myself, after six weeks of very little postnatal sleep bolted on to quite a lot of previous prenatal insomnia, doing a mad and awful thing. I put my baby in his cot at what the book seemed to say should be one of his naptimes and I went away and left him there whilst he screamed miserably and continuously, wide awake and understandably outraged. I think I went away for twenty minutes; I fear it may have been longer. I have erased the details. When I went back his face was glazed with tears and set in horizontal lines of woe like the Duchess's baby in *Alice in Wonderland*. I held him tight and wept whilst he continued to sob convulsively. He was inconsolable; I could not console him.

The book didn't actually tell me to do what I did. I just lost it. I thought I was damaging him and myself by allowing us to carry on in the way we were (and funnily enough we weren't unhappy that way – he was just a tiny baby and I was just a bit strange). I subsequently read another book about abandonment and stress hormones and psychological development and convinced myself that this one incident had psychologically scarred him. Forever. Neither of the books I read helped me to be a better parent or him to be a happier baby.

I think many people, like me, found Mumsnet in the early days of our parenting in bewildered retreat from one book or another we had snatched from the shelves, too tired to read it properly, too tired to apply it, too tired to exercise our critical faculties about what it was telling us. Too tired not to feel like we were failing miserably at times.

So we found a website. Where other folk told us it was OK to be exhausted, to feel at times like you had the wrong emotions for your baby, to fail to have a routine, to impose a routine if it was right for you and your baby, to make mistakes, as long as you tried to do better next time: that they had made mistakes and life had carried on and their children were fine.

And a couple of years down the line, when we couldn't get a three-year-old out of nappies, we found some ideas for bribes, and a little later some reassurance about the baffling testosterone-fuelled rage of four-year-old boys. And when we had seven-year-olds who went upstairs to get their clothes on for school and were discovered twenty minutes later reading the *Beano* in their pants, there were other people's stories to laugh at and their tips to try.

Because, at each stage of your child's development you tend to realise there is a whole lot of stuff you fretted about at the previous stage which you probably didn't need to.

'God, I did it all though. But it's like having a wedding and then realising you should have just eloped or had your immediate family. Once you KNOW you KNOW.'

(codjane)

Which perhaps makes this rules thing seem rather paradoxical. Why rules? If we are in retreat from gurus and experts, if we are saying that there is a broad spectrum of good-enough ways to parent, why do we need rules? And where do they come from? After all, on controversial issues – sleep, feeding, vaccinations, schooling choices – Mumsnet posters often shout in the internet language of capital letters. They occasionally insult one another, they sometimes flounce from the site altogether. So what is the wisdom of crowds, how can there be any rules when everyone is sitting at their computers disagreeing with everyone else?

The answer, we think, is this – that by reading a hundred different people's views on controlled crying, on the contents of party bags, on how to help a child who has no friends, you find that there is usually a common-sense consensus around the important things. But there are also boundaries to what works and what is OK, and sometimes we need a (virtual) village to help us find those boundaries. *The Mumsnet Rules* maps out both the areas of consensus and the boundaries.

And the goal of the *Rules* is to make you into the person you would be if you had had two or three children to practise on before the ones you actually have. So that when you hear your toddler singing (from the back of the bike on which you are ferrying him to nursery), plaintively and to the tune of 'Twinkle Twinkle Little Star': 'Mummy, Mummy, Mummy, Mum. Mummy, Mummy don't go to work . . .', you can laugh a little rather than falling off your bike.[i]

Of course the truth is, looking at Justine's four children and my three, that we miserably fail to apply most of these rules most of the time. A fact that rather came home to us when we were bouncing the rules off Justine's twelve-year-old daughter, who variously laughed uproariously and suggested that in respect of most of the rules, the opposite rule would be more appropriate. Or when we had plonked all of the children in front of YouTube in order to get the book finished on time. Or when one of Justine's children suggested that were he to win the lottery he'd buy his dad a boat, his siblings the contents of the Arsenal shop and his mother a new computer, because that's what she likes to do. Writing these rules has, to an extent, been like a daily mortification of the parental flesh for us as we confronted our own deficiencies.

But what it has not been is a pointless wallowing in guilt of the kind that newspapers and experts sometimes seem to invite. Because what we hope you will find in this book is reassurance: a buoyancy aid to help you keep your head above water. These rules are about finding your bearings, doing things in ways which make your life a little better and easier, forgiving yourself for being barely adequate at times but recognising when you are heading towards genuine awfulness and learning to put the brakes on.

And there is a metarule here, which came to me when my four-year-old, during a complicated conversation about single-sex unions, asked, 'But if there are two ladies, who will do the driving?'[ii] And that rule is: when you can, try to take things lightly. Have a cackle at yourself and at all the other parents muddling along beside you, and remember to laugh with – and about – your own children. Because one of the best things of all about being a parent, about living with children, is that it is really very funny. Part of the time.

Although not so much when eavesdropping on a crowd of four-year-olds telling poo jokes.

i) This would be Justine, with her fourth child.
ii) Justine would like to make it clear that she, however, is a very good and experienced driver.

GOLDEN RULES

You don't have to bake with your children

THE RULE OTHERWISE KNOWN AS:
DON'T BELIEVE THE LIFESTYLE JOURNALISTS

'I remember when my mum knitted me a school cardigan.

Christ, it was awful. Luckily she saw sense and bought me the polyester one that everyone else had. Knitting is just a thing, it's not a way to be a good mum. It's just wool.'

(Ozziegirly)

Unless you live up a tree in the rain forest, it is probably impossible to avoid Jamie Oliver and his kids. Or many another celebrity plus offspring pictured in their lovely homes. Baking and doing craft activities. Or just looking radiant and fluffy in soft sunshine and cashmere cardigans. And it's not just celebrities – we have too much access to all sorts of other people's prettified versions of their own parenting, too many books and blogs and tweets. (Although you have to wonder about some of the blogging mummies – when do they find the time and how bored must they be to write those blogs? Why do they never post about their bad days? But let them blog – we all have to get through the day somehow.)

It sometimes seems that what all of these people and Sunday supplements and catalogues are selling is the one truly good and wholesome way to bring up children, a way that probably involves picking berries and visiting baby farm animals and messing about in streams. And a great deal of contentment. And not very many reconstituted meat products in a breadcrumb coating or cartoons. Or screaming.

So those of us who regularly fall by the wayside with packaged entertainments and packaged foods and don't holiday in our own reclaimed crabshacks full of the children's oil paintings and converted crabpots, or whatever it is you catch crabs in, sometimes feel like we are not managing to be particularly good parents. That we do not spend enough time with our children and that the things we do with them are crap.

But actually, the stuff your kids will remember fondly (apart from the many, preferably illicit, things they did with other children) is the stuff you both loved, the stuff you both enjoyed, not the stuff you endured because you thought it was what you were supposed to do to be a good parent. OK, some stuff along the way you do just have to endure – no adult person wants to play with Thomas the Tank Engine or talk about Dora the Explorer. Almost no adult person wants to hear about the different kinds of battle droid or watch *High School Musical 3*. But you might all enjoy walking or swimming or riding bikes. As they get bigger, you might all want to make stop-motion animations. Or pretend you are on *MasterChef*. Or eat pizza in front of *X Factor*. Or you might all love to bake and paint china. We are many and various and so are our children; no one's relationship with their children can really be much of a model for anyone else's. And, whatever activities you get up to, some days there will be shafts of great happiness, unexpected exchanges of kindness. And other days they will tell you they hate you, that you are the most unfair mummy in the whole world. And you will bore them and they will bore you.

Because the truth about parenting is that it is not some perfectible edifice you are building in which you will keep your babies safe from the outside world until they are strong and clever enough to emerge. It is an unpredictable, often worrying, occasionally revelatory relationship with one or more other people, who are themselves changing all the time. And sometimes it is just hard graft for all the parties involved. If you can let go, if you can realise that no childhood is nirvana, but is at best a sometimes random jumble of good and bad and boring, then you and your children will probably find some unexpected adventures in unlikely places. And cupcakes won't be some ghastly symbol of an unachievable lifestyle. But a kind of small cake which you might bake some time. Or you might buy some Mr Kiplings instead.

What, no cupcakes? Mumsnetters' happy childhoods

'I think the important thing is to think back to your childhood – what do you remember? I found out recently that for quite a few years my dad worked a six-and-a-half day week doing overtime to meet the mortgage when interest rates were high. This means my sister and I must hardly have seen him. I have absolutely no memory of that. What I do remember is looking down the road to see him come home for lunch sometimes. That and that awful yellow haddock my parents fed me, Princess Di's wedding, a holiday in Sussex, lilac blossom and the buddleia covered in butterflies, coming downstairs on Christmas morning and seeing my new dollhouse, the day the neighbours went waterskiing leaving a casserole in the oven and the oven caught fire . . . nothing, *nothing* to do with how much my parents worked or spent time with us. I hope and trust it's the same for my kids. I've no reason to think otherwise.'

(NorthernLurker)

'I remember candle making and "science experiments" with my mum, and fingerpainting when younger, and having friends around to play in the garden, and every year we'd pick all the blackcurrants and try and make blackcurrant jam but my mum was hopeless at it and it would always end up being blackcurrant syrup, and I remember having a chest freezer where the yummy puddings were stored (like premade chocolate eclairs) but she would never remember to take them out in time so if we had one as a treat it would always still be half frozen which didn't stop it being delicious. And sometimes there'd be parties at our house (we always had lodgers to help pay the mortgage) and I was allowed to stay up a bit and try the (cheap) camembert on baguettes. She detested cooking, so we lived on fish fingers and Findus pancakes and bad stew, but sometimes on weekends she'd make flapjacks or eggy bread, and every Halloween she'd try and make treacle toffee and sometimes get it right.

The thing is, my mother was a single parent working horrendous hours, and we grew up in a cheap horrible neighbourhood, with a titchy back garden mostly concrete, and I had to share a bedroom with my brother until I was ten because we needed lodgers.

But I don't remember that, I just know it now. My memories of my childhood are idyllic, because my mum loved us so.'

(tortoiseonthehalfshell)

Don't fret about milestones

'It's not a modern thing to be worried about development of speech etc. . . . As a child, Einstein seldom spoke. When he did, he spoke very slowly – indeed, he tried out entire sentences in his head (or muttered them under his breath) until he got them right before he spoke aloud. According to accounts, Einstein did this until he was nine years old. Einstein's parents were fearful that he was retarded. One interesting anecdote, told by Otto Neugebauer, a historian of science, goes like this: As Einstein was a late talker, his parents were worried. At last, at the supper table one night, he broke his silence to say, "The soup is too hot." Greatly relieved, his parents asked why he had never said a word before. Albert replied, "Because up to now everything was in order."'

(*jenwyn*)

The Cloud of Parental Anxiety

Our initial impulse is just to say 'get over yourself' in relation to milestones (milestones are things your child is supposed to do around a certain age: rolling over, smiling, talking, reaching developmental stages right through to puberty and beyond). But 'get over yourself' is the parenting advice no one can ever take, except retrospectively, because really some degree of hyper-attentiveness is part of the human parenting condition. Parental insouciance only works for species like seahorses which wander around in a soup of offspring and can afford to have a few wander off.

For those of us with any tendency to worry, hyper-attentiveness means living with the Cloud of Parental Anxiety. The Cloud of Parental Anxiety is by no means always obscuring the sun and sometimes you will hardly notice it at all, but it is always floating somewhere, just casting its shadow over a different part of the landscape. So if I reassure myself about my non-walking twenty-month-old by starting a discussion on a parenting website in which a hundred respondents tell me that their children didn't walk until that age or later, the Cloud of Parental Anxiety will drift slowly away from the swamp of late walking before stopping at the little hillock which is that bump my baby has always had on the back of her head. And the Cloud, which was really quite pale and wispy and cirrus for a while, will darken and thicken as I google the bump. And it will swell with rain and sizzle with lightning bolts as I discover obscure conditions which the bump could be but almost certainly isn't . . .

So we do need to attend to milestones, to an extent, without becoming hysterical about them. They are there for a reason and they have a role to play in alerting us to problems our children might (but statistically probably do not) have.

'Our son did have language delay and spotting that he was lagging behind on the development charts meant we picked it up early and got the involvement from a speech and language therapist which he needed. It might well have been nothing, but in our case it was not. Now he is 6, you'd never know he'd had a problem. He never stops talking.'

(*Mumasaur*)

Some thoughts about milestones:
- Places where new parents congregate tend to be hotspots of anxiety over milestones. There is sometimes little else to talk about on slow news days, which are many of the days of infancy. Parenthood turns you into a kind of scientist who specialises in your own baby. You watch him so much of the time. And there can be so little to observe. So you are driven to compare what he is doing (or not doing) with what other babies are doing. Consider hanging around with people with older or no children to distract you from ruminating about why your baby isn't rolling yet. Although these people may avoid meeting your eye.

'It's BORING. Find some different mates that talk about shoes or plants or the economy or Corrie. ANYTHING.'

(*Mallory Towers*)

- Don't constantly be reading books about child development, and be especially wary of those which give very narrow ranges for particular skills.
- Remember that there are many areas of development where the range of 'normal' is vast – walking is one.
- Many milestones are meaningless – some children never crawl, for example.
- Once basic skills have been acquired, there is a lot to be said for enjoying the achievements of today and not looking ahead to the ones which may or may not occur in the future.

'The whole planet might get eaten by a Giant Goat before he ever makes it to managing director, but a complicated jigsaw done upside down today is still Good Stuff and something to be enjoyed.'

(*cory*)

- Constantly comparing one child with another is a mug's game.

'Two things I have noticed since having children is firstly that pretty much *all* children have something they can do amazingly well. My goddaughter could do jigsaw puzzles at about eighteen months, both the right way up and upside down (i.e. with no picture showing). That was it – in every other respect she was entirely "normal", but if you judged her on that alone you would think she was astonishing. My son and daughter have both been very early talkers – much earlier than their peers, clear diction, full sentences etc. But that's all, and in fact in my son's case, all his friends at four now speak exactly the same way and you certainly don't look at him and think he is freakishly advanced, in the same way that I don't expect people say about me "Wow, doesn't Anchovy speak well – so clear, and in sentences".'

(*Anchovy*)

- Anecdotally, many parents report that children who do things late often do them very quickly. They have just been figuring out exactly what to do in their own heads before having a go. Perhaps it is a pride thing.
- Remember your child is the product of your own dubious genetic material and is compelled to express it. One of the great pleasures of having a child is seeing similarities and being struck by how he or she differs from his or her parents.

'My son was very funny about clapping. Can't remember the age, but everyone else's baby could already clap. He watched very closely while I clapped. Then he rubbed his hands together, while smacking his lips to make the sound. We figure that with both parents being people who cannot run/jump/throw a ball or do anything that requires physical coordination, that is just the way he is.'

(fisil)

- There is a crude tendency to associate early development of particular skills with intelligence. So a lot of clever mothers peer doubtfully at their largely inert infants and wonder where their DNA went.

'Sleeping through the night, potty training, walking, these are NOTHING to do with intelligence, are they??
I can litter train a *rabbit* in a day.
Dogs have really good motor skills.
Hamsters sleep a lot.
Not relevant.'

(harpsiheraldangelssing)

- And let's be frank – some of the anxious watching and comparing is not just about reassuring yourself that your child is 'normal' but about nourishing your guilty hope that she is somehow spectacular. This is probably why people love those Einstein stories about how he didn't do anything at all as a child and then suddenly discovered the theory of relativity. It's the 'if we only have "normal" children what did we do "wrong"' or 'I'm clever so why isn't my kid clever, too?' kind of thing.

Then we wonder if others are exaggerating about their children's talents.

'I'm bummed my kids aren't gifted; but I'm also grateful they don't have any major problems, either (other than being burdened with me as a mother, but that's another going back to wondering what I'm doing "wrong", again).'

(zebratwizzler)

There are of course some developmental delays which are worth check-ing out. If a child seems to be delayed in many areas or is particularly slow at one thing, take your concern to your GP rather than looking it up on the internet. Chances are everything is fine but if a child does have special needs, early intervention is likely to be a good thing.

'Also it often depends on whether the milestone is just late or whether it is disordered as well. My two-and-a-half-year-old has very unclear speech – and I've lost count of the number of people who have told me about late speakers. The thing is though that his speech isn't delayed, it is disordered – he is trying to put it together incorrectly – speech sound development should follow a fairly set pattern, he's all over the place – and that is often more of a problem than a delay and usually doesn't get better by itself (and can indicate other problems).'

(*Jimjams*)

Don't buy a guinea pig for your child

OR A GERBIL, RAT, HAMSTER, CAGED BIRD, RABBIT, AFRICAN LAND SNAIL, STICK INSECT, GOLDFISH . . .

The guinea pig acquisition scenario

Maybe your eldest child is three, four, five, six and you become a bit pet broody. You start to think that it would be nice for him to have a little furry or scaly thing for which he is responsible. The whole longing for some novel baby thing in your house disguises itself as a potential educational experience – he will learn to look after some small rodenty scrap and it will be character building, teaching him about life and death and hygiene. You feel a little bit pastoral about it. And so you think you might just pop into a pet shop or degu breeder, just for a look.

And at that stage it is all over, because once you and the child have been in the presence of the cute furry thing, you will surely be taking it home with you. Along with an attractive array of consumer durables – cages with pipes coming out of them and chewsticks and big bags of woodshavings and stuff for nests. It's the whole baby-goods-buying fest all over but a little cheaper and less fraught.

But almost as soon as you get the pet home, the cracks start to show. You don't even get to use up any of your great baby names or the witty pet names you had been mulling over, because the children insist on calling the furry cylinders Brownie and Yellowy. The children gaze adoringly at the sleeping fluffy things and then drift off after ten minutes of waiting for them to dash around in their wheel.

One week later

You are feeding them every day after fruitless nagging followed by forgetfulness on the part of your progeny. You are mucking out their cage. You are trying to tame them and make sure they have some company.

And you are thinking:

Hamsters: OK, you knew they were nocturnal but everyone loves the way they stuff all that food in their cheeks. If you ever saw it happening . . .

African Land Snails: why don't they move? Are they dead?

'The way you tell if they're dead is to pick them up and sniff – when they're dead they smell *vile*. (Or if you've left it too long to perform the sniff test all their innards fall out as you pick them up.)'

(*RubberDuck*)

Gerbils: why are they fighting so much?

Birds: should never be in cages, what were you thinking?

Goldfish:

'They are dull and totally non interactive. They take up space which could be better employed. They need cleaning and feeding which is a pain. They will die or get fin rot. The pump things waste electricity.'

(*Miggsie*)

They get constipated and you have to handfeed them shelled peas and put them on rigorous diets. Goldfish, which are popularly but wrongly regarded as low maintenance pets, are constantly being nursed through one illness or another or thinking of new ways to cark it – fin rot, hole in head disease, suicide by tank-jumping . . .

Lizards: why did you buy something which has to exist on a diet of live crickets?

Because the truth about pets is that they basically mean more cleaning and it is cleaning with consequences:

'You have to get up to your elbows in fish poo water and siphon it off to a bucket. You have to scrub algae off the sides of the tank then you have to clean out the filter. Gross.'

(Passionflowerinapeartree)

'I have seen this so many times when I worked as a vet. Neglected bunny rabbits, stuck in their cages to rot – literally, in some cases, as we had to treat so many poor bastards with fly strike (maggot infestation basically eating them away). Where they have been left to fester in their own shit all day. I've had to put down too many bunnies who were too far gone to save. But when I used to get people ringing me and saying, "My rabbit has a shitty bum, what can I do?" I would say, "Bring it in, we will clip and clean it for you – it will most likely have urine scold and that is incredibly painful, also there is the risk of fly strike," then I would get, "Well I can't come at this time because I have to take little Jemima to ballet, I can't get there, how much?" Yes, well it's expensive owning a pet and there are time commitments, get used to it.'

(lucyellensmum)

Two years (hamster, gerbil) plus (guinea pig, rabbit etc.) down the line

Your children are sobbing at the rodent graveside. You are filled with the guilty fear that it died of boredom and/or loneliness. If you have goldfish, you have probably been committing identity theft all the way through:

'I've given up with them. We've had 3 lots and done absolutely everything for them and they just die. Garry 1, 2 and 3
Mr Squidward 1, 2 and 3
and
Patrick 1, 2 and 3.'

(Nbg)

'Get him two. Replace them before he notices when they die. That's what I do. My son thinks his goldfish are five years old. Well they're not.'

(cornsilk)

'Agree with Cornsilk, we're on Dorothy #2. I made the stupid mistake of getting "that lovely one with the black bit at the end of her tail" – cue panic when she kicked the bucket and I had to try and get an identical one. Get a plain orange fish, if you want to avoid the headache of "matching" or making up stories of how she's changed her looks.'

(Carnival)

Conclusion

No small/caged animals for your children, ever. If you really love small animals yourself, have some and let the children hang out with them.

'Surely any parent should realise that when they buy a pet for their child the child will ultimately get bored of it and it is the parent who will end up looking after it. We have lots of animals (dogs, cats, birds, rabbit) but although some of them (budgie/rabbit) are my son's, the only reason I allowed him to have them was because I am a huge animal lover and have no issue with being the one left to look after them. I was the one who spent hours with the budgie getting it tame enough for my son to be able to let out, I am the one who goes out in the rain to feed/ clean the rabbit. If I wasn't prepared to do that then we wouldn't have the animals. And if I'm honest we have the animals as much for me as for my son.'

(wannaBe)

Pet substitutes

If your children are pining, try these ideas. Retrieve some tins from the recycling. Fill with sand and seal open end with duct tape. Upholster with fun fur and stick on googly eyes. Use some small sweetcorn tins for baby ones. Place in box with woodshavings etc. Squeak when children come near box. Far less labour intensive and only fractionally less entertaining than real guinea pigs.

Furry animatronic pets, robo dogs, tamagotchi etc. Total duration of play value averages one hour. What is that telling you?

If you have the resources in terms of time, space, money and energy and you yourself are happy to look after it, get a real pet, i.e. a cat or dog, something with which you and your children can have a substantive relationship, one that is like a relationship with a human being but with more slavish adoringness and no personal criticism.

And if you truly truly must have a rodent, get a rat – consistently rated top for intelligence, hardiness, longevity and handleability:

'Had a pet rat (Noel) after the hamster and he was FABULOUS. Like a tiny person in a rat suit, huge character, intelligent and friendly.'

(NomDePlume)

A tiny person in a rat suit, what more could you want?

Postscript: some guinea pig eulogies, in case you get one anyway – we can't stop you . . .

'In moments of profound grief such as this I find the Haiku the most fitting tribute:
    On a brighter note
    In Peru you would have been
    Someone's roast dinner'

(Hassled)

'Noble furry pet
You roam eternal lawns now
Unfettered by size'

(Wingandaprayer)

'Here's one from my dog.
    Natural prey
    Bedecked in hay

    Awesome squeak
    And yet so weak.

    I heard you munch
    I yearned to crunch.

    Carrot eater
    Jaw cheater.'

(Threadworm)

'Thro' Heav'n's gate you pattered ere
I caught your glance this day.
Where guinea pigs a' frolic in

Th'eternal fresh-placed hay.
Aboon them a' ya tak your place
We'll ne'er see you mair.
We'll ne'er look upon your face
Nor stroke your sleekit hair.

Whate'er sleekit means, you chose
This day to limpe away,
Or crowl, or crepe, howe'er you left,
You've gan agley'

(VintageGardenia)

'Farewell fat pig
you pushed your luck
you ate too much
now off you fuck'

(pagwatch)

'Guinea Pigs graze all day through
So make an awful lot of poo
It's an unfortunately common fact
That this poo becomes impact(ed)
You mention Beetle wasn't fit
I'd guess your pig was full of shit
Upon you, Threadie, was the onus
To push down gently on his anus.

It's too late, the pig is dead
But keep that nugget in your head
In case you get another one
Always monitor its bum.'

(Boco)

Post-postscript: Don't look after anyone else's pet whilst that person is on holiday – it will die on you.

Ignore unsolicited parenting advice from old biddies on buses

(GET A SENSE OF HUMOUR)

This rule is about all the things people say that offend you and which are largely just social noise. You are left standing there grinding your teeth about some affronting toad that has emerged from a person's mouth whilst that person wanders off innocently whistling, *with nothing at all going on in his/her head.* Because the thing that affronted you never even went through his/her brain. It was just part of a grand communal stock of point-less verbiage that floats about and alights in people's mouths.

Here is a list of examples of the kind of thing we are talking about:

- Birth
  'Oh, what a shame you didn't manage to give birth naturally.' (And variations.)

- Baby gender
  (If you already have a baby of a different gender.)
  'Ooh, you must be pleased.'
  'Ooh, now you've got the perfect family.'
  (If you have a baby of the same gender as your previous one or six.)
  'Ooh, you/your husband must be disappointed.'
  (If you have ten boys and are pregnant again.)
  'Trying for a little girl, then?'

- Size of bump
  'Ooh, you're huge.'
  'Is it twins?'
  Often followed the same day by:
  'You're very small.'

What we like in this department are the kindly white lies:

'I loved "Aren't you blooming?", too. And "you are glowing" and all that shit. I knew I had greasy hair and looked like a milking cow, but it was nice that people cared enough to lie.'

(*ReasonableDoubt*)

- Size of baby
  As above.

- Appearance of baby
  'Ooh, it doesn't look like you at all.'
  'Oooh, it looks just like its dad.'
  'Ooh.'

- Baby names
  'Oooooooh.'

- Baby's 'goodness'
  'Is she a good baby?'
  'Is she being good for you?'

- Baby's state of dress
  This category often shades into irritating *advice,* a large category of inane discourse you need to let flow over you.
  'Your baby is too hot.'
  'Your baby needs a hat.'
  'Your baby has lost a sock.'

'And someone says, "Your baby is cold." And these over-sensitive mums all go BANANAS. I often see over-heated babies and feel sorry for them.'

(*SuSylvester*)

Often the advice strikes at the most inopportune possible moment, when you are struggling a tantrumming toddler into his buggy as the contents of his changing bag scatter themselves across the bus floor and his older sister attempts to exit the bus and possibly this life altogether.

Sometimes folk are just trying, maybe a little clumsily, to make some contact. A benevolent impulse you could easily squish with a glare or a smart retort:

'I loved chatting with the older ladies while I was on maternity leave. I remember one in particular telling me to be careful about taking my daughter out in the cold. Now I could have been very offended by this but she went on to tell me all about her sisters who died from flu and her little babe who had lung problems and I understood totally where she was coming from and we chatted for quite a while after that, funnily enough, out in the cold. I think she enjoyed chatting and I know I did too.'

(*tarantula*)

Other people's opinions are particularly hard to bear if you are an advice magnet. Some of us cannot step from the house without being assailed by detailed and insistent advice from the postie, other mothers, all the old people within a mile radius and a few concerned gentlemen of the road. Maybe we just look especially gormless.

Really, you must relax about this stuff. The only person you hurt by gnashing your teeth and beating your breast is yourself. And a world in which you rounded on all the people who said something inane or even objectively offensive to you would be a more trying and confrontational one than the one we have already. Jeremy Kyle world, we could call it.

The 'just you wait' school of vacuous remarks

We admit these are especially irritating:
    'Just you wait till labour.'
    'Just you wait till he's a toddler.'
    'Just you wait till he's a teenager.'
    'Just you wait till [insert normal developmental stage here].'
    (Always accompanied by a 'she'll learn' look.)

'The way people talk, you'd think I should be preparing myself for a lifetime of hardship, coming in stages that are each worse than the last.'

(*TheFruitWhisperer*)

But try *internally* substituting these:

'Just you wait till you hold your own real baby in your arms.

Just you wait till he learns to smile at you.

Just you wait till he tells you he loves you.

Just you wait till he is old enough to bring you tea in bed. I waited . . . and it was worth waiting for <big silly grin>.

Just now I am waiting for my ten-year-old to come home from school. I am feeling a bit off colour today so he can run down and get me something comforting from the corner shop. Then if I wait a bit longer the thirteen-year-old will come home from her Shakespeare audition and tell me all about that. And if I wait yet a while, we will all sit down to dinner and have a chat and a laugh about the day. Waiting's good . . .'

(cory)

Or this:

'Just you wait until the sun expands into a huge gas giant and the seas boil and we all burn to a crisp.'

(Jasonthunderpants)

Travel hopefully, though, and you may find you mostly hear the nice stuff and the irritating stuff washes over you:

'I've never had any adverse comments either – not for breastfeeding in public, or tantrumming children, or anything.

Quite the reverse, actually.

For example, my son was enjoying a little strop in the queue in Waitrose the other day. Behind us was a very staid-looking man in a suit. He looked at my son, bent down and started whirling the "PLEASE WAIT HERE" sign round and round for my son's amusement. The whole queue was smiling.

Maybe that's Waitrose for you . . .

Mind you, I do know I can look rather scary. Perhaps people are afraid NOT to help . . .'

(Shodan)

'The best "interference" we experienced was when my daughter was two days old. We'd walked to the co-op but the pram was too big to get into the ridiculously small shop so I went in and left my husband with the pram.

An elderly lady came up and cooed at my daughter. Two minutes later the woman had tapped my husband on the shoulder and shoved a tenner into his hand saying, "That's for the baby, mind, don't go spending it on beer." Still makes me smile to this day (actually making me cry a little bit now, fecking pregnancy hormones).'

(Bumperlicious)

Don't give up work for your children

Young mothers assemble
At swing and sandpit
Setting free their children . . .
Something is pushing them
To the side of their own lives.

Philip Larkin, 'Afternoons'

Well, Larkin always manages to tap into our more lugubrious thoughts about parenting, and work and everything else besides. And some of us actually feel, in the early months or years after having children, quite the reverse of this, thrust suddenly into the very centre of our lives, or something important about life. And if you have been doing work which is very consuming but not necessarily satisfying, being at home with a little child can be a kind of liberation – time to walk in parks and watch the world and think aimless thoughts which might nonetheless wander somewhere interesting, whilst still having an underlying purpose to your days. Larkin, you think, didn't realise how the playground also set the mothers free . . .

Up to a point. But the novelty does wear off and even parents who don't feel pushed aside at the beginning (and some certainly do), may begin to feel a bit Larkinesque as their children get bigger and particularly when they go to school. The ways in which your children need you become less immediate and all-consuming, more subtle. They have relationships with more people, interests which don't necessarily involve you. They need you to have your own interests and your own independent life and *you* need to have these things as well.

As a generation of parents, we seem to struggle with all of this, those of us who have the (very considerable) luxury to do so. We struggle to find the balance between the demands and satisfactions of worthwhile and interesting work (and hobbies and other interests) and the demands and satisfactions of raising children. How much time can we, should we devote to each? Can our careers survive if we take the time we feel we need to be with our children? Can our children survive the hurly-burly of our careers? Can we survive without our careers? Contrary to the generalising nonsense we read in newspapers, there are no universal solutions to these problems. Sometimes you have to cobble together something which works reasonably well for you:

'I hated being a SAHM and felt like the least maternal person in world once my son was born. This was despite my entire career/game plan in life being "be a mum". I joined the gym when he was six weeks old (having never been before) and went for two hours a day, every day just to get rid of him in the creche for two hours. By the time my daughter was born 2 years later things improved slightly and I started my eBay business. I still had to keep busy even if it was only walking to the post office every day with parcels. I wasn't a playdoh, organic type mum. I love my kids, keep the house tidy and on top of the ironing but it doesn't fulfil me. Now that they are both at school I have all day to work on expanding my business and go to the gym (old habits die hard). Then I concentrate on the after-school activities and the mummy time from 3 until 7 when they go to bed. What I'm trying to say is that me being a SAHM is good for my family but wasn't the best thing for me. I worked around it and made it fit. If you can crowbar a few hours a week of time for yourself into your life it may make you happier. IME a happier me equals a better mum.'

(ebayaddict)

Don't give up a career you love *for the sake of your children.* There are lots of reasons to stop doing a job, to curtail it, to change direction. Maybe you *want* to be at home more with your children. Maybe you want to be a stay-at-home parent for a particular period or indefinitely. Maybe your family cannot manage with both adults at work all of the time. Some people, by the time they have children, are fed up with the particular job they are doing and welcome a chance to break with one career and look at other options. But no one, male or female, should chuck their career away because they think their children require them at home. And many of us are far nicer, calmer and therefore better parents when we don't spend all our time with our children.

'It isn't very nice, as an adult (but I remember feeling like this as a teenager too), to feel somewhat responsible for the regrets and lack of fulfilment of a person you love so much as your own mother. Of course she gave up work willingly, and she has never made us feel responsible for her choices (far from it). I still wish she'd maintained some kind of professional identity, she'd be happier now, she'd have been happier for many, many years, and that would make me happy too.

It's never black or white though, really. You are still very present in your children's lives even if you are at work nine hours a day. Conversely, you can be absent from their lives even if you are at home all the time.'

(TheMysticMasseuse)

'The trite old saying "No one on their death bed wishes they'd spent more time at the office" is just meaningless. It implies that going to work means sitting in some dull office, being bored out of your mind, doing a pointless job. I hope on my death bed I look back over my life and feel contented and fulfilled with my life – and yes, the most important chunk of that will be about family, my children etc., but there will also be a lot of other things to feel fulfilled about – places I've visited, books I've read, people I've met, things I've learned . . . and quite a lot of that comes from life outside the nuclear family.'

(violethill)

There are costs to all of our choices and a period of full-time parenting can not only be financially debilitating, it can make you wonder who you are and what the hell happened to your life. The financial dependence of one parent on the other can put terrible pressure on the providing parent and on the non-earning parent. Viz the providing parent is plagued by nightmares in which she is naked in a public place and being pursued by the mortgage. And the non-earning parent feels like she has disappeared into some kind of childcare black hole as she pushes her buggy about wearing the Manky Old Fleece of Invisibility. And experiences mild panic when faced with the question 'What do you do?' at dinner parties. (Although we have always liked and would recommend Lisa Kudrow's line in *Romy and Michele's High School Reunion* about inventing Post-it notes.)

And of course it can be hard to try to resume a career when everyone else in your old office who didn't stay home with kids has become your boss. If you can even go back to anything like the job you had. Or, you think in your more apocalyptic moments, any job.

The truth is, we think, that in the prevailing social and economic circumstances there is simply no perfect or even very good solution to the work/childcare balancing thing for the majority of people. There is only a choice between a number of ways of doing things each of which is crummy in some respects. The thing to do is to choose the one that seems to you the overall least crummy and then not make yourself too miserable about the bad aspects of it. And you will probably have to choose between crummy options a number of times as your children increase in age and number and your other circumstances change.

But always bear this in mind when you are choosing: everyone in the family matters and one person should not be sacrificed for the perceived good of the others. Whatever you do by way of paid or unpaid work, you need to do something other than parent.

Other interests for SAHMs and SAHDs

If you do stay at home with your children for a period, there are many non-job things you can do. Some people are delighted to find the time to do gardening and proper cooking and crafts. Here are some examples, but substitute stuff you like; beadweaving doesn't float everyone's boat:

'You need a project. I find that having a project on the go helps me to see that I am making progress each day/week. It's so hard to see your efforts paying off with kids. I do mosaics, but I also like to have other arty craft projects on the go too. I don't get a chance to do them until the evening or the weekend, so progress is still slow. But that's what helps me.'

(*Dragonbutter*)

'Yes, the projects! I've been a SAHM for the last 6 years and I'm not bored at all! Have so much to do all the time. In the last 5 years I've built an aviary, built a chicken run and coop, redecorated both kids' bedrooms, the dining room, laid new flooring in dining room and extension, built a playhouse, relandscaped the garden (front and back). Also I've done voluntary work for Meals on Wheels for a couple of years until they disbanded, done gardening for the elderly for Age Concern, helped out at local playschool and last year did part-time work in the evening and weekend as a home carer. There is always plenty to do, just got to think outside the box. I've also been collecting beads and trinkets to start doing beadweaving in the winter when I can't get out into the garden and tend to my vegetable plot.

When I was at work it was just get up, on train, catch other train, walk one mile, work at computer and talk all day (call centre), catch two trains back, cook dinner from 7 p.m., eat, go to bed. Being at home means you have freedom to do the things you dreamed about whilst stuck at work!'

(Ripeberry)

Getting back on the horse

Some people use a period of stay-at-home parenting to retrain for a new career. Although some of us, it must be said, wait patiently for a brainwave and not much occurs:

'I assumed I'd get a burning desire to do a particular job or learn a particular skill after some time at home (in fact, thinking about this has often got me through a bad phase in the past), but it hasn't happened.'

(OurLadyofPerpetualSupper)

In those circumstances, you may just have to try a few different things and see what appeals. If you're fortunate enough not to have to earn ready cash to support the family coffers, voluntary work can be a good way of trying out new things:

'What sort of thing did you do when you were at work? Not all voluntary work is making tea in the local hospital or clearing woodland (which is fine if that is what you are after – a bit of structure to your week and some adult company). But if you are looking for more of an intellectual challenge, many charities are desperate for trustees: they basically run the business side of the charity, make decisions on staffing, funding, finance and strategy. They often meet in the evening, too, so it's easier as the other parent may be at home to look after the children.'

(wonderingwondering)

Doing voluntary work can be also be a good way to rebuild confidence if you have been a long time out of the workforce. As can finding a course which helps you get ready for the job market.

'I was lucky in that I found a course at the local FE College for "Women Returners". It was one morning a week for 10 weeks and was partly practical (CVs/forms/interviews technique etc.) and partly about yourself – highlighting your strengths and so on. Really, really useful on many levels.'

(GreenShadow)

BUT *do not both work eighty-hour weeks*

Reluctant as we are to generalise too much in this horribly fraught area, we think that if at all possible, whilst children are growing up, at least one parent should not be working what we would call full-time plus, i.e. jobs which involve being in the office/in Hong Kong from before your kids get up until after they are in bed. We know that posh parents of the past would go off abroad for months and leave the children with the nanny or at boarding school. And those people carried on ruling the world, in their emotionally weird way. And we also know some people have to work all the hours they can to keep their children fed and housed. And who could have anything but respect and admiration for parents in that position? But we still think that it is better for children and for the relationships between parents and children for at least one parent to spend some time with those children every day.

So, if you are both working 80-hour weeks because you are corporate lawyers or bankers or hospital doctors or whatnot, one or both of you should scale back whilst you have little children. Maybe you can serially downsize your careers so that they take roughly the same sort of beating. You have, after all, the whole rest of your lives to be working stupid hours. You can just retire later; you'll probably have to retire later. Look at it this way – the hours you spend with your children now are hours you can't spend playing golf in your twilight years. Hours you can't spend on cruise ships eating round-the-clock dessert buffets and listening to lectures on dinosaurs. Work when you are old and save yourself from the horror of old-person leisure time.

'I think most parents have a gut feeling for whether they are spending "enough" time with their children. You know as a parent when your children are contented/ settled or anxious/unhappy, and you respond accordingly, whether it's spending

30 minutes chatting, or making more radical changes to your lifestyle such as reducing your work hours. Also, you need to differentiate between what you as a parent may feel you're missing out on, and whether this actually bothers your child. If your child is having a really happy afternoon with a childminder and other children, for instance, then feeling negatively about that is nothing to do with the child, it's about the mother perhaps *needing* to feel totally irreplaceable – which is clearly nonsense, as from the moment a child is born, it begins a life-time of forming relationships.'

(violethill)

Cut all their hair off

We are not going to pretend we did this ourselves. With this rule we are seeking to help you profit from our errors. In fact we have between us at least seven sons who variously resemble Farrah Fawcett, Cousin Itt and the Hair Bear Bunch. And daughters who could be cast as Rapunzel without the aid of wigs or hair extensions. And we are martyrs to haircare products and specialist tangle brushes and have purchased enough nit treatment lotion to suffocate the insect population of South America. And wasted hours of our lives, armed with said products and tangle brushes, chasing bushels of hair with skinny legs poking out around the house to a sound-track of wailing.

It all started so benignly – with the soft little curls which appeared in the night like snowdrops and relieved the absolute and scaly baldiness that we briefly feared would persist into adulthood. And the curls were so adorable as they lengthened and multiplied, what harm could there possibly be in letting them grow? Who knew it would end with school-age children who screamed at the sight of the scissors? And whose features were barely visible behind great drapes and swags and jalousies of hair?

Long curly hair, it's so lovely when you have no responsibility for it, but who wants to look after someone else's long curly hair? Especially when the hair is attached to a child scalp so sensitive it could detect a Tangle Teezer concealed under fourteen mattresses? And who wants to go hunting for headlice hiding out in an accidentally formed dreadlock? Or shave off a whole head of real dreads because you can't get the nits out any other way?

'I think every schoolchild in the UK should have a stage 1 haircut. Louse-free education. Wonderful.'

(*Ecomouse*)

So if it is not too late for you, be stern with yourself and say this – no child of mine shall have high maintenance hair until he/she is able and willing to look after it him/herself:

'I don't like short, short hair on boys if I'm honest. I hate seeing little lads with bullet heads, and my son does have the most beautiful thick, soft, golden hair . . . but . . . it only looks really nice just after it's been washed and if I'm honest I prefer him to look like somebody owns him.'

(OrmIrian)

Some hair martyrs to frighten you off

When you are hesitating with the scissors, consider whether this is the life you want:

'My daughter has fine, waist-length, although not curly, hair which matts easily. After towel drying I put serum through it and that helps with detangling. When it's been really bad, I've detangled while she's in the bath. I slather the washed hair with conditioner and serum and use my fingers to get the worst knots out, followed by a comb. When it's done, I give her hair a quick rinse with the shower, making sure I don't ruffle it up again. It comes out beautifully soft and shiny!'

(suedonim)

'Ahh the matted back problem. We had that one.

I tackled it by using mega type conditioners, the Aussie 3 Minute Miracle was very good, and teasing as much of the matting out with my hands while the conditioner was in as I could. Always put hair into a ponytail or plait to sleep in. Finally, when attempting to detangle when dry, I use a bit of serum rubbed through with fingertips. You can get a lot of tangles out that way, using the flat of your hands and fingers before the dreaded comb even comes out.'

(slug)

But there is something worse, we think, than being enslaved to a really lush head of hair on a small child. There is the imposition of fashion hair-dos on tiny children.

So we say no gel on small boys, no tram lines or Mohicans or highlights:

'Dressing up for a party is one thing but dressing your small child up like a Guess ad for school is all about the parent wanting to gain some weird kudos. And if the child has absorbed these fashion rules at the age of seven then they are not getting out enough. It is just the extension of the child as a fashion accessory – so beloved of Katie Holmes and others. Let them be little for fuck's sake. They will want to look like pimps and hookers soon enough without having to be started early.'

(pagwatch)

'Somehow I feel that children and fashion (within reason) should be kept separate until around the age of puberty if at all possible.'

(Countingthegreyhairs)

Some parents get a bit narked at school uniform rules which include rules about hair. We say, unless your child's school is insisting on universal buzzcuts or baldness, relax, your child's freedom of expression is not being interfered with in any meaningful way. There are plenty of interesting ways to express yourself which do not involve you pledging allegiance to some hair tribe or other. And hair tribes are bad for schools. Helping the school to enforce these rules may make you feel like a complete repressive totalitarian fun-squelching pig. But you are a parent and sometimes it's your job to be a repressive totalitarian etc.

'Just say no. If he wanted to carry a knife because he thought it looked "cool", would you let him?'

(Pixiefish)

'Unfortunately, kids with "extreme" haircuts often actively use how they look in school to intimidate others and create a gang culture. Having rules about hairstyles can discourage this. Also, the vast majority of kids have basic hairstyles. Kids who do dye their hair crazily or have mad cuts do attract a lot of attention from other pupils and love it – it can be quite disruptive in a lesson/form time. Finally some of these more extreme hairstyles can actually be a health and safety risk – the kids with tons of gel and hairspray in their hair need only lean slightly over a Bunsen burner to go up like a deodorant can!

Schools have to have rules so that everyone essentially looks the same so that we can try and instil the same codes of conduct for everyone – kids only actually spend about six hours a day at school for just over half the year – they are free to be as hair expressive as they want outwith these times!'

(*Haggisfish*)

Don't think about the future

If what is keeping you dancing attendance on your children's barnets is fear of their adult bitterness at not being allowed to have their hairstyle of choice, we say, give up, this is a fight you cannot win. There will always be something to be bitter about in the parent/child relationship and if it's just hair or not being bought a Mr Frosty or a SodaStream (seventies child) or a FurReal or a DS (noughties child) then you are doing pretty damn well and should buy yourself a SodaStream to celebrate.

Because for every sense of hair grievance which looks like this:

'I had long ringlety red hair as a child and because my mother hadn't thought of using conditioner – I was given a bowl cut rather than her putting up with me crying every morning while she tried to comb my hair. Not that I am bitter.'

(*Bigmouthstrikesagain*)

There is one which looks like this:

'I was fobbed off with a fake spray conditioner called something like "No tears, no tangles". It didn't bloody work. The pain. My mum wasn't gentle with a comb. Oh and elastic bands in hair that ripped it out from the roots, not these lovely soft toggly things these days.'

(*NOTHEROLDIE*)

Or this:

'I am the opposite to some of you, as my gran took great pride in my long blonde hair. I hated my long hair, my gran gave me some money to go to the hairdressers to have a *trim*. I told the hairdresser that I wanted the lot chopped off in a boy type haircut and yes, my gran had given her permission (he knew her). She was furious when she saw my cropped hair, and went storming into the hairdressers and shouted at him. Sorry, Tony. Mind you, she got her revenge when it had grown a few cm, and gave me a Toni perm. I looked like Vera from Corrie.'

(GetOrfMoiLand)

And if it's not hair, it will be something like this:

'My nan used to knit my Sindy's clothes. I wanted shop-bought ones, but oh no, my Sindy had to go around looking like a refugee from some war-torn Eastern European country.'

(ShirleyKnot)

But don't cut it yourself

Unless you are a gifted coiffeur/se. Get them to a hairdresser once they are past babyhood, particularly if you are taking the hair shorter than bob length. Unless you know what you are doing, it's almost impossible to do a good short haircut rather than some pitiful moth-eaten mess. And chopping off those long ropes of dead skin cells doesn't mean banishing all child beauty from your life. *Au contraire*:

'Have just realised that I actively love *short* hair on small boys as much as some of you like the long hair. Long hair can't do that gorgeous summery thing of hair gone delicately silver at the nape of a brown neck. Obviously it can do other things but not that.'

(Bink)

Let them eat cake

On the one hand you walk about these fine isles and everywhere children with tiers of tyres of fat like those stacking ring toys for toddlers are merrily consuming crispy deep-fried yellowish carbohydrates of one sort and another. And when you see a group of fine and lithe teens on the beach, they turn out to be French. And on the other hand some schools are banging on about healthy eating in a way that causes at least one eight-year-old boy whose ribs already stick out like those of the crucified Jesus to shudderingly refuse to eat cheese. And in other schools, nine-year-old food police are condemning a piece of homemade sponge in a packed lunch.

Because sometimes the zeal to combat obesity causes the healthy eating message to become oversimplified. And children are themselves past masters at oversimplifying and garbling the messages they get. Many children come away believing whole food groups are inherently bad for them or that other foods are essentially unexploded bombs:

'My friend's little boy (age six) was hysterical one night thinking he was going to have a heart attack because he's had a piece of chocolate cake after his dinner – "and chocolate cake makes you fat and then you have a heart attack and you *die*!"'

(*DrMarthaMcMoo*)

And we have all met the somewhat lugubrious tot whose mother makes a birthday cake out of rice cakes sandwiched together with raisins and puts a carrot stick in a party bag filled with hummus. And felt a little dampened by the joylessness of it all.

And yet, and yet, the constant eating of deep-fried battered stuffed-crust crisp-flavoured pizza nuggets washed down with that blue pop which is the same colour as de-icing fluid is clearly no good either. So we are saying, not too surprisingly, that moderation, a bit of this and a bit of that, even when that is sometimes a refined sugar product or a sausage roll, is the way to go with food. Being too hardline and banning whole genres of food (sweets, chocolates, crisps in particular) tends to have one of three deleterious effects:

1) Child becomes six-year-old Woody Allen, enquiring anxiously about the fat content of food and asking for salad at birthday parties.
2) Child reacts violently against restrictions once of an age to purchase foodstuffs:

'My mum was a sweet denier in the seventies (before it was fashionable) . . . so when I left home I lived on Topics, pints of full-fat milk and cream crackers. For weeks. As someone who's been on the receiving end of Puritan Parenting, I would say let them have everything in moderation. Otherwise you create this air of mystery and desirability round all the things you don't want them to have, and as soon as they can choose for themselves, they'll choose them.'

(*PreciousLillyWhite*)

3) Lifelong vacillation between the first two positions. This is you, isn't it?

Some practical thoughts on how to create a healthy non-extremist kind of diet

- Let them have some chocolate, some sweets, some crisps, some ice cream. Work out what is a rational amount. Don't generally keep the stuff in the house – have it be a treat for when you are out.
- With older children, talk about what healthy eating means – how it is not about excluding whole food groups but about achieving an appropriate balance between them. Kids need to eat a reasonable amount of fat but some sources of it are better than others. You can talk to older children about food labelling so that they can help choose the best options in the supermarket.
- Explain about advertising. Someone wants to sell you some cheese rope so they are going to try to make it attractive to you. It doesn't mean it's nice.
- Continuing to cook and serve a range of healthy foods (and enthusiastically eating them yourself) is likely to lure even children who go

through 'only ham and strawberry yoghurt' phases into eating a more rich and varied diet.

- Don't do that fifties thing of making a child who is already full finish everything on his plate.
- Do provide sensible-sized portions. Better to serve a second helping than an over-large first helping.
- A healthy meal needn't be a huge faff:

'Healthy food doesn't have to mean hours slaving over a hot stove, not at all, in my opinion. For example pasta, beans, crudites, peanut butter/marmite sandwiches, hummus, fruit, toast, cereal are all quick and healthy.'

(*wickedwaterwitch*)

- There are ways around the desperate rubbish often served up as children's food by eating establishments:

'My personal bugbear (very apparent when we were on holiday in Devon at the start of August, and eating out for lunch a lot) is the abysmal fare served up as the "Children's Menu". Sausages, chicken nuggets, burgers and the ubiquitous chips. Both mine could have had that in every place we ate – thank goodness for the few places with imagination that offer things like pasta, roast dinner etc. My son asked for the "homemade mushroom soup and crusty bread" in one place we went and the waitress wouldn't believe it was for him!'

(*marthamoo*)

Try getting a half portion of something less yellow and fried off the adults' menu. Or a decent starter.
- Helping to choose and prepare food is an absolutely brilliant way to increase a child's interest in trying new foods. Watching cooking programmes like *Junior MasterChef* can inspire some children.
- A party is a party is a party. Let them eat cake:

'Parties & Christmas I relax the rules. I loosely try to enforce a "You must have some proper food first" rule – which basically means eating at least a small portion of anything not crisps or sweet, before they are allowed to stuff themselves on cake. I snitch all but one choc and sweet out of their party bags, too. This tactic will only work until my son learns to count.'

(zebra)

But just in case the packed-lunch police turn up at your school . . .

'I liked one Mumsnetter's experience where a lady had put on her child's lunch-box in huge letters "JUDGE NOT, LEST YE BE JUDGED". Eight-year-olds are the most judgey as well. My daughter comes home telling me about X in her class, "All she eats is sugar. Sugar, sugar, sugar. She has sugar for snack and sugar for lunch." Then she folds her arms across her chest and makes the same face Les Dawson used to when he was in drag.'

(MadamDeathStare)

'Start putting joke items in. In little tupperwares, neatly labelled for the inspector's benefit: cold snail porridge, carrot toffee bombs, frog-meat sandwich, oxtail tart, mackerel-flavoured angel delight.'

(hatwoman)

'My husband suggests taking it a bit further:
   half a pound of lard
   20 lambert and butler.'

(hatwoman)

Boycott World Book Day

(AND DECORATE AN EGG DAY AND MAKE AN EASTER BONNET DAY ETC.)

So, World Book Day. Those of you with babies and toddlers only will be wondering why anyone would suggest boycotting anything so manifestly worthy, something which is about *reading books*. But, as many a parent has discovered, her eyes descaled, World Book Day is basically onerous and unrewarding homework for (mostly) mothers. The majority of schools seem to respond to World Book Day by sending a note home with the child (usually but not invariably on the eve of World Book Day) suggesting that the child attend school dressed as a favourite character from a book. The mother who stays up much of the night fabricating a Hungry Caterpillar costume out of an old sleeping bag will then discover that child herd mentality means the playground will look like a rerun of the *South Park* Halloween episode in which Cartman dressed as Hitler and everyone else came as Chewbacca. The Hungry Caterpillar, probably unable to eat, learn or move in the transformed sleeping bag, will suffer social death as the classroom fills with a synthetic fabric frenzy of Asda Snow Whites and pound-shop Spidermen and may thereafter be unable to go to the loo. Or, conversely, your child will crackle proudly into school dressed as a Power Ranger and you personally will be shamed by coteries of homemade Cat in the Hats.

Apart from the fact that teachers have not worked out that many of us have no skills and no time to be a-making costumes, they have not thought through the myriad varieties of Hell the whole exercise puts parents and children through:

'My daughter is going as a poo. 'Tis social suicide.'

(*SawneyBeane*)

'My son has decided. And now I'm going to look like poncey mcponce of ponceville. He would like to go as Theseus (and the minotaur). Still I s'pose a toga should be easy . . . shouldn't it?'

(Twiglett)

'It reminds me of the time my mum sent me to a fancy dress party with a really c**p costume at the age of seven. Everyone else was dressed as cool animals, princesses, super-heroes . . . I got sent in dirty clothes . . . apparently she thought it funny for me to be the Persil kid from the then TV adverts . . . not realising that seven-year-old kids don't get irony. Oh the shame.'

(Indaba)

Contrary to what you might think, you cannot escape from World Book Day misery by being a talented craft-doing parent with a sewing machine. If you do have creative tendencies, an unseemly ambition to do something really clever and fancy will overcome you. This is fine and well if you are making your child a diorama or somesuch, or writing a poem for their homework or really anything they do not actually have to *wear*. The problem with costumes is that the more effort you invest (e.g. the mother who made the anatomically correct iguanodon costume) the more likely it is that your child will baulk at wearing the costume at the last minute and wail to wear a mass-produced Spiderman costume. Possibly adding insult to injury by later remarking, 'But well done for making such a good costume, Mummy' in your own most patronising tones. On the other hand, if you spend money on a costume, your child will change her mind about it once you take the labels off.

'It takes me back to the nativity play. I spent a whole weekend fashioning a giant papier mâché dove's head by wrapping zillions of sticky bits of newspaper round a balloon, painting it, cutting out a face, sticking on millions of little white feathers and a beak, making a feathery dress with wings. My daughter got into position on stage, decided she couldn't breathe wearing it, and literally bounced it off the stage and into the audience.'

(Boco)

Ah, but surely, you ask, it is worth making a little parental effort to inspire children to read books? The sceptics amongst us question the methodology:

'I have a grade A A-level in biology, all without ever dressing up as the digestive system . . . and I feel sure (I hope) that gynaecologists complete their training without unseemly fancy dress providing motivation for their studies.'

(Blu)

A canny and well-organised parent with connections on the PTA may be able to redirect World Book Day energies into other channels – children might bring their favourite book to school, for example. Young children might come to school in pyjamas and have stories read to them. Although the latter project can and does go wrong when children decline to wear pyjamas or you realise they have only unsightly rags in their pyjama drawers.

If dressing up it must be, old hands at the World Book Day game suggest that you reverse engineer a costume by choosing something from your dressing up box and finding a character to fit (Dracula, miscellaneous fairytale princess, a knight from some book about knights etc.). This creates less misery all round when the child wakes on World Book Day and refuses to wear the selected item. Some schools, however, try to ruin this tactic for you by imposing a book, author or theme. In which case, we can only suggest an enlightened minimalism in your approach. Remember the World Book Day Formula: $W^2 = S + s$, where W is work invested in project, S = duration of screaming by parent and s = duration of screaming by child.

Minimalist costume ideas (in ascending order of effortfulness)

- No costume: child going as self, i.e. character in own forthcoming autobiography
- No costume at school with school uniform: child going as a character in any school story, e.g. Mallory Towers etc.
- No costume on red-haired child: Ron Weasley from *Harry Potter*
- Use eyebrow pencil to fill in space between child's eyebrows and draw moustache on lip and eye 'tattoo' on child's ankle: Count Olaf in *A Series of Unfortunate Events*
- Child in ordinary school uniform involving a blazer plus plastic martini glass from pound shop: James Bond
- Child holding bucket with plastic dinosaurs: Harry and the Dinosaurs
- Child plus several rolls of loo paper: mummy in *Horrible Histories* or *Scooby Doo* or similar

A minimalist approach can be applied to any competitive craft activity devised by your child's school, e.g. Easter bonnets, nativity costumes and Easter eggs.

Minimalist Easter bonnetry

Go to pound shop and buy Easter chicks, coloured paper, other tat as appropriate. Give child materials, plus old hat/baseball cap/paper plate and glue. Retire for fortifying cup of tea. Stick results on child's head.

And here are some moderately fancier ideas for the Easter bonnet enthusiasts amongst you:

• 'The easiest way to do it is a fez-shaped hat (cardboard) with a hollow in the top of the crown (I'd *never* condone use of a Kentucky Fried Chicken Family Bucket but it is the right shape). Cover in glue and roll in straw, hay or All-Bran to simulate bird's nest. Glue plastic chicks, decorated brown or plastic eggs etc to top. Can also do nest using turban-type arrangement of brown fabric round any old hat, but gluing All-Bran is more fun!'

(*MrsBadger*)

• Stick some hot cross buns to a baseball cap.

Minimalist nativity costumes

Nativity plays can be more vexing, however, because the school imposes the role on the child. Minimalism thrives on creative choice. You will have mastered sheep (white jumper, black tights, headband with ears) and stars (large cardboard star stuck to child sandwich-board style), wisemen/shepherds (dressing gown, tea towel, for shepherd add toy sheep), angels (white nightie, tinsel round head) and then your child will be cast as a mince pie, a 'friend of Mary and Joseph', a chocolate Santa, a Christmas cracker, a dish of Brussels sprouts.

These literary devices might save you:
Synecdoche (part represents the whole): so a Brussels sprout attached to the child's forehead alludes to the whole bowl of Brussels sprouts and the child is synecdochically representing a bowl of Brussels sprouts.

Metonymy (something is represented by something associated with it): so a child required to dress as a Christmas pudding could instead wear his brother's old brandy butter costume. Wibble.

Minimalist Easter eggs

These often have to be characters from books so try this: Hard boil egg. Put in box. Seal box: Schrodinger's cat.

Don't hit your kids

(BUT IF YOU DO, TRY VERY HARD NOT TO DO IT AGAIN)

'There are times when I just have to quote Roseanne Barr: "If the kids are alive at the end of the day I've done my job."'

(madamez)

Sometimes Philip Larkin's words ring in your ears with dismal inevitability, not just 'They fuck you up, your mum and dad,' but the old sucker punch 'They fill you with the faults they had / And add some extra just for you.' Maybe at the end of day when you have found yourself offering to rehouse a three-year-old who won't stop whining or screeching at an eight-year-old who is laughing at your escalating hollow threats and sneering at you and your tinpot authority. When you are paradoxically confronted by your powerlessness to improve the situation and by the awful power you have to reduce your children to a state of cringing misery. And there is a giddy moment when you are unsure where your brakes are. Who died and made you king of these children, dictator of this small and feud-riven nation? They surely shouldn't have.

'Just had a bit of a lightbulb moment where it struck me that all the old cliches about parenthood are actually TRUE and that it is tremendously difficult to be a good parent all the time and no one really thanks you even if you pull out all the stops? And sometimes, just sometimes, you get tired of putting the needs of your child before your own?'

(bibbitybobbityhat)

And frankly sometimes it is a terrible struggle to forgive a child who has been rude to you or physically hurt you or broken something you value and to move on and be the grown-up.

'I think I know what you mean – that nothing is yours – it's pointless liking a nice dress or special wine glass, as it will get wrecked. It doesn't matter in the grand scheme of things, but it is hard to come to terms with.'

(*oranges*)

And for a quite a large proportion of parents who don't believe in corporal punishment there is a grim moment when they smack or yank or push a child in anger. And are visited by a terrible and unremitting remorse. Because physical violence towards children is never OK. And all you can do is try very hard to make sure it doesn't happen again.

And it's not just moments of crisis which can make you feel helpless and useless and that you've failed, sometimes it's the dragging attendant anxiety about the whole course of what you are doing, the postnatal background noise of the whole rest of your life:

'I'm permanently terrified something is going to happen to the children or to me or I'm going to screw them up for life.'

(*Meglet*)

The great crevasse of doubt about how you are performing is likely to be larger and craggier if you are engaged in the relentlessness of being the full-time carer. Bringing up a child is such a long game – with so many dreary groundhog days. And it's underpinned by a feeling that you should be keeping an eye on the big picture which is almost entirely obscured by trivia.

There's no universal panacea for feeling like a crap parent. At some stage most of us do behave badly – shout when there is a better way of coping, say something nasty in anger, make a poor judgment call. And sometimes you get into a dispiriting pattern of doing those things. And it is more likely to happen, of course, when you are tired, stressed or ill yourself.

But, but, but, but . . . there are ways of thinking about what you do generally and about the ugly moments of crisis which can help to make you feel happier and more relaxed and therefore better able to cope. So below we've suggested, firstly, some ways of getting some perspective – generally getting philosophical about the whole business. And secondly, we've looked at how to be better – avoiding doing the stuff you don't like (and shouldn't like): screeching and hitting and losing control. We aren't saying that sometimes people aren't doing intervention-grade bad parenting. Of course they are. If you really don't know how to cope, you can get help. Or if you just want to learn to do some things better. See the second section below, 'How to be better' for some detailed tips and sources of support.

Getting some perspective

Here are some things to think about which have helped us, sometimes, to cope better.

For a start you need to try to recognise and accept your own strengths and weaknesses as a parent. Some people struggle badly with some ages and stages. Nature has not made us all happy nurturers of babies and toddlers. Sometimes that is something you can address by the way you divide up childcare between parents. For some people it may be a question of recognising that you are a better parent if you go out to work and don't attempt to be a full-time carer. If, however, you can't change the situation in externals, you can only do your best and stop comparing it with someone else's best.

'When he was at the height of the two-year-old stage I felt really disconnected from my son, having felt very connected to him as a breastfed baby. I didn't know how to deal with a two-year-old, nor the anger and frustration some of his behaviour evoked in me. I didn't know how to empathise with him and see the world through two-year-old eyes. My husband seemed to do some of this instinctively and my son and husband seemed to have a more special bond. It made me sad.

I realised in the end that some of it went right back to son's birth and early feeding problems and difficulty I'd had "bonding", whatever that means. So I took some steps to address that, to put it in the past and it helped.'

(*Grendle*)

'My mother was fairly perfect with small children (from anecdotal evidence, I can't remember that far back) and awful with teenagers (I remember that only too well). So I had an idea as to what "Mothering" was about, and prior to having children knew perfectly well that wasn't me. I'm not patient and I don't enjoy arty stuff or make believe or repetition. I like my own space and I have a strong need to achieve. So I knew I was no earth mother, and that I'd be going back to work and leaving the children with someone who was good at and enjoyed baby stuff. However I still found a huge pressure (from me, not anyone else) to be this great mum, and not surprisingly I really wasn't and got frustrated when I tried to do the things I thought I should. It was my husband who reminded me that it wasn't in me to mother babies in that way. I can do it, but I don't enjoy it, so after a short time it makes me very grumpy. He's much more laid back, enjoys the children doing little things more and just isn't driven the same way that I am. So he is better at some aspects of parenting than me. Yes that's irritating, but that's how it is. For me going back to work confirmed that that was the right choice for us, and indeed when I took some time out of work a year ago too. But my children are happy and we have a good relationship.'

(nooka)

It helps to remember that all children are not equally easy or equally easy for you personally to deal with. Once you are the parent of several older children, you tend to have had this vividly demonstrated to you. A robust pugnacious parent may relish a combative six-year-old, but struggle with an anxious neurasthenic eight-year-old. And so on through all the different and complex varieties of parent and child.

And children's conduct varies too. You cannot remake a toddler or a teenager or any child so that he behaves well and delightfully all the time. You can only survive until he gets older. Most children go through some extremely difficult phases. During those phases, try to make sure you conserve energy to cope and cultivate a state of mind such that your whole day is not wrecked by a tantrum or some surliness, rather than constantly and wearingly trying to *mend* a child whom only time will change.

You shouldn't compare yourself unfavourably with a parent who does less childcare than you. The more time you spend with your kids the more time you have in which to feel like a terrible parent. And the more time you spend with a child, the more he will feel he can lavish his less attractive behaviour on you – it is a compliment of sorts.

Similarly, it is often the day of delirious treats which culminates in the most filthy behaviour. The unfairness of this can stick in your craw, especially when you have fondly imagined the infant delight which will be created by the enjoyments you have elaborately constructed. And like many things about being a parent yourself, this can reconfigure your view of your own parents and their methodology:

'I am compelled to quote my own parents:
   "It's been a long day and you've had a lot of treats and now you are starting to show off!" I swore I'd never say it myself <<sigh>>.'

(MiladyDiScorchio)

Sometimes the answer is to reduce your ambitions for fun for a while at least and let your children experience what one parent described as 'low-grade misery' and others call productive boredom. Every single day at the weekend or in school holidays need not be a fiesta of fun. And don't expect too much from the gala events – the parties, the days at theme parks and the late-night-with-DVDs-hot-chocolate-and-crisps-fests, or, God help us, the sleepovers. Especially don't expect gratitude.

As a parent, sometimes you will be crap, so don't set the bar too high. Which is not to say you don't pick yourself up and try not to shout the next time but don't lie awake picking over the harm you think you've done. Make mistakes, *apologise*, and move on. (And see 'How to be better' if you think you are likely to repeat the mistakes.)

And it can help you to keep your pecker up to bear in mind that your children won't remember what you think they are going to remember. You can't programme beeyootiful memories for them:

'My dad always laughs that we remember family holidays so nicely and he remembers them fraught, full of cross words and embouteillages. I remember the poppyseed by my grammy's gate to this day. My mum couldn't remember any poppies. You can't control memory. You are parenting today not for tomorrow, that's very Hallmark.'

(AlaskaNebraska)

'I hardly remember ANYTHING of my childhood. Imagine if my parents were doing year-round water fights and pizzas and stuff so I could have happy memories. And all I remember is my toy farm and a nasty kagoul I didn't like.'

(CoupleofKooks)

Remember that your partner brings different things to the whole parenting ragbag; it's not a competition between you. And perversely, being a kinder more patient parent doesn't always make you a more popular one:

'My husband is a gifted parent. He plays gently, imaginatively and with total engagement in a way that I find trickier. He is also a teacher. It is a standing joke with us now that he is at his most perfect as a parent in June just before the schools break up here. By then, confined mainly to post-dinner playing, he is prone to undermining the team. A few weeks into the summer, when he is working but in the house more, his patience is tested regularly and his ideas about how parenting functions become more realistic. He is a better parent than me because he is calmer. But I work damn hard as a parent and my children adore me too for different qualities than the ones he has.'

(*UndeadLentil*)

'My partner is a full-time dad and I work full time. He is pretty perfect. He draws with our daughter (age four), does crafts, takes her out, is fantastic with her. I am grumpier, more boring, can't draw and am knackered after work, and keep trying to make her read and grilling her about school. I'm the one who does time out, he distracts her (usually successfully). And yet when I come home from work she's all over me and pretty much ignores him. Often she starts saying "Me and Mummy will play at the weekend . . . and Daddy can't come." He's even fine with that and says it's natural she should want to be with her mum. I could never be so gracious if I'd been at home cutting out pictures of Madeline all day.'

(*AllyOodle*)

The bottom line is you can't be someone else altogether. You can adjust the way you do things and try to do them better. But even if you read all the parenting books and utterly reprogrammed yourself, you would be a hollow shell of a person talking sanitised parent-speak. And your kids would see through your manufactured cyborg self anyway.

'I do almost all the bad stuff everyone has listed.
    Surely the most important thing is to be a human being and recognise that your child is a human being? Human beings are riddled with faults, flaws and insecurities . . . and you go on loving them anyway. Bugger off all of you with your over-earnest, listeny, listeny, humourless parenting. Be sympathetic and

loving when they make mistakes, encouraging when they do well. But most of all, teach them how to laugh, at life and at themselves.'

(Swedes)

How to be better

Turning around a situation which is rapidly going bad

These are some Mumsnetters' techniques for dealing with the red mist which descends and leaves you shouting at, saying something horrible to, or deliberately hurting a child. If you have gone beyond the occasional loss of temper with a bit of shouting and have actually hurt a child physically, or the shouting itself is out of control and is frightening the child, you need to make a concerted effort to break the pattern.

* Identify flashpoints and plan how you can avoid them if possible, if not, plan what techniques you might use when they arise:

'I've come to the point where I know I am going to do something stupid and I have had to call my husband home from work. But I have done that. I'd rather call him home from work/meetings than slam my children against a wall, which is frankly how I felt at those moments. There were times when I had a crying baby and a three-year-old with night terrors and although rationally I knew I COULD deal with it, I just felt the anger rising.'

(morningpaper)

* Sometimes you can avert the crisis by early intervention:

'So much bad behaviour is attention seeking. When my children are making me mad, the most effective way I know of improving their behaviour is to give them my absolutely full attention. Turn off the telly, sit down with them and read a book, or embark on some craft activity, or play hide-and-seek with them. It need only take fifteen minutes or so and can be incredibly effective at improving everyone's mood.'

(policywonk)

- But don't break your heart and lose your temper if this ploy doesn't work – it doesn't always. Try something else.
- Stop and think before you respond to some piece of infuriating behaviour:

'Two things that have helped me in the past have been: child says something infuriating – leave five secs (1001,1002 . . .) before you respond – enough time to have good-parenting-refresher thoughts . . . or at least to rethink some of the nastiness of your initial reaction. Ask yourself question: is this Very Important? Quite often answer is yes. But sometimes it's no . . . so let those ones go, if you can, sometimes.'

(onebatmother)

- Step away. Have yourself some time out when things get too much for you. Lock yourself in the bathroom. Sit with a coffee and a newspaper. Put on a DVD and bribe your children to be quiet with sweets.

'I think you have to just run the fuck away, don't you? Leave them to destroy the house/each other and go SOMEWHERE ELSE until you can calm down. I have been known to lock myself in the conservatory or go out into the back garden and shut the door so they can't follow me – it wouldn't win me any prizes for parenting but it's better than pushing them about or screaming, I guess.'

(policywonk)

- Find ways of releasing anger safely . . . exercise, beating up a pillow:

'Maybe a timeout would be even more effective if one went out into the garden and ran around it ten times, or did ten push-ups or star jumps or something – would dissipate the adrenalin and have the bonus of making your kids so surprised that they forget to behave badly?'

(policywonk)

- Try to change the mood (yours and theirs). Stick on some music you all like and dance about, or:

'If you feel yourself getting wound up just attack them and tickle them or something, diffuse the situation with laughter.'

(CountessDracula)

'Also the "disarming myself" method – whereby I reach the end of my powers
of containment, and find the only way out is backwards, so to speak, so I drop
my weapons and surrender – hug him, or cry, or just go floppy, as it were.'

(flightattendant)

- Try some fantasies (include TV celebs of your choice). These exercises
  work surprisingly well:

'Imagine yourself as a beautiful, lentil weaving, Ma Walton type mother and after
a while, you start to become the imagined mother! Well, OK, so Ma Walton I
am not BUT there are things I do now which stemmed from this exercise/tip
and now I do them or think them without giving it any thought.'

(RedMist)

'What I find very useful but you may think me a raving nutter for doing, is I imagine
that I'm being filmed for a programme about parenting. I particularly do this at
bathtime, when I'm at a bit of a low ebb, knackered, bored of having the children
all day, and desperate to get them into bed – and they are splashing water over
the floor, refusing to brush teeth, hitting each other with bath toys etc. It was
becoming a bit of a screech-fest and so now I imagine that I have a camera crew
in the corner of the room. It is miraculous. Instead of screeching, "Oh for God's
sake LET ME BRUSH YOUR TEETH – look I'm bigger than you, I'm going to win
even if I have to put you in a headlock, just GIVE UP and LET me," I find myself
saying, "Come on! Shall we sing 'this is the way we brush our teeth'?" in a bright
and happy tone. It really works. For some reason I imagine the person with the
camera crew is Kirstie Allsopp, I don't know what THAT is about . . .'

(PalomaPicasso)

- Debrief after a bad day:

'Oh and we talk through at sleep time. We talk and I say, "You know mummy
was horrible today" and he nods, and I say, "It wasn't your fault. I really do love
you but sometimes I feel worried about . . . and . . . and that means I need to

think and sometimes when you are being noisy I get cross. I should not do it and I am so sorry." Like that, and we hug, and I tell him how much I love him and make silly faces and he laughs, spraying milk everywhere.'

(flightattendant)

- And remember that it's OK for your children to see you expressing negative emotions sometimes, as long as you can (mostly) keep it within limits. That includes sadness as well as anger:

'But, there's a world of difference between *occasionally* shedding the odd tear, or feeling sad and being able to explain to your worried child why you're crying/sad, and very soon restoring your equilibrium (well, at least until after the children have gone to bed when you can cry to your heart's content). It's perfectly possible to be sad, and still be in control of yourself. As opposed to sobbing uncontrollably and being visibly distraught, on a fairly regular basis.'

(LeQueen)

If things are going very wrong

- Recognising that you, rather than your children, are the problem is the first step:

'I think RAGE is much more common than lots of people let on, and when the red mist descends it is very difficult to control it. The first step is acknowledging you are responsible for your anger, the anger is all to do with you and nothing to do with your children or what they do.'

(ahundredtimes)

- Consider whether you have issues to do with your mental and physical health. Depression can often be accompanied by anger.

'I had rage gushing up through me like a volcano when I was depressed.'

(Blu)

Is your anger caused or exacerbated by PMT or perimenopause? Are you affected by Seasonal Affective Disorder? Go and see your GP. We know this is not some instant solution and that you may have to push hard to get the medical attention you really need.

- Do you get enough time to yourself – to exercise, read a book, think, socialise without children? If you don't work outside the home, is that a possibility and might that help?
- Is your diet contributing to your mood? Do you drink too much caffeine or eat too much sugar?
- Make sure you get some exercise:

'Quickly start running. Physical exercise is great for destressing and getting your endorphins working for you. Time to yourself, and control over something – your own body.'

(Blu)

- Sometimes there are practical changes you can make so that you are less stressed generally. If, for example, the problem is that you are stressed and made miserable by mess and lack of organisation in your house – find ways to deal with that. Make a sanctuary – a room in the house which is tidy and orderly and where the children can only go with your permission.
- Share the problem and possible solutions with your partner and/or other family members. What practical and emotional support can they provide to help you get back on track?
- Sometimes the answer is professional intervention – counselling or anger management classes.
- With older children, clarifying the rules and responsibilities can provide a base for improved relationships. Try writing a list of rules and go through them with the children. Hang them up in a public place.

Here's a first draft you might adapt to your own circumstances:

Some general principles

- The grown-ups are in charge. The grown-ups love the children and want what's best for them, even if that's not always obvious.
- Fun activities (including playdates, parties, TV, computer, PSP, football, rugby etc. and anything else the children enjoy) are treats, not entitlements.

- Family rules are for everyone's benefit and everyone has to live by them.
- If the rules are broken then there will be consequences and treats may get taken away, at the discretion of the grown-ups.

Rules and responsibilities

- Children respect the grown-ups, who are in charge. Grown-ups respect children. We all listen to each other and respond appropriately.
- We do not behave violently or aggressively. This includes hitting, punching, kicking, pushing, screaming, yelling etc. and also using threatening behaviour.
- We use good manners. We ask nicely for things and we thank people when they have done something for us. We sit at the table and eat nicely at mealtimes. We wait until it is our turn to speak. We do not interrupt each other.
- We communicate nicely and use nice language. We do not swear or say rude things or call each other names. We do not shout. We talk in a pleasant tone of voice.
- We treat each other kindly. We care about each other's feelings. We are not mean or unkind to or about each other. We look after each other and try to make sure that everyone is happy.
- We do not lie. Especially, we do not lie about our behaviour and whether we have broken the rules.
- We take responsibility for our behaviour. We understand that there are consequences for breaking the rules. If we do break the rules, we accept the consequences without lying or complaining (though we are welcome to negotiate in a grown-up manner).
- We understand that although other people annoy us sometimes, we probably annoy them too. In a family, everyone has to put up with everyone else and get along together.

Some very good parents have fought their way back from horrible losses of control and have come through the tunnel of being very bad parents. We are not great fans of guilt but maybe this is an area where it plays a useful role – because unless you recognise how wrong it is to hurt a child, you are unlikely to start the hard work necessary to make sure you don't do it again.

Put away your mobile, turn off your laptop and don't even think about a BlackBerry or an iPhone

The more there are together, Togetherness recedes.
Louis MacNeice, 'Babel'

Internet twitch – a diagnostic test

Do you ever deprive yourself of sleep because you are looking at Facebook/eBay/Mumsnet/Twitter, playing World of Warcraft, googling old boyfriends/people you were at school with?

Have you ever introduced yourself by a posting name you use on a website? 'Hello, I'm MrsNorksynorkhausen.'

Do you ever dream about other posters on websites or about chat threads?

Do your children think you work on the computer when in fact you have no paid employment?

Have you ever logged on during Christmas dinner/a child's birthday party/a dinner party/sex?

Do you quote posters on websites thus: 'Oh, yes a friend of mine says that you shouldn't wean until three years'?

Do you find yourself thinking in website acronyms?

'I find it difficult not to write DH, DP, DIL on medical notes at work.'
(*Nevergoogle*)

'For every slightly controversial thought or emotion you have, you picture the four letters "AIBU" in your head.'
(*foureleven*)

When your foot spontaneously combusts or your spouse runs away with a colleague, is your first thought 'I must post a thread about this/blog about this/tweet about this/announce this on Mumsnet'? Do your children suggest consulting websites you (over)use?

'Even my son tells me to ask Mumsnet when we're not sure about something, or when he things I am being harsh or unfair.'

(overmydeadbody)

Do your children plead with you to stop being on the internet?

'When my son keeps coming up to me and trying to lift my hands off the computer, saying, "Mummy, no! Computer away."'

(thumbwitch)

'I overheard my daughter telling the baby to hush because "Mummy doesn't like to be disturbed when she is doing her emails."'

(DuchessofAvon)

Has a child of yours ever eaten catfood/matches/contraceptive jelly whilst you were checking your email?

This is you, isn't it? You are reading this book with one eye on Facebook. You are probably drinking Diet Coke with the aid of your third hand and sending text messages with your nose . . .

We understand – we know it crept up on you. It was perfectly virtuous at first – when your baby was new you just turned on the computer to research cures for nappy rash. Then you got involved in a little chat about weaning. You MSNed some people you met on a chat board. And tweeted them. And texted them. And facebooked them. And read their blogs. And before you knew it, you were on the computer/mobile phone pretty much ALL DAY, cosy in some internet granfalloon ('a group of people who outwardly choose or claim to have a shared identity or purpose, but whose mutual association is actually meaningless' – Wikipedia). It was like the funniest notes you ever sent at school. ALL THE TIME.

And your children were wringing their bony hands and trying to open tins of beans with their milk teeth. You may even have done Ironic Posting:

'Many a time I have been reading or posting about "communicate with your child . . . gives lots of attention . . . marvellous mother, me," blah blah blah whilst telling my daughter to "Hush . . . in a minute," whilst she's drowning in the bath.'

(*Tinker*)

There is seemingly no end to our desire to communicate with other adult beings. And we are the first generation for whom there are not merely channels of communication but a veritable ocean of the stuff. For some of us, the internet has become an addiction which is eating up the time we could spend paying attention to our children and our real-life friends, seeing to our abodes and our jobs. And which is depriving us of the productive boredom we need to do something more creative with our hands and brains and hearts . . .

This is not (just) parent-bashing. We have said elsewhere that your children need you to let them be sometimes. They need to wallow in their own boredom and find their own entertainments. But they also need, a reasonable proportion of the time, your focused attention. This will not always be entertaining for you, far from it. And yes, you need to have a cackle and a break and chat to someone who isn't in nappies. But not all day. And you don't need to be in the park constantly texting and messing with your BlackBerry/iPhone either.

And this is not just about your children; it's about you. It's fine to find some comfort and support in the electronic vastness of the world wide web, but you will probably be happier if you find some 'real life' comfort and support as well.

True confessions

'*Every day*, I try to avoid putting on the PC, but always manage to come up with an excuse to myself – bill to pay . . . train time to check . . . important email to send . . . then inevitably, I get sucked in. I'm ALWAYS sneaking away to have a wee read . . . my kids call me and I'll be like "Just a MINUTE!" . . . "I'll be down in a second, just going to get some towels", (yeah, and read about stuffed pasta and imaginary erections with a raised eyebrow). I just can't bloody turn it off, and know I have no self-discipline and am selling my kids short. I do love playing with them too, but when I'm down on my hands and knees building a train set or colouring in, I've still got my next fix at the back of my mind, and am not giving them my full attention, there's no denying it.'

(*OrangeSpacedust*)

'I am currently struggling to maintain a conversation with my husband, who has had an iPhone for about three months. He appears to be addicted to using it (for no discernible goal or good). He simply cannot put it down. He attempts to hold conversations and look after our children whilst playing with it and any spare time he gets is immediately filled with iPhone activity. I think he prefers it to real life. He has always had a short attention span and this new phone has filled the previous gap between his concentration and the demands of real life.'

(*Contra*)

Recovery plan

Be of good cheer. You can claw back intimacy, time for work and time for concentrating on your children. Follow our nearly-twelve-step plan:

1) Set 'computer time' for yourself, just as we suggest you do for your kids:

'Set yourself a time when you will go on the computer, and set a time limit – so after I've done (whatever) I'll take a cup of tea up and play on the computer for x minutes then after that I'll (list something else you need/want to do). Stick to it – and try to do it when your children are in bed/out.'

(*jambutty*)

'Just don't turn it on. Play with your children. Go on Mumsnet in the evening.'

(*Oliveoil*)

2) TURN IT OFF when your time for use is over. Do not think of internet footling as something you can do simultaneously with a load of other stuff like cooking and Lego and freelance work. Confine computer usage to solitary leisure time. If you are at home with the children and badly addicted, get your spouse or partner to take your laptop to work with him/her.

'I get my husband to take the laptop to work with him so I can't waste my time on it. Of course, if you have a PC, then that isn't very helpful – unless you are married to the Hulk.'

(pooter)

3) Plan things to do with free time/time with children OUT OF YOUR HOUSE. Do not bring technology with you.
4) Think about what you are missing:

'I reminded myself that my kids are young and fab and I am spending too much time online and not enough with them.'

(Enid)

5) If your children are absorbed in independent play and you are at a loose end, do not always reach for the laptop. Read a book or newspaper, knit, repair a bike, write a book, make bread, plan a cupcake business, file your bunions, work on your tax return, consider starting a commercial space travel company, paste stamps into an album, lift weights, groom a dog, talk to your spouse or partner, learn Russian, do découpage . . .

Because books and hobbies actually are better:

'If you're reading a book and someone starts to speak to you, you put the book down and give them your attention and eye contact. If you're on the PC and someone starts to speak to you, you may listen and answer them but half the time your eyes will still be on the screen. It's the same reason driving while talking on the phone is not a good idea – you are still giving the other person on the phone your attention even when you need it to be on the road. Screens and phones are interactive in a way that books and other hobbies are not.'

(FrannyandZooey)

6) Have another baby. Kidding.

IN THE BEGINNING

Have a baby, not a birth

(YOU CAN HAVE THE DRUGS
IF YOU WANT THEM)

Any of them – crack, smack, skunk, errr frog.

Well, no, you can't. Especially not frog because we made it up. But you can have: gas and air, pethidine or diamorphine, an epidural. OK, they don't sound as much fun (except in the minds of some pharmaceutical enthusiasts amongst us who still feel nostalgic about the pethidine) but you might want them and there is no shame in taking them. THERE IS NO SHAME IN TAKING THE DRUGS.

We are certainly not saying that everyone needs the drugs. And we recognise that some births are unnecessarily medicalised and that one intervention can lead to a cascade. And of course some people have the drugs and hate them – they would prefer the pain to the numbness of an epidural or the trippiness of pethidine. 'Drugs scare the crap out of me,' as one mother delicately puts it. But you certainly shouldn't feel pressurised *not* to have the drugs. Or that you have somehow failed because you didn't manage your pain by assuming the downward dog position and controlling your breathing. Some women seem to be pre- or postnatally dogged by:

'Birth bores who think any analgesia is a failure, oft heard muttering "why can't these women chant an incantation and breathe really deeply like the *madeup-picus* tribe?"'

(*scottishmummy*)

Perhaps, though, many of these 'birth bores' are just making conversation, albeit somewhat ineptly. And sometimes, as we have gently suggested elsewhere, the newly-delivered-of-offspring listener is just a little oversensitive:

'I personally love to stop mothers, complete strangers, in the street and tell them that I had no pain relief for my labour. Similarly, at parties, I make a point of slipping into conversation, apropos of nothing, that my birth was drug-free. I'm just desperate for that extra validation.'

(independiente)

The truth is that every birth is different and everyone experiences pain differently. And you cannot really know how it will be for you until you are in the midst of it. Nor can you really plan for the complications which may lead you to want analgesia or to require intervention in the form of induction, caesarean section, forceps, ventouse . . . This is an issue which is larger than the drugs but interrelated. Many women hope for a birth which is free of both analgesia and intervention. And it is undoubtedly the case that a relaxed mother who is properly supported is less likely to require some types of intervention. But although you can tweak the odds a bit, in the end birth is a crapshoot.

So what we say is this – it is disappointing not to have the birth you had hoped for and a difficult birth may be very traumatic. Hell, a perfectly common-or-garden birth may be very traumatic. But you have not failed in some way because things didn't go the way you hoped. One woman may feel proud because she has given birth with the minimum of help. Another woman is equally entitled to feel proud because she got through an intrusive, painful, medicalised birth. There are no medals in these events – 'most intact perineum', 'smoothest second stage', 'least sweary contractions', 'complete absence of faecal emission' – a healthy baby and a healthy non-gibbering mother = a good outcome in this arena.

'With my first son I had an epidural, and felt like a failure afterward, and thought "OMG how can I tell the NCT group?" I have also had a drug-free birth, which was nothing to do with me being better/stronger/having more guts. I don't feel big or clever for having a pain-free/drug-free birth, but I do feel incredibly lucky. I didn't have any drugs because I didn't need them. I was lucky not to need them.'

(LynetteScavo)

'I love that childbirth is about the most macho thing anyone can do and it's only women who can do it.

Let's all recognise that's it's effing hard however it's done. Well done everybody.'

(*chequersandchess*)

There are lots of techniques which *may* help you cope with pain without drugs – hypnobirthing, breathing and relaxation exercises, the use of water, being able to move around freely during labour etc. Research the options and look at the pros and cons of the various kinds of pain relief. Look at the place you are going to give birth. Find out about the kind of monitoring which is carried out. For many women, knowing a reasonable amount about what is going to happen helps them to feel more in control. Some women do fine with a kind of blind insouciance and their babies slip out on to the kitchen floor whilst they are doing the washing-up. But if you have any tendency to worry you are probably better off educating yourself. And keeping an open mind. You cannot plan for every possible eventuality.

'I think that it is incumbent on us to fully inform ourselves, ask questions, read books, attend classes, read MN, talk to other mothers, midwives, doulas, health-care professionals, and really get to grips with birth.

I always ask my clients to do a worst-case birth plan and a best-case birth plan and then we can meet somewhere in the middle, but it is really important to cover all bases and to think about the "what ifs" of birth.'

(*lulumama*)

'For what it's worth I hated my natural birth, well I hated the medicalised one too, but both hurt and had their bad side. Birth is pretty sore whichever way you do it. But the difference was that after the first one I felt I had "cheated" and after the second I got a lot of "respect" from various people for doing it without anything (not even gas and air). I only refused the gas and air because I didn't reckon it would touch the state I was in! I was begging for an epidural. There wasn't time though.

So in retrospect, yes I got my "no holds barred" experience, so I have exorcised that "failure" demon, but really I shouldn't have had the feeling of having cheated in the first place. I don't know why I did. Perhaps other factors in my own self-image. I hated feeling like I'd done it that way, not the "proper" way. It does feel like a sort of "club" when you've experienced it without any sort of blocking of the pain, no idea why – I suppose like people who have jumped off tall buildings might feel a sense of comradeship (if they are still alive that is!)'

(flightattendant2)

Lock visitors out after the birth

As a social occasion, the arrival of a new baby can be an uncomfortable mixture of, say, a wedding and a gallbladder removal (including the run-up thereto): a lot of anxiety and pain, hopefully much euphoria, some flowers and some bloody sheets. On the one hand there is a lovely life-changing family celebration and on the other there is what may have been a medically difficult birth or a major operation. The result can be that family and friends of the new parents are excited about the former without really giving proper consideration to the person at the centre of the latter. And people often do just want to be close to the everyday miracle of birth and to see the newborn whilst he is still new, before he loses his first squashed alien look or the golden tan of mild jaundice. All of which can cause some tension, some missteps and for some women a disappointing or stressful experience of the very early hours or days after giving birth.

Some women find they are euphoric with adrenalin, hormones and whatever is left of the drugs and are delighted to have company and to show their babies off. They have families who come at convenient times bearing food and gifts, make them feel good about themselves and their baby and stay long enough to make themselves a cup of tea and unstack the dishwasher. Before we get into moaning too much about the inept or downright terrible visitors we should be clear that postnatal visitors can be a very great joy. It is happiness they have come to share.

Other women report ghastly experiences of postnatal visitation – the colleagues who turn up whilst you are being stitched, the crowd of in-laws who sit about in your home expecting supper to be cooked for them and not letting you hold your own baby. Whilst the new mother is struggling not to bleed all over the furniture and cry because her mother-in-law is telling her she is doing it all wrong.

'A random man from my husband's work came shooting into my room just as I was attempting breastfeeding. He is 6.7 billionth on my list of people I want to see me topless. My only previous contact with him was when he poached one of my best technicians without even the courtesy of setting up a transition period for a replacement. Just thinking about him makes my blood pressure rise so you can imagine my joy when he showed up, and I still don't know why.'

(*MadamDeathStare*)

So you need to think about two things:

1) The fact that you don't know before it happens what the birth will be like and how you will feel.
2) The fact that families and friends vary enormously in terms of tact and helpfulness and indeed relationships with family members are all different.

Bearing the uncertainty in mind, it is usually sensible for you and your husband or partner to tell most people that you would like to play it by ear as to how and when you would like to be visited after the birth. Rational people will understand; irrational people are probably best kept at a distance until you have re-gathered yourself.

Don't have anyone you don't want at the hospital whilst you are in labour

This really is an area where you are entitled to say what you are comfortable with and no one else has any 'rights' which are worthy of even passing consideration. You are the person who has to get a baby's head to emerge from her vagina or have major surgery. This is not a social occasion. You should not feel that people are waiting for you to perform. Or listening to you. If either you or your husband/partner have the sort of relatives who are likely to turn up at the delivery ward uninvited, you may have to adopt the old ploy of simply not telling anyone anything is going on until the baby is born.

'It is the wishes of the labouring woman that are paramount. Women need whatever they need in labour (and you have no idea until it happens how you will feel). Interference or anything that makes you feel anxious can inhibit labour, e.g. even things like bright lights that can't be turned down can have an effect – we are animals, after all, and most animals go somewhere dark and quiet and safe to give birth.'

(edam)

'I would hate for someone to be waiting like this. It would be like sitting on the loo trying to do a poo and a queue of close relatives/friends right outside the door. Most unsettling.'

(LauraIngallsWilder)

And crowds of relatives may be banned from the delivery ward by the hospital in any event (or you can tell them that this is the case). It is good to think about this before the occasion arises and make your wishes clear because there may come a stage in actual labour when you will be welcoming the hospital cleaner in to express a view on how dilated you are. Someone needs to protect you from yourself and if your husband or partner is a bit daft or likely to have freaked out by that time, the only available person may be you – *before you go into labour.*

Home

Folk have very different ideas about what they want in terms of home visitors. Some want to have a 'babymoon' with just the immediate family and the new baby for a week or two. Other new mothers are frankly desperate to have their mothers or their friends around to help with practical things and to make them feel they are not alone with this new dependent creature and the responsibilities which go with it.

Once you know what it is you want, be very clear about what that is. We know that with some families this will cause offence, so try to get your husband/partner to act as the gatekeeper. This may be the first time in his life when he has had to be firm with his parents about any unreasonable expectations they may have (and what parent doesn't have unreasonable expectations sometimes?) It is good for him to practise.

'I know someone who put a red tape cross on their door (like the plague) and a little note saying "Strictly no entrance, new baby in the house, visits by appointment".'

(mumofgiants)

So: if you need visits to be short, if you don't want any home visits at all for a period, if you only want visitors at certain times of day, if you are most certainly not providing meals, these things need to be communicated. Unless you have very tactful and intuitive relatives and friends. Which some people do.

Houseguests

No one should be staying at your house in the early days unless you would find them a help. The likeliest candidates are your own mother or sister. Even if you think you and your mother might be a bit itchy and scratchy together living in the same house, you may well find yourself deeply grateful to have on hand an adult who knows what she is doing vis-à-vis the baby, has seen you naked and having temper tantrums before and with whom you can discuss your need to manually evacuate your bowels due to post-stitch-up constipation.

It can be very difficult to say no in particular to in-laws who are travelling long distances, but if you do not feel it would be helpful to have them as houseguests immediately after the birth, you should be firm. Oftentimes husbands or partners may simply have failed to think through what the situation will be like. Whilst it may cause offence to ask people to stay in a B&B, it will almost certainly cause less damage to the relationship between you and your relatives or in-laws than the resentment you may feel if having them as guests spoils the postnatal period for you. Although try not to get too precious about all this either – some wrongheaded buffoonery by a new grandfather, some tactless interfering by one relative or another, is all part of the great postnatal circus and, whilst it can feel like you extruded your sense of humour with the placenta, it's worth trying to grow it back as soon as you can.

Call your baby
what you like

The naming process, which should be fun, can be surprisingly fraught. And we think it's important because it can be a little rehearsal for some of the bigger decisions you will soon be having to make in relation to your baby, with the same pressures – the desires and opinions of other family members (the other parent in particular) and the unsolicited views of the world at large. So here are our thoughts on how to handle all the opinionators in your life, now and into the future . . .

You don't have to name your baby Reginald even if every male in your husband's family has had that name since 1066

Many mothers feel a kind of visceral indignation when they discover that their partners are expecting to have a significant (or any) say in the naming of the forthcoming child. The primary reasons for this indignation seem to be that:

a) It is the mother whose body has suffered the various ills that pregnant women are all heir to in some degree or other – whether this be some discomfort and stretch marks, continuous vomiting, turning yellow and itching, inability to walk, life-threatening high blood pressure etc. This is before we begin to think about the birth with its accompaniments of pain, tearing, defecation in front of medical staff . . . Surely, we cry, extreme bodily suffering confers some rights?

b) It is likely to be the mother who has devoted time and pages of her diary during adolescence to planning names for her future children. Why should someone who has devoted absolutely no imaginative energy to the topic and who stands around saying 'Er, I quite like

Charlotte [substitute name of old girlfriend here]' expect to be given any air time. WHY???

Some real-life examples of the names we wanted in the days when we still read Just Seventeen

- Bowie and Christabel
- Pagan, Roxanne and Shyloh
- Jasmine Viva Thea Tamara Roxette Taurean Star
- Bliss and Fallon for girls, Miles for a boy (from a Dynasty fan)
- 'From a diary in 1978:
  Patsy Alice
  Joshua Harvey
  Piers Henry
  Theodore James
  Portia Scarlett'
  (*MrsSchadenfreude*)
- 'Zhaine. (It's Jane but with a French-sounding 'j/zh'). (In my defence, I was eleven.)' (*Adair*)
- 'I wanted twin girls: Liberty and Britannia, and a boy: Vinny-Kingston. That's just embarrassing.' (*ChynaDoll2006*)
- 'I wanted two girls – Indie-Mo Mackenzie and Destiny Mae. God knows what I was thinking.' (*flibberttigibbet*)
- 'Sage, Paisley and Ezekiel. I still like Ezekiel. My husband is not having it.'
  (*MPuppykin*)
- 'Had an elaborate game as a teenager with a few friends where we planned (theoretically) to repopulate the world using a gene pool only made up of our 6th-form mates and doing our best to avoid interbreeding. Of course all the hypothetical children needed names. Macbeth and Acid were two I recall, although my personal favourites were the twins, Welwyn and Hatfield. Never used them, of course, though might do in the future with cats!'
  (*LadyWellian*)
- 'I was going to have six children all with a different arty, creative (rock star maybe) father: David (after the statue, the perfect male), I was an art student! Tamar, Salvador, Camellia, Marley, Kestral.' (*Magdalena*)

- 'When I was very very young I thought Silvia was the most glamorous name in the world, but that there should have been a name Goldia too because that would have been even better.' (*fluffles*)

All of which leads one to reflect that perhaps the condition of adolescence is in some way similar to the condition of living in the United States . . . And that possibly the world would be a more entertaining place if we were all compelled to use the names inscribed on the back of our GCSE maths homework.

Perhaps worst of all is when the father of the baby doesn't just lamely (yet persistently and stubbornly) keep raising the small collection of deeply dull names which strike him as an acceptable subset of the names he came across when he was at school, but trots out some family name (his own, his dad's, his grandmother's) which he announces is traditionally always conferred on male/female infants in his family. And that his parents will be sad forever and possibly languish and die if your child is not saddled with this horror.

Now we try generally in this volume to be proponents of compromise, particularly as between parents and with regard to intergenerational tensions. On this topic, however, we say that you are entitled to stand firm, on first names in particular. If you do not want to call your child Gerald, don't do it.

Some things to say to you partner on this topic:
- How would he like it if you insisted on imposing a family name he didn't care for? The traditions of two families come together in the child and there needs to be a compromise.
- Insisting that children be named after fathers is patriarchal crap.

'Tell him your family tradition is to choose a name you like. My ex-husband was the third "blah" and I was briefly put under pressure to have a fourth blah. But I just said I didn't like that name and didn't think it was a good idea to continue a name. The surname is continued, their surname!! Not mine!'

(*ChoreDodgersOnHerBreak*)

- Try to get him to understand why it is important to you to choose:

'There's nothing like the excitement of choosing a name that you and your partner choose to give your child. I found it the best bit of being pregnant, thinking of names! Because lots of stuff is tied up in it; you tend to choose names you love the sound of (obviously) but also I think names say a lot about how you see yourself, and the hopes and dreams you secretly have for your child and what they may be like, what they may do or where they're heading in life . . . it's a lovely gift to give them, I think, their name. Such a shame just to blindly follow traditions that other people have imposed.'

(*CirrhosisByTheSea*)

'I think I would say "you get the piles and you choose the name".'

(*codcodcoddycod*)

- Fuggedaboudit.

This is also, perhaps, a useful time to consider whether your partner needs to start standing up to his parents on issues which are ultimately for you and him to decide. Otherwise you may find yourself facing a series of trivial but enervating battles with your in-laws, flanked by a partner who is struggling to find a way to reconcile his new role as a father with his old role as his parents' child. We are not suggesting you fight with your in-laws. But you can usefully discuss with your partner whether he finds it difficult to contradict/disappoint his parents and how things may arise in relation to your child (names, christening or not christening, the incidence of Christmas visits, the child's haircuts, methods of discipline etc.) in relation to which they will have to be contradicted/disappointed (as tactfully and pleasantly as personalities and circumstances allow). And you can work out how you might deal with these issues. And he may raise similar issues in relation to your own family. But he will probably be wrong about those.

'Frankly, this kind of mother-in-law behaviour needs to be nipped in the bud, or she'll be giving him secret bottles of formula while you try to sort out breast-feeding, choosing nurseries and schools for him, or nipping him off to the hairdresser for a quick restyle.'

(*frogs*)

But back to names. Your secret weapon here is middle names. Middle names are the graveyard where ugly family names go to die or at least to be preserved until a future generation finds them alluring again. It will be difficult for husband/partner/in-laws to maintain the moral high ground if you accept a family name as a middle name. Conferring on a child a middle name which is not your absolute favourite is not really such a hardship, particularly if it makes people in your family very happy. And children themselves are often interested in the connection with the past a family middle name gives them. Even if that name is Gordon. And if you have some entertaining frivolous names you want to use somewhere, bung them in as well. But maybe not too many.

'Our son has an epic name, poor kid (!) – a first and middle name we chose ourselves, then two additional middle names (the names of each of our fathers). I'm glad we did it, though. His additional middle names are rarely if ever used, even on official documentation, but they're on his birth certificate and our families were both chuffed.'

(MrsMattie)

'I think along the lines of "my baby", but if I can do small things which cost me nothing to please others then why not?"

(Communion)

'I like having my grandmother's name as a middle name, and have given it to my daughter as her middle name. I hugely regret not giving my son a family name. I think the *Who Do You Think You Are* programme shows how strong the pull of your family history is. History is what we are.'

(aloha)

If the proposed family names strike you as too gruesome for use even as middle names, consider doing some digging about to see whether there are any more acceptable candidates. Oftentimes your family/in-laws are just looking for some piece of the family to be carried forward and will be pleased and grateful if you achieve this.

'My father-in-law offered me a choice of Reginald or Aubrey as family names. Managed to evade Reginald by pleading a deeply unpleasant Uncle Reg, but Aubrey was looking to be a middle name until my husband and I did a bit of digging and found the family tree was full of Williams. Phew.'

(ravenAK)

'I've used grandparents' names as middle names for my first three, but with number four the last name left was (IMHO) horrible – Ronald (apologies to any Ronald-lovers). So we quietly went back a generation and used Ronald's father's name – everyone's happy and I do like keeping the family name thing going. I'd like to think there will be a little Hassled in a couple of generations' time, and I like that my mother is remembered in my daughter's middle name, especially as she never met her grandchildren.'

(Hassled)

How to arrive at a first name you both like

Some people suggest that one person gets to name the baby if it turns out to be a girl and the other if it is a boy. Or that one of you gets the first child, the other the second. These methods can easily go wrong and lead to bitterness. What is important, we would suggest, is that you arrive at a name neither of you actively hates.

'I disagree with the "she labours therefore she gets carte blanche on choice of names" view. While I would fully support the labouring woman getting the final say in the event of a mild disagreement on names that both partners like, names that one partner actively hates should not be used, in my view.'

(Skegness)

'We have been in the situation of not agreeing about names every time. I think you (we?) DO have to compromise. Because the alternative for us has always been one of us having a name that we loved and the other having one that they hated. Which also didn't seem fair. I like names like Elijah and Otto. My partner likes names like Martin and Geoff.'

(FillyjonkisCALM)

Some things to try:

- One of you drafts a reasonably long and liberal list (so not: Star, Starletta, Starlina) of all the names you like and the other chooses from said list. We suggest you draft the list yourself. This often does not work but it is worth a try. One wheeze is to insert the name you really want amongst contenders you know will be unacceptable, thus:

  'Duke
  Melvyn
  Spongebob
  Thomas
  Chappy
  Beelezebub
  Kermit (as a frog, he was a better man than many men are)'

  (copperjar)

- You sit down together with a baby name book shouting out any name which you like. Other person must count to twenty before providing a considered response to the name. Or you both draw up lists from the book, exchange the lists, cross out all unacceptable names on each other's lists and create a master list which you both consider together.
- Just talk and talk. You may feel you will never get anywhere at all with a man whose first suggestions are Janice and Graeme, but days and weeks of debate will eventually move him on. A bit.
- Remember that even if the name you end up with is a compromise name in the sense that it isn't the one you have lovingly cherished since childhood it will be the name of your child and chances are it will just come to *be* that child and therefore lovely.

And finally, and entirely contradicting the above: a little trick to get past the wrangling over names

This trick requires you to be a little more mentally collected postnatally than you may turn out to be. Nonetheless we are convinced it has worked for many many mothers. Simply assume an air of sweet reasonableness about the name issue in the lead-up to the birth but be vague about what name you might (collectively) ultimately select. If you are convinced your personal best-beloved name will not find favour, keep it confined within your swelling bosom. Then when the baby is born and handed to you, cry (preferably with tears in your eyes) "Kestral!" It would be quite a stubborn and mean-spirited husband/partner who then sought to reopen the issue (although at a rough guess, perhaps 35 per cent of husbands/partners will, despite having witnessed this affecting scene, continue the argument up until you are sitting in front of the registrar six weeks after the birth). Some people suggest that if you have no success in the first instance, you could bite your husband/partner whilst you are having your perineum stitched up but we are not necessarily endorsing that approach. Do watch out for this trick being performed in reverse, bearing in mind that husband/partner will have his wits more about him at this sensitive moment . . .

'Stick to your guns. My personal opinion is that men have dreadful taste in names. Think about clothes, home furnishings, you name it. Heterosexual men have dreadful taste in everything. Previous generations of women evolved many devious and ingenious strategies for dealing with this tactfully.'

(*Cloudhopper*)

Ignore people who hate your baby's name . . . or batter them

'Aren't great-grandparents great . . . my nan (eighty) kept telling family and friends that my daughter was called "Lasagna" for the first week of her life. Her name is Isabella!!'

(*cauiflowersarebuffy*)

There are two scenarios here. In scenario one, you discuss potential names excitedly with people on the bus and post candidates on internet forums. And then every single name you like is trashed because someone thinks it sounds like a name of a vaginal deodorant or someone else had a smelly dog with that name. In scenario two, you announce the name of your new baby to your nearest and dearest and they variously greet it with a pregnant silence, remark that it sounds like the name of the vaginal deodorant or insist on referring to your baby by some other name which they prefer.

Before the birth

Generally speaking you should keep schtum. Why expose something important to you to the world's random memories and musings?

'Most people will be more polite once the baby is here and named. If you are telling them before the baby is born then they still feel they can offer an opinion to change your mind. Moral of the story, as has been said many times on here, is NEVER tell anyone the name before the baby is born.'

(Eglu)

Or try a little bait and switch:

'When I was having my daughter I told everyone that she was going to be called T'Shaaundra after a woman I had seen on *Maury* trying to DNA test sixteen blokes to find out which was her child's father.
     After that, when I told them her real name, they loved it.'

(pagwatch)

Not bouncing your name off everyone you meet doesn't prevent you from doing some necessary research:
- If you are worried about selecting a name which is too popular, consult the top 100 lists for the past few years. But names also tend to breed in little geographical pockets. So if you want to get a feel for what is popular in your neighbourhood, you may have to hang around playgrounds a bit . . .
- Test the candidates out with your surname and be alert for unintended effects such as comic alliteration (Peter Piper) or rhyming (Norman Gorman) or an unfortunate homophone (the perennially hilarious Wayne King . . .) or bad initials (Sarah Teresa Daly).
- What does the name mean? Look on the internet. A surprising number of plausible-sounding names mean 'hairy sword carrier' or 'bringer of darkness'.
- No brand names.
- Can you really face the hassle (for you and your child) caused by an idiosyncratic spelling of a well-known name (e.g. Meghenn)?

- Make sure you are happy with all the customary nicknames for the name you have chosen. If you call your child James, somewhere along the line someone will call him Jim. Do you care?
- Try the 'shouting in playground' test. Will you feel comfortable shouting, 'Come here, Coriolanus!', 'Stop biting that little boy, Agrippa!'?
- Call us stuffy, but we say don't put a nickname on the birth certificate (Nick, Archie, Millie). If you cannot bear the long form, think again or see if there is an alternative (vis Bertie can be Albert, Herbert, Bertram, Bertrand . . .) . You give the child more options and they can use the full version for situations when they require a bit more gravitas.
- In a similar vein, give your girl children names with some dignity. Certainly a girl named Honeychile Flufflepot can grow up to be a High Court judge, but what are you telling her about your expectations?

'I don't like names that remind me of serial killer weirdos in beige macs with fat stubby fingers either. (But there's only one name really does that to me.)'

(*Bucharest*)

Postnatal rudeness

'A friend of mine couldn't get her head round the fact we'd called our son Ned (he's Edward on his birth certificate). For months and months she would do those silly inverted commas in the air with her fingers whenever she said his name! And she didn't even have the excuse of being old . . .'

(*sphil*)

Mostly we would just suggest you just live with postnatal name rudeness. Relatives and close friends are much like the Duchess in *Alice in Wonderland*'s baby – they only do it because they know it teases. If you laugh with or at them, the fun will go out of it. And anyway, what is the point of family life if we can't all wind each other up a bit about matters that are really sensitive and important to us?

'My mother got it into her head that we should call my son Brian (no offence etc. to Brians and Brian-mums, just not my cup of tea) and kept banging on about how he looked like a Brian and calling him Brian BUT it did all die down in the end (although she does occasionally call him Brian still). I am still not sure if she was taking the piss.'

(*GhostofNatt*)

If your family/friends are persistently refusing to use your child's name and it is getting you down, some folk recommend some concerted training:

'My real advice is to just start being very firm and consistent with them. So every time they call him "the baby" or "titch", or whatever they say instead of Elijah, you should butt right in and say loudly, calmly and confidently, "HIS NAME IS ELIJAH." If they make remarks about not liking his name do not attempt to reply to these remarks in any way. Just repeat, loudly and calmly, "His name is Elijah." If possible enlist your husband to say the same thing after you say it to reinforce it. Keep it simple for them and *never* get into any arguments or discussions about his name. They might be old dogs but you can still train 'em. Be persistent, consistent and calm and you will get there.

Elijah really is a lovely name. Nan and Grandad will realise eventually that you were right all along although obviously won't actually admit it. With enough persistent training they will probably think it is a brilliant name that they cleverly suggested to you in the first place.'

(*Podrick*)

Don't buy a
Moses Basket

If, by the time you get pregnant, you have been out in the job market for a while, are a bit jaded by shoes, handbags and iPhones and are relatively cashed up, it can be easy to see the arrival of a baby as an exciting new retail opportunity. Tiny biker jackets! Suede slings! £500-plus buggies! Many women on maternity leave are apparently struck by the notion that what everyone really wants and needs is, for example, a baby codpiece, and so they start a small business through which to sell it. And you are their target market. You are a marketer's dream, virgin territory, marinated in hormones and wildly credulous. And so the world of things you could conceivably buy for a baby increases daily . . .

If you are feeling poor on the other hand, the ranks of appliances, toiletries and soft goods available for newborns can seem like a great mountain of unaffordable buying. And the marketing of it all can leave you feeling baffled and sad.

Either way, we would firmly suggest, you really do not need to buy very much at all. And only buy the bare minimum before the birth because what you actually require in the crucial areas of sleeping and feeding will probably only become clear once you have brought your baby home and experimented with his ways. There is also a reasonable chance that you will receive as gifts some of the more esoteric and adorable items, so stay your hand. Remember that having children makes you poor, poor, poorety poor.

Small is not necessarily beautiful: frivolities no one needs

And these are just representative examples. By the time you read this, someone will have invented an electronic nappy airer or a sling which converts into a stroller with its own integral changing bag.
- Moses basket: a frilly nonsense on a stand suitable for keeping kittens in. A big baby will seem to fill it almost immediately and be busting

out by about ten weeks. Try to borrow one for the early days if they really call to you at that tender stage of pregnancy when you find yourself weeping over a poorly pigeon. There must be millions cluttering lofts and garages across the land.

- Bottle warmer: too slow and a waste of electricity.
- Nappy wrapper bins: tardis-like contraptions for containing used disposable nappies and drowning them in a fragrance created in a lab which is exponentially more offensive than the smell of baby urine and faeces.
- Baby wipe warmer: if it's really that cold, you could always store the wipes on the radiator.
- Top and tail bowl: if you really feel you to have a dedicated vessel for the washing of faces and bottoms, consider some cheap Tupperware from the pound shop.
- Changing table: a whole piece of furniture designed for a task which can be done anywhere at all by whipping out a cheap changing mat. Even if you have back issues which mean you need to change your baby at height, you can stick a changing mat on a chest of drawers.
- Cot bumpers: pointless dust-gathering tat you stick round the bars of the cot. Older babies can use them to vault out of the cot.
- Most baby toiletries: new skin doesn't need all the chemicals to be found in most of the commercially available products. Plain water will generally do for washing in the early months. And a big tub of aqueous cream for dry skin.
- Baby bath: most people get on better with a little stand or (later) a seat you just put in your actual bath. If you have back issues and need to bathe baby from standing, a sink is a better bet if you have one large enough because then you don't have to hoick a large heavy tub of water up to waist height.
- Designer togs and cashmere jumpers: we are all wired to respond to miniaturisation by saying 'awh' and extracting our wallets. But those tiny and beautiful clothes will be worn by creatures who spend much of the day curled up like prawns and simply don't show the garments to any advantage. And many of them will constantly leak curdy sour milk from their mouths onto the cashmere cardigan. Which will then have to be soaked in a bucket of cold water with some special cashmere-preserving cleaner. This is not the life you planned for yourself.

So here, divided up into the various areas of baby activity are our pared-down, after-the-shipwreck bare essentials:

Eating

If you are breastfeeding, you need:
- Breasts, preferably contained in a decent maternity bra (which ideally you have fitted after the birth, but if this is unattainable at least something not uncomfortable that you have ordered off the internet).
- Breast pads, disposable or washable.
- Wait and see what happens with feeding before you rush into buying a breastpump. You may find that you do not end up expressing milk at all.

If you are formula feeding, you need:
- Bottles – you may end up experimenting quite a bit to find a bottle and teat you really like so don't buy a stack before the baby is born.
- Formula. Because formula milk has to comply with government standards as to the basic mix of nutrients, the different brands are probably much of a muchness in terms of quality, so again you can experiment to find one that suits your baby.

Sleeping

- Cellular blankets for swaddling, covering, putting in a pram if you have one.
- If you are sure you don't want to co-sleep, a cot. And cot sheets. Buy a cot-bed for longevity and if you get a second-hand cot make sure that you have a new firm and well-fitted mattress.

Wearing

Don't buy too many outfits – just basic sleep suits, vests and maybe some cardigans. You may well find you get a lot of clothes as gifts.

Cleaning

- 'Definitely get a plastic changing mat. A really simple one is fine. Don't bother with liners, covers, fancy things etc. It's just good to catch the runny newborn poo that will otherwise get all over your floor/bed.'

  (*RuthChan*)
- Disposable wipes or flannels/muslins/reuseable wipes. Or for the early days: cotton wool and water.
- Barrier cream.
- Some small white towels are useful for bathtime.

Travelling

If your baby is going in a car, a modern, age-appropriate car seat. This should either be new or have a verifiable history (i.e. it belonged to your sister or friend). Otherwise, what you need in this department depends a lot on your lifestyle. People who travel much in cars often like 'travel systems', heavy machinery which does the job of car seat, lie-down pram and pushchair all in one. People who travel much on buses ultimately generally want a lightweight foldable stroller unless they are dedicated long-term sling users. If this is you, try to borrow or buy cheaply a lie-down pram you can perambulate slowly in the park with in the early days.

'Entertainment'

Bouncy chair or baby gym or swing – somewhere you can safely put the baby down so he might not scream whilst you go for a wee. New babies don't need much in the way of 'toys' and actually you can provide a lot of toy variety by visiting a toy library.

That's all folks, almost . . .

'Actually, that's reminded me, I made a box of "essentials" for my friend after her son was born that included a travel mug for drinking coffee over a baby's head, that's another essential IMO!'

  (*Chrpygirl*)

Don't heed
the gurus

Do I contradict myself?
Very well, then I contradict myself,
(I am large, I contain multitudes.)

Walt Whitman, 'Song of Myself'

If we could rewind you to the beginning, we would say: don't buy the books. But we suspect, if you are sitting reading this book, that it's too late for you and parenting books. So, if that onion is already irretrievably fried, what we want to say is look at those books with a very cold and critical eye and borrow from them only that which is genuinely useful to you.

In no other area of your life, we suspect, have you gone to the book-shop, selected a book and applied its philosophy and method in its entirety. 'Yes, we are applying the John Snodgrass method to our holidays! It's marvellous. We are never bored and subject to existential angst on the beach these days!' 'I am a Carol Snookist in terms of how I organise my relationships with my friends! I think we are all much happier for it.' No.

Parodying the whole market only a little, the books tend to fall into two camps:

a) The sort-your-baby/child-out-with-some-stiff-scheduling-and-firm-boundaries style
b) The child-centred, wisdom-of-ancient-peoples style

Here are our reflections on these broad styles and what might be in them for you.

Parenting book type 1: Don't feel you have to do a routine

So what is a routine anyway? Many of us may think of ourselves as spontaneous routine-free kinda guys. But we have nothing on newborns. A very brief if mildly discomfiting thought experiment which makes this point is to imagine an adult behaving as a newborn does. Start with any hour of the day. You wake up on your sofa or perhaps in your car, maybe on a park bench or in a supermarket after a half-hour's sleep, start snacking on some toast (which is handily dangling in front of your face, although you might have to bash at the bag it's in or shout to get it to come out). Then you fall asleep on your bag of toast. You wake up again, possibly now somewhere else completely, after twenty minutes and weep, then start eating toast again. You stare at some stuff for a while then fall asleep for a couple of hours, during which time you wet yourself. And so on, round the clock, with no distinction between night and day. Actually, that's quite scary.

At its most minimal, then, a routine is just a fragile, barely-there structure to the day such as pretty much all adults possess. There is a part of the day (night-time) when sleeping generally occurs in a block. And some rough slots when meals take place. That's all.

But a *baby routine* as set out in some childcare books may be a veritable cathedral of a structure compared with the little huts of routine which most of us live in (outside of the imposed warehouses of organised time represented by work and school). Some books offer very elaborate routines with very laudable goals – that your baby will have the right amount of nutrition, will have the correct amount of sleep for health and happiness, will develop properly and will sleep through the night at the earliest reasonable time. Feeding, napping (and sometimes your own consumption of liquids) are timetabled in these routines.

The problem with some of the books written by parenting 'experts' is simply that the subject matter is so very sensitive. If someone produces a book telling you how to regrout your bathroom which suggests that there is a much better method than the one you used when you actually regrouted your bathroom six months ago, or is so complicated and hard for you to follow that you splodge along regrouting in the slightly shite way you thought you planned to do before you bought the book, you may be annoyed but you are probably not going to find the book personally wounding. But if the book is about your *baby, this tiny human being for whose health and happiness and future development you are primarily respon-sible*, it can seriously mess with your mental health. Any piece of advice can feel like a devastating criticism of what you are in fact doing/have done.

And some of the books are very keen to warn you about bad habits you and your baby might develop or 'traps' you might fall into or bloody rods for your back you might unwittingly construct. Because why would you buy the book at all if you weren't at risk of doing stuff wrong in the first place?

'I read one of the better-known books in the last twenty-four hours before my son was born, and spent six weeks worried because I couldn't express six ounces of milk before my slice of toast at 7 a.m. . . . .'

(*alibag*)

So here is what we say about routines. Some mothers and some babies thrive on the routines in the books (almost invariably tweaked to suit). If you like order, structure and control and your pre-baby life provided you with these things, it can be hard to throw it all away:

'Both my children thrived on routine and so did I. It is an unpopular view but the baby does have to fit in with the rest of the family to a degree. The best thing you can give your children is happy parents. Some people hate the idea of a routine, however relaxed, and some people, like me, couldn't really cope without one. I really don't think there is anything wrong with living by the clock unless you take it to a ridiculous extreme. (I don't think there is anything wrong with not having a routine either.)'

(*alucard*)

'Ha, well get your head round this. I fed my son on demand purely because I had never heard of Gina Ford, and the midwife had told me that that is what you do. You feed them on demand. So I did. Within two weeks the little blighter had put himself into a Gina Ford routine. I don't know how, and I don't know why. Actually an airy floaty easygoing baby would have suited me better. My point? None at all. My conclusion? Babies do whatever the hell they want to do, and if you don't let them, they make your life miserable until you do.'

(*colditz*)

However, if you do follow a very set routine or your baby makes one up for himself, expect the routine to periodically dismantle itself and a new routine to emerge. Growth spurts, teething, weaning, illness and vaccinations all mess about with routines.

For other babies and mothers, the off-the-peg routines are hopeless. Some babies are too hungry to wait as long for feeds as a prescriptive routine might require. Or have no intention of sleeping at the proposed naptimes. Or in anything remotely resembling the suggested pattern. If you are not attracted by the routine books, don't touch them. Don't buy them, don't get them out of the library, don't let anyone leave one at your house:

'I spent ages trying to get my son into a routine when he was a baby – wrote everything down obsessively, read all the books and was a slave to getting him into a routine that frankly prevented me from just getting on with life. My daughter has been routineless from the start and I've enjoyed it so much more. She had to fit in around the school run routine anyway but just does what we're doing when we do it. A ring sling, breastfeeding on demand, co-sleeping and baby-led weaning have all made life so much easier. Hurrray for hippy parenting!'

(*treacletart*)

'I see that your TERROR occurred AFTER you had read the book. Your mistake was to READ THE BOOK. I have a toddler who has a dummy and still occasionally co-sleeps. But I also have a five-year-old who does neither. They grow up – make the most of your baby time! It doesn't last very long.'

(*morningpaper*)

And remember: not having a set routine may give you much more freedom to be out and about with a baby who happily sleeps and eats wherever he is at whatever time he is hungry or sleepy. In any case, without following any book at all, even the most free-range baby can usually be gradually nudged towards what may feel like a more civilised pattern of sleeping and feeding. After the first chaotic weeks, many parents want to develop at least some minimal fixed points, an actual bedtime, for example. Remember you can have a bit of a pattern to the day without having a rigid timetable. And some babies themselves seem to yearn for a more structured way of living which they need your help to find:

'We nudged both sons into a routine of feeding every 3 hours. It was loose in the sense that if they wanted feeding less than 2 hours after the last feed, we distracted them (and then fed them if they would not be distracted!!) and didn't let them go more than about 4 hours between feeds.'

(*SoupDragon*)

Similarly, the little bits of daytime sleeping some very young babies do can be gathered up gradually into some longer naps. This stuff really tends to happen anyway if you wait:

'I'm of the opinion that until twelve weeks, do nothing, then after that, watch the child and try to spot what his natural routine is, and go with it as much as possible . . . when they are at about six months, have worked out their routine and you are used to it, then tweak it to fit *your* needs.'

(*Flamesparrow*)

Whatever you choose or don't choose in terms of your management of feeding and sleeping, remember that it is absolutely right and proper to consider your own health, well-being and sanity in all of this:

'I parent in the way that I consider to be focused on the well-being of my children, in the short and long term. My children's well-being wouldn't be served by me getting very little sleep, or them being unable to self-soothe, or me not having sex with my husband, or feeling utterly unable to have any time to myself.'

(*Jamieandhismagictorch*)

And finally, do not forget that breastfeeding 'advice' given in many routine guru books is pants. Consult a specialist breastfeeding book or counsellor for good advice on breastfeeding.

Parenting book type 2: You don't have to 'wear' your baby all the time

Those of us who get squeamish about neologisms get particularly squeamish about 'babywearing'. Which sounds like you are toting your baby about like a handbag or somehow putting your arms through him like a cardigan.

But all it really means is carrying him in a sling of some sort. Although when people actually call it 'babywearing', they may be referring to the constant carrying of the baby in a sling as part of some overall philosophy of parenting, probably 'attachment parenting' or its anthropological fore-bear the 'continuum concept'. Here's a brief synopsis:

'There aren't that many differences between attachment parenting and the continuum concept. Both include babywearing, breastfeeding, co-sleeping and generally being close to the baby. However, attachment parenting tends to be a bit more baby-centred, and the continuum concept tends to be a bit more parent-centred, if I've read them both right. In the continuum concept model you do carry the baby around with you but it's while you get on with the rest of your life, so that the baby is almost a satellite to the mother. You'd get on with your housework with the baby in a sling but not be too fussed about having to interact constantly with the baby.'

(*MerryXMoss*)

But carrying your baby in a sling does not need to be part of some grand philosophy. And we would venture to suggest that how you move your baby about is not actually terribly significant as a parenting choice.

'As for thinking products define you or add heroic qualities. It is only a fucking sling, it doesn't make you earth mother. Get over it.'

(*scottishmummy*)

There are, of course, some very good things about slings for sling-lovers:
- You have your hands free to do other stuff whilst baby sleeps or feeds in his sling.
- You can nip about with the baby attached to you without worrying about the Horror that is Taking a Pram on Public Transport.
- If you have a baby and young toddler you can get about without using a double buggy.
- Some parents find a sling indispensable with a very cuddly baby:

'I used to because it was literally the only way I could do anything. My son had to be held twenty-four hours a day.'

(*NineUnlikelyTales*)

- Wearing a sling can be a good upper body workout but make sure you are not doing your back in with the wrong sling or the wrong 'carry'.
- Slinging the newborn can also allow you to spend more time with an older sibling:

'My older daughters far preferred the baby being quiet and snuggled in a sling so that I *could* get on and read books/play games/do craft/cooking etc. with them as opposed to the alternative. Which was the baby screaming her head off upstairs with me tense because one of my kids is upset.'

(*Loopymumsy*)

- A sling is useful for doing the colic dance with a colicky baby.

But some people go off their heads being strapped to their babies all day. It is not wrong to want some physical free time. Some time to rest. There is a balance to be struck between your needs and the baby's. And a wretched, exhausted, fed-up parent is not the best parent anyway:

'I don't want to be clung to, that's why. I *hate* being clung to. So I decided early on that I wasn't going to be clung to. And my children (and I know this is at least partially luck) don't cling. I am pretty certain that if my second son had been allowed to be carried everywhere, he would have been perfectly happy to be carried everywhere. But I didn't *want* to carry him everywhere. I wanted to put him down and do something *else*.

It doesn't mean I don't love him – I do. Deeply. And I would kill for him. But demand feeding past the age of one – Not Happening. Ditto being carried everywhere.'

(*colditz*)

And some babies are like some grown-ups – they want to be in their own personal space. Some babies just aren't that cuddly:

'I know all babies are different. My first son got held until he howled to be put *down* (after about five minutes) and I don't know why he was like that.'

(*colditz*)

'Most of us do what WE can do with the personality of the baby we get – there are very few parents who struggle against the grain of either their own personality or the child's, with heroic results.'

(*Prunerz*)

Other people find that it's just uncomfortable carrying anything other than a very tiny baby. Don't walk around with a bloody great toddler tied to you for the sake of some parenting notion.

How you convey your baby from place to place (and whether you are in constant physical contact with him) just isn't the be-all and end-all. And remember that, even with very clingy babies, the period when they want to be attached to you round the clock is likely to be relatively short. After that they need some time to exercise their muscles independently.

There is a larger message here. The need to find some kind of accommodation between the kind of person you are and the kind of person your baby is applies to many other areas including the overlapping and sometimes overwhelming issue of sleep:

'I think that you have to recognise that different babies and different parents are different. I had one baby who liked to be swaddled and left on his own to go to sleep, who enjoyed rolling around on the floor and was all in all very independent. He did scream a bit when left to go to sleep, but to a definite rhythm, so that you could pretty much predict when he found his thumb, and when he'd go to sleep (took maybe five mins). If you tried holding him during that time he'd flail around and not go to sleep at all, with the result being one tired and cranky baby. With my daughter on the other hand she was very very clingy, she'd cry for what seemed like ages (not in a screamy way, just persistent) and not only did she want to be held, but she wanted to be walked around (she'd scream in your arms if you tried to sit down, or just stopped walking/swaying etc.).

For me, my son was an easy baby, and my daughter was a nightmare. Now if I'd been a "isn't it lovely my baby needs me so?" sort of person, then I might well have felt the reverse, but I'm not terribly keen on babies (I much prefer children) and I found my daughter suffocating and frustrating. It's all very well to say that everyone should love to have their child attached to them at all times, but what if you hate that? If you find permanent feeding exhausting and sharing a bed = no sleep at all? I watched my big sister and my aunt take a demand/attachment approach, and saw how totally exhausted they were and thought "not for me".'

(nooka)

And a word about prams

Prams are not, contrary to the pronouncements of some opinionators, 'mobile baby prisons'. Some babies love their prams, they stretch out their curly arms and legs and sigh themselves to sleep as the wheels gently bounce over paving stones and ditches and dogshit. Think of the bliss of sleeping on a train. When they are awake, they watch the sun making patterns in the leaves overhead. Prams can be lovely.

And buggies, even the much-maligned front-facing buggies, are the means by which child and parent may be enabled to travel long distances and have greater adventures than are available to you in your own immediate neighbourhood. They are ecologically friendly. Pushing one is good exercise.

And you know what, we say use them as long as you damn well like. If you regularly walk long distances which your three- to four-year-old can't manage, you can take your buggy. And you can hang your shopping on it. It is nobody else's business and using a buggy sometimes for a preschool child doesn't mean you are going to end up with a morbidly obese kid who can't walk. As long as you have a modicum of sense and let him out sometimes.

You don't have to 'get your figure back' six weeks after the birth

There is a widely held belief that French women go for their postnatal medical checks and the doctor talks to them about how swiftly they can fit back into their bikinis and thus preserve their marriages. They presumably then go away and live on cigarettes and low-fat *yaourts* as advertised on French television by slim naked women and thus avoid *le divorce* (which sounds quite glamorous in French, but we digress). This may well be an urban myth. Or maybe it is not even a widely held belief and is just something we made up in our heads whilst on holiday goggling at lithe French mothers tossing their toddlers about in the sea. What is undoubtedly the case is that every starlet and TV presenter and WAG who has a baby is pictured in the tabloids within six weeks, looking 'curvy' (= tabloid for fat, lazy and bad) after childbirth or, having pilated and personal trainered her way back to her prenatal shape (= vain, evincing lack of care for her infant and bad but good but bad).

So what we say is that in the early days you should let yourself be. Let your body recover. Let your life recover. Establish breastfeeding. Get used to your new sleep pattern. Or to never sleeping again until you are quite old. And frankly, 'early days' means different things for different people – it may be the first six months, it may be much longer. Otherwise 'I must fit back into these jeans' turns into yet another stick you beat yourself with. And you may either be back at work with no spare time or at home with baby with no spare time and no energy.

'I was still more than a stone overweight when my son was nine months old, and to be honest the thought of exercising/dieting up to that point was furthest from my mind, I just felt so tired and lethargic looking after baby.'

(*Jodee*)

Breastfeeding has different effects on different people. You might think that the baby is really just sucking those doughnuts out through your breasts but it ain't so. Breastfeeding, for some of us, engenders the most profound hunger, a hunger not satisfied by a baked potato and a salad but only slaked by a whole bag of truly delicious funsized choc bars (and really chocolate of any size is never more fun than when you are breastfeeding). People in this category tend to gain rather than lose weight during breast-feeding. Sometimes many doughnuts-worth of weight.

And then there are people like supermodel Giscle and some other simi-lar folk who find the small vestiges of baby fat literally slide from their person and disappear in a greasy trail down the gutter. Or something like that. Not that any of us on the funsized choc bar end of the spectrum feel any resentment about this disparity of outcomes. No.

Having said that you mustn't feel you have to rush to lose the extra weight, for many people there does come a time when one's postnatal body seems an affront to one's sense of oneself and a bit of tweaking is OK too. As long as you don't become frenzied about it.

So we say go for a gradual approach. Try lots of walking with the pram – this is good for both mental and physical well-being. So is swimming. Yoga classes can be good for toning and relaxation if you have a hope of getting to one. Otherwise exercise DVDs are good unless they cause you existential angst or simply make you feel foolish. Exercise you enjoy is exercise you will keep doing.

And some thoughts on eating:

- Don't do a very low-calorie diet or one which involves cutting out whole food groups.
- Don't keep crisps and sweets and biscuits etc. in the house. At least if you have to walk to a shop to get them, you have time to reconsider.
- Keeping a food diary can be a shocking revelation as to quite how many slices of peanut butter toast you are consuming.
- Having a day off from watching what you eat once a week is appar-ently a good thing.
- Some folk thrive at slimming clubs. If you think you would be helped by some group support, give it a try.

Whilst you are transitional, finding some clothes that don't make you look like Humpty Dumpty will probably make you feel better. Dresses and tops which come in somewhere under the bustline and drape around the flappy floppy abdominal region are good. With leggings, tights or narrow trousers (jeggings even). And some attention to peripherals will distract attention from your middle – a haircut, some nice boots (winter) or sandals and some nail varnish (summer). Accessories if you are an accessory person (but if you weren't one before you gave birth, you aren't one now and if you try you are just going to look like mad-scarves-and-bangles-woman so don't do it).

Although you might just want to heed the lugubrious words of one suspicious mother:

'I don't trust women with small children who look good. I think they must lock the children in the cellar while they get ready or something – I could never manage it.'

(*BananaSkin*)

Don't feed your baby in lavatories

We live in a very odd society in which our children see naked silicone-filled breasts intended for the sexual titillation of adult men on the lower shelves of newsagents but many adults think a woman should only breastfeed at home or in a lavatory or a room specially designated for feeding babies and wiping their bottoms. So we say, loud and proud: public breastfeeding is a feminist issue. Women should not stay at home becoming depressed because they feel they have to put themselves into breastfeeding purdah and daren't venture too far from a baby feeding and changing room. You are entitled to feed your baby anywhere he needs to be fed and where it is safe for you to do so. But it is also true to say that many of us reach the childbearing stage of things having got used to keeping our breasts under our jumpers. So public breastfeeding mixes up our feelings about our right to feed our children when and where they need to be fed with our feelings about our bodies and privacy in ways which can make it difficult to know how to go about what should be a straightforward and natural activity.

The discretion thing

So here's what we think about scarves, pashminas, 'hooter-hiders' and the whole question of feeding discreetly in public.

It is a great and good thing that some women don't feel the need to be excessively covered up about breastfeeding in public because we are never going to be a society where children see breastfeeding as a normal and natural thing and adults are unembarrassed by it without lots of public breastfeeding going on *which people actually notice*. Unlike the very large amount of it which nobody notices because it is done 'discreetly':

'I prefer to lob the whole breast out wherever possible. Just in case someone at the back of the bus may have missed the chance to be offended, I sometimes remove my top and also my bra just so they can get a really good look.'

(*FrannyandZooey*)

Sometimes, total discretion is impossible anyway, usually because the baby is small and/or the mother is inexperienced at breastfeeding and they are both getting used to latching on:

'Ha. I'm also one of those who could never be discreet. Just couldn't do it, I was too incompetent. I remember once when my son was about three months in Orpington High Street, when he just went mental and sucked and sucked and sucked, then came suddenly off my breast and the milk just arched out in a fountain. Orpington woman was shocked. But what would you do if your nipple just sent out a fountain of milk? TBH I was so surprised by it and busy making sure the milk didn't go all over my clothes, that it was only about thirty seconds later I realised that I wasn't being discreet. Who are these women whose first reaction to something unexpected is an immediate, effortless, strategic draping of an elegant pashmina? I'd love to be like that, but never was.'

(*Caligula*)

And some older babies like to stand up for their mother's right to publicly breastfeed in their own small way:

'My little one likes to whip himself off without any warning but with a great flourish as though he is pulling a rabbit out of a hat, exposing a nipple to the assembled company and beaming widely. He then makes a great fuss about going back on, thrashing around and gulping and snorting loudly in case anyone at the other side of the restaurant/shop/train hasn't spotted the breastfeeding mum.'

(*Squirmyworm*)

For many of us the practice lags behind the theory and whilst we applaud other women stripping to the waist to breastfeed, we aren't quite there yet ourselves. For the likes of us, it is often (subject to the early days and oversupply issues described above) perfectly possible to breastfeed almost everywhere without showing anyone our nipples.

For an awful lot of women the initial shyness about public breastfeeding completely disappears over time. Some women say they just experience their breasts differently during this period:

'I needed to expose my tits quite a lot to get my daughter latched on, because I was never very good at breastfeeding. I swear, you really Do Not Give A Shit when it's your milk and your baby who is crying. I would be mortified to expose my breasts to my pals now, but I know they copped an eyeful when I was feeding the girls. It's a very different thing, your breasts aren't really the same creatures. Or at least that's how I felt anyway.'

(*Aitch Two Oh*)

Remember that although you read the odd horror story about women being asked not to breastfeed or evicted from public places, the anecdotal evidence is that the vast majority of women do not get any hassle at all:

'I keep meaning to print out a stack of business cards saying "thank you for sharing your opinion about breastfeeding" on one side and "now f@@@ off" on the other. However, no one has *ever* approached me anyway and if they did I would ignore them.'

(*SoupDragon*)

'A lady caught my eye as I fed on a bench in the town centre and she veered more towards me and said "That's the most beautiful thing in the world" and walked off. I was beaming for days.'

(*ASecretLemonadeDrinker*)

'A friend was breastfeeding in John Lewis and someone (a woman I think) told her she was disgraceful and should be ashamed of herself. She was quite upset and mentioned it to a passing member of staff. A few minutes later there was an announcement over the store loudspeakers along the lines of "John Lewis fully supports and welcomes breastfeeding mothers in our stores . . . we will not tolerate any harassment of breastfeeding mothers within our stores and we will ask offenders to leave."'

(*marthamoo*)

You don't have to go to baby groups

You are on day seven of being at home alone with an angry pink maggot and a crotch that feels like a road traffic accident. Breasts as taut and as sensitive as colossal boils. Nipples crazed like antique plates. You are a woman on the edge and danger is your middle name. So you hobble down to the health clinic for baby massage class, the maggot dangling in his sling like a larval astronaut. You have to take the maggot's nappy off and you realise he has filled it with mustardy faeces which are also speckling his legs and his back right up to the hairline. And you have no wipes or spare nappies. Or friends. Or any kind of life. Or the will to carry on.

So look, you don't have to go to baby groups. You really don't. Baby groups exist for the sake of parents and carers who want to get out of the house and perhaps chat to someone in similar circumstances to them. Babies themselves have no need to 'socialise' or indeed to listen to music or be massaged en masse on grungy gym mats in a municipal setting. Try asking them whether they want to go. Bear in mind that if you do go to baby groups, you can easily find yourself afflicted by acute social paranoia. Check out the School Gates Rule later on in the book for our theories on the reality of the politics of schools, baby groups and other places where people are brought together on the basis of having offspring of roughly the same age. Remember that a proportion of new mothers won't be their most sparkling or outward-looking selves in these environments.

'She is a fairly recent mum exactly the same as you and quite possibly feeling less than adequate. Cut her some slack, stop judging, don't seek out the bad in people – and you might eventually find one or two kindred spirits to hang out with while you get acquainted with motherhood.'

(*bibbitybobbityhat*)

Another feature of these groups which disturbs some new mothers is the presence of Insane Boasting Mums. These are women who apparently constantly ask other mothers about the size, developmental stage and bowel movements of their babies in order that they can then triumphantly share their own child's statistics. Probably the world population is rich and varied enough that there are genuinely some women who take great pride in having a baby who is a bit bigger than someone else's baby or who feel like grinding their heels in the faces of women whose babies haven't rolled over yet. But we are willing to bet that they are a teeny-tiny proportion of the whole population of new mothers and that there is not a large clique of them in every baby group in the land. We reckon that the vast majority of people asking other people about their babies' nutritional requirements, sleep patterns etc. a) are just desperately trying to find something they have in common with the other person to talk about and b) don't really give a shit what you say about your baby and possibly aren't listening properly to your answers anyway.

Actual conversation:
Insane Boasting Mum: 'So, has your baby started smiling yet?'
You: 'Er, no, she's only two weeks old.'
IBM: 'I am sure Gerontius was smiling around a week . . .'
But inside the heads:
IBM: 'She looks nice, must find something to say. Er . . . Fark, I think this maternity pad is leaking. She looks like she hates me. I hate it here, I want to go back to work, waaah.'
You: 'Argghh, there is something wrong with my baby. Why won't this mean competitive bitch leave me alone?'

Even those who are actually boasting may well just be talking to reassure themselves or because somewhere in their heads they are still delivering a presentation about added value customer solutions.

'One of my friends from NCT classes does the competitive thing. The rest of us smile and ignore it. Because we know her, and know it doesn't mean anything, and because none of us care anyway – she's a nice lady and her little one is a nice child.'

(*cyteen*)

And remember that talking about choices like childcare and weaning is always going to be like two people with no skin poking each other with feather dusters, at least until you all toughen up a bit:

'Personally I find it's really difficult to talk about any of the choices we make as parents without sounding like we're putting someone else's choices down. We all need to cut each other some slack and lighten up.'

(WhatFreshHellIsThis)

The advantage of getting over the initial horror is that baby groups can be a source of pleasant company and reassurance and a way of getting out of the house. They can also be plain old dreary and dispiriting. If you have lots of mates with kids to hang out with, or you like taking your baby to galleries and on long walks, or to lunch with work colleagues, do these things instead. But remember that eventually some of the people at these groups will shuck off their cocoons of baby-induced dullness and potentially be just like you. And if you do want to witter on about rolling and grabbing objects and the pros and cons of bananas as a weaning food, who else is going to listen?

'Re: the constant talking about children – I was so frazzled for much of my son's first 9 months that I couldn't get enough thoughts together for anything else! Even now I find it hard to grab a thought and cling on to it; back when he was waking five times a night for milk there just wasn't space in my head for anything other than banal observations about his latest funny noise.'

(cyteen)

But remember you don't have to stay, if the group is bad or mean. Just because you are paranoid doesn't mean there aren't some socially unpleasant baby groups:

'It's five years since I last did baby groups and I still get twitchy remembering the horror . . . I remember at one particularly impenetrable one asking a group of laughing, chatting mums: "Hello. I don't know anyone else here. I see you all have older babies. Can any of you give me some advice about teething?" (or something innocuous) and they looked at me, said: "No" and carried on talking . . .'

(filthymindedvixen)

It's OK to do controlled crying

(THE RULE WHEREIN WE ALIENATE LOTS OF PARENTS)

It's a terrible name – anything with crying on the tin is going to upset people. If only it could be called rational comforting or something like that. But there it is. Some people on parenting talkboards seem quite sincerely to consider it to be a form of infant torture. Reading a thread about how bad and misguided you are to have tried it can seem the final cruelty as lack of sleep loosens your grip on the shreds and tatters of your parental self-esteem:

'I consider that helping my child to learn to sleep is a gift to him, not cruelty. I have been called evil, cruel, child abuser, all the usual hysterical bullshit, but hey, my child is brilliant and loves me and we're all happy, and get plenty of sleep, so who gives a toss what other people think? Do what you think is right.'

(krang)

You are not a modern-day Torquemada if you do controlled crying. Controlled crying is just a sleep training technique which you might use on a baby over six months old (and some experts say not before twelve months) who is not sleeping for very long periods (i.e. is waking multiple times in the night and compromising your will to live). It is not the same as 'crying it out' which essentially means just letting your baby cry until he falls asleep (we and many other folk consider this to be a bad plan). There are many versions of controlled crying but it usually goes like this:

'In controlled crying, babies aren't left to cry.
    Baby cries.
    Parent comes.
    Parent checks baby is OK, and soothes baby.
    Baby stops crying.
    Parent leaves.
    The whole "controlled" thing is about limiting crying to short intervals, comforting a distressed baby, but not cuddling/feeding/rocking one to sleep.'

(Perkin Warbeck)

'Controlled crying is about reassurance. You put the baby down, it cries. You comfort the baby. Put the baby down, it cries, give it a minute, comfort the baby, continue for however long it takes. It's a process, which might take a long time, it might be over in twenty minutes. If the baby wakes in the middle of the night, you don't necessarily leave him or her to self-settle, you'll listen to the cries, maybe wait a minute or two, use your instinct and common sense.'

(ohforfoxsake)

The best-known version of this technique is found in Dr Richard Ferber's book *Solve Your Child's Sleep Problems*. The Ferber version involves returning to the baby at set intervals over a period of nights and not picking the child up. Ferber doesn't recommend controlled crying for all children and he is not opposed to co-sleeping where it is done with appropriate precautions and suits the family involved. We think he comes across as sensible and humane and open-minded.

Why some people don't like controlled crying (*the super-condensed version*)

There are a variety of experts who expound versions of the following ideas (we have simplified the arguments, as you will see if you have a brief google):
- Lack of response from a carer raises the levels of the stress hormone, cortisol, in the brain.
- The infant brain is developing rapidly and excessive quantities of cortisol can influence the way it forms in potentially devastating ways.
- Controlled crying methods are therefore dangerous.

In fact, a little digging around suggests that neuroscientists don't at present know all that much about the detail of how brain formation is affected by experience. And that most of the hard evidence about the effect of deprivation on brain development comes from studies of Romanian orphans subjected to extreme emotional deprivation and neglect. What can we properly derive from those studies? As a neuroscientist called Steve Petersen remarked: 'Don't raise your child in a closet, starve them, or hit them on the head with a frying pan.'

A number of experts have nonetheless hypothesised that much lower levels of deprivation (including crying as a result of controlled crying) can cause problems in later life such as susceptibility to mental illness. With the result that many parents find themselves feeling aghast when they are occasionally clumsy or insensitive in their handling of their babies. And just terrible if they did controlled crying before they came across the views of Penelope Leach. All of which is not particularly excellent for everyone's mental health.

Basically, what it seems to us (as educated non-scientists) to amount to is that there are theories about how controlled crying might damage your baby but no hard evidence that it does. What there also is is a recent Australian study of 225 children from babyhood to age six who had had sleep training. The results of that study suggested that there was no adverse effect on the emotional or behavioural development of the children involved. And the mothers of those sleep-trained children had significantly reduced depression rates. Because actually a parent who is not utterly befuddled from lack of sleep is usually going to be a better and more responsive (and happier) parent:

'On a personal level, I know for a fact that leaving my son to cry for twenty minutes one night, then five minutes the next, when he was six months old meant that I was a far better parent than I had been for the previous two months when he was waking up every forty-five minutes. In fact had I left him to continue on waking me up I think my inability to parent effectively would have been far more damaging.

(*noonki*)

If you decide to sleep train

Look at the different methods available. It's worth reading Ferber, looking at some other techniques such as Tracy Hogg's (*Secrets of the Baby Whisperer*) 'pick up/put down' method of sleep training and having a read of Elizabeth Pantley's *The No Cry Sleep Solution*, which offers a variety of techniques to help a baby or child sleep better without employing any form of controlled crying. Think about what might work best for your baby and for you, the parents. Some people just don't have the stomach for controlled crying.

If you decide to use a controlled crying method be sure that you have understood it properly. We say this as parents who have ourselves struggled to read to the end of sentences and still remember the beginnings whilst battling sleep deprivation. And try to understand why your baby is crying – always make sure that a baby is not crying because of hunger, pain, a dirty and uncomfortable nappy. Many parents say they can distinguish between a distressed cry and an overtired grizzle.

If you are lucky, you will have a child who sorts out his own sleep and you will never have to think about controlled crying or any kind of intervention, or you may be able to do a very mild version with complete success:

'I say I do controlled crying, but in reality I am blessed with a very easy sleeper who usually goes down awake without a peep, but sometimes cries for a few minutes before drifting off. When he cries I'm not going to go in to him because I know he's on the way to sleep and going in would interrupt that. He has slept through since four-five months and before that we co-slept.'

(*kallo2907*)

Others find controlled crying can be done relatively painlessly by structuring it around the baby's sleep patterns:

'A lot of people who use a form of controlled crying DO use the baby's sleep pattern. That's why you wait until they're older. They've shown you when they need to go to bed. That becomes their bedtime. You don't just pick a time. Our babies seemed to be ready to go into their cots between six and seven. So that's where we started. They seemed to like to wake up at half-four or five. So, to start with, we worked towards getting them to sleep from about seven to half-four. The fact that it worked for both of them, so quickly, indicated to me that we were simply nudging them along a route they'd already chosen. They are both very affectionate, demonstrative children who are quite articulate about their needs. I don't think we've harmed them in any way. I also think I could give them more because I wasn't shattered all the time.'

(abraid)

But all babies are different and for some people controlled crying just doesn't work:

'It didn't *work* for us. We had five nights with hours and hours of crying each night, a frightened and hysterical one-year-old who began to panic at the beginning of his bedtime routine and general misery all round. *But* there have been *no* lasting ill effects at all, and at eighteen months the same child is only waking once a night now (down from 6–8 times), done to his own internal timescale. I'm not sad I tried it (I was at the end of my rope with it all), but it was a nasty experience and did no good.'

(GreenGlassGoblin)

Others find they have to 'retrain' after changes in the child's life – illness, a change to routine, a holiday, a change in the weather.

But some parents remain lastingly glad they did it:

'I didn't regret it. It is a very hard thing to do. But I *needed* to do it. My daughter was tired and irritable. I was tired and irritable, getting ill, and making mistakes at work. Our lives improved immeasurably afterwards, after a little upset for three nights. I admire those who can soldier on through the crappy broken nights. But I reached my breaking point, and that's really not a good place to be.'

(MarthaFarquhar)

Don't let your toddler kick all the babies at playgroup

If you attend toddler groups of any sort, you will almost inevitably find yourself on both sides of this situation:

a) A two-year-old kicks your crawling or just toddling baby. You are overcome by the instinctive maternal reaction – you have hurt my child, now I have to kill you, never mind that you yourself are still in nappies. You are also overwhelmed by judgey-pantsitis in relation to the mother of the kicking, running about, screeching, out-of-control two-year-old. You would never be the mother of such a horror.

b) One year later. Your own out-of-control two-year-old bites a baby on the face. The mother looks at you accusingly and tells your child off. You are hit by the kind of shame and desire to deny any responsibility which somehow swamps one's better impulses in these situations and you make your excuses and leave . . .

This is the sad sad tale of toddler groups everywhere and at all times and there are two basic precepts for surviving – be understanding about other people's kids and deal effectively with your own.

Other people's kids

Toddlers are like weather systems, they are subject to great clouds of passion and frustration, cyclones of aggression and monsoons of grief. Mostly over trivia. And a toddler group where there are many other toddlers and babies competing for toys, space and attention, or just being in the wrong place at the wrong time when you are overcome by rage, is likely to provoke some of the worst toddler behaviour. Apart from the inevitable running about mindlessly whilst someone is trying to read a story or get you to sing 'Sleeping

Bunnies'. So you really have to expect and accept that there will be a fair amount of wild behaviour, some toy snatching and occasional violence. And not get too irate when your child is on the wrong end of the bad behaviour. Unless he/she sits at home and waits it out, the parent of a volatile toddler is going to lose control of that toddler in public from time to time.

'There is a child like this – and a mother struggling with it at every group I've ever been to. Yes it's annoying when your child is hurt – or persecuted – as when your baby is followed round by a toddler who 'just wants to give her a love' (aaargh). I think the best thing to do is to intervene and distract where you can and otherwise breathe deeply. Mums and dads who are struggling need support not condemnation in my personal opinion. But I do agree that it is very annoying nonetheless.'

(*NorthernLurker*)

But you also have to take some responsibility for your own kids

Don't be the oblivious mother who sits with a really poor-quality hot brown drink reading *HaveaChat* whilst her child rampages through the playgroup like Godzilla through a cardboard city. Yes, you are knackered and yes, part of the point of a toddler group is that your child can play independently with other children. But you must keep at least half an eye on your child, especially if he has form for poor behaviour.

'I *have* a difficult child, I know how hard it can be to stop a child rampaging, but you have to make the effort!'

(*colditz*)

Because part of the point of being thrown amongst your peers is that you are there to be socialised. If you are biting and kicking your peers unchecked, you are probably not learning much or at least not learning anything which will assist you in future.

It is very tempting to do 'display discipline' when you are being looked at accusingly by the mother of a bitten or battered infant, who seems to expect you to cuff your child and take him to the police station or dish out an on-the-spot ASBO. Usually 'display discipline' means shouting. Try to retain enough composure to deal with your child in the way that would seem most appropriate if you could beam your way out of the gruesome social context. Two strikes and they are out may be a reasonable rule with a child over two who understands what you are saying to him. So the first time he batters a baby, he gets a warning and you discuss how he hurt the baby and that's not OK. The second battered baby and you both leave hurriedly.

On the other hand there is also such a thing as an over-controlled toddler group. Sometimes run by a do-gooding volunteer who hates children. And who gradually bans everything until the children are only allowed to sit in a circle singing 'Wheels on the Bus'. Quietly. If you happen to stumble across a group like this, just move on and find another. People are often running these groups on a budget of just about nowt and having to make do with what voluntary help they can get, so you will inevitably get some weirdos who don't like toddlers/people.

Dealing with the unchecked violent toddler of another

There is one uncontrolled toddler causing havoc in any toddler group at any one time. But the problem is he can spoil it for everyone else:

'I don't bother with toddler groups any more. Camel-back-breaking straw was when my eldest was four and a little boy kept thumping her, and all the mother did was laugh and say "Boys will be boys!" I didn't particularly want to hang about with a woman who thought it was fine for boys to smack the crap out of girls myself, let alone have my kids around hers.'

(*SueBaroo*)

Do bear in mind that people have a range of opinions as to how exactly to deal with issues like violence and 'not sharing' and so forth. The fact that someone's notions as to exactly when and how to intervene in toddler politics are different from your own does not mean they are wrong. No, the parents and carers who can make toddler group life hellish are the ones who do nothing at all. If the parent/carer won't do it, we hereby authorise you to tell the child off yourself (and by 'tell off' we mean deal with the behaviour in an age-appropriate way). Unless the parent/carer is very scary.

But don't go round picking on every bit of crap behaviour – just deal with things which are serious and affect your own child. And make sure the carer isn't already struggling over with a baby dangling from her breast to do the deed herself before you get stuck in. Also, cathartic as it is to shout at a small child, don't react in a way you wouldn't with your own child. Remember that a child who seems so much bigger than your own is still a very little child and may be developmentally in a place where he really doesn't yet understand why snatching toys and punching those who are holding them is wrong. Weirdly, you may find that the offending child follows you around adoringly thereafter, having decided that you are its mother.

'My response in these situations is to speak pretty sharply to the child, on the basis that somebody ought to let them know that their behaviour isn't on. Little Jemima-Epiphany's mummy is usually so surprised that she forgets to call me on it.'

(*rowan1971*)

Some parents recommend that you roar "WHOOOSE IS THIS CHILD?" whilst keeping a firm claw on the malefactor in cases of egregious unchecked bad behaviour. You may or may not welcome the social friction which will inevitably ensue. Also other toddlers are likely to assume you are the enforcer and come to you with all their tales of woe so unless you want to be the group's Mr T figure, we wouldn't necessarily recommend this approach.

It is possible to set things up in such a way that babies are protected to some extent from the depredations of toddlers:

'I used to run a M&T group. Clearly boisterous toddlers charging around could endanger smaller children. So we used to put the mums' chairs in a circle and the babies and "crawlers" would play in the middle. The bigger ones would run round – pretty much unsupervised – outside the circle of chairs. The mums got time for coffee and chat, the babies were safe and the older children had fun charging about.'

(*fortyplus*)

Some parents just don't seem to realise that they ought to be intervening when their children are harming other children or destroying play equipment. It genuinely hasn't occurred to them. If you think that is what's going on, it may be that the group organisers would be willing to have a general word about rules and dealing with unacceptable behaviour, which message might penetrate the carapace of an oblivious parent/carer. Or here is one parent's proposal for dealing with the wafty mother who just excuses crap toddler behaviour and doesn't establish any boundaries:

'Punch their lights out then say, "Sorry – just tired." Nick their rich tea, dunk it in coffee and say, "Sorry, am just exploring." Smack them, then ask if they will come round for coffee next week. When they look at you bizarrely, tell them that after the primeval tasks of washing, feeding etc. one of THE most important jobs a parent has is that of socialising their children so they can become well rounded, sociable likeable, well-mannered, affable, wonderful, compassionate human beings.'

(custardo)

Or you could cultivate otherwise undesirable acquaintances:

'I have a blunt acquaintance, whom I try to avoid.
    One day she followed me to a toddler group where there was a v boister-ous, violent child with a semi-comatose mother. "Christ!" she said to his mum. "He's a right nightmare, how do you cope?" Comatose mum never seen again. This is why I tolerate blunt acquaintance. Sometimes you need someone with the social grace of a hand grenade to state the bleedin obvious, very loudly.'

(Wandering Trolley)

DOS AND DON'TS

Avoid loud (otherwise known as 'performance') parenting

OR: 'A POTATO IS ACTUALLY A TUBER, ANDROCLES.'

This is perhaps a speciality of parents of preschoolers in public places. It often takes the form of a didactic monologue:

'Oh look, Ella, what are the duckies doing? Are they SWIMMING? Yes they ARE! And WHAT do we call the duckies' mouths? Yes, their BEAKS! And what is beak in FRENCH? And what species is the duck? And what about the duckies' FEET? What, why is that duckie chasing that other duckie? Oh, look, it's on its back, yes, you're right, maybe it's being unkind. Hmm. Shall we look at these SQUIRRELS instead . . .' etc.

'Or worse – reading a book REALLY LOUDLY to a kid on a train. No need to shout – the kid is on your lap.'

(*MrsShu*)

Or the loud parenting may have a more exculpatory character, the voice going higher-pitched but not shouty as the mother of the tantrumming toddler explains the reasons why she is not giving in to the toddler's demands, allegedly to the toddler but patently for the benefit of surrounding shoppers (ah, we've all done that). Also common: 'Yes, you can have that one sweetie, as a SPECIAL TREAT. Then you will be having lots of lovely free-range organic broccoli later for supper, won't you?' Sometimes people use their children, usually ineffectually, to advertise their credentials:

'I overheard a woman in the supermarket recently doing this kind of thing with her around three-year-old.

The child asked for tomatoes and picked some up, the Mum said, "Oh no, we don't have those unless they are in season", really loudly. The daughter replied, "But Mum, we have them every week". I actually sniggered at her, and wandered off with my out of season fruit and veg.'

(muggglewump)

There are some enormous caveats here. Obviously it is a good thing to chat to small children about the world around them, to speak clearly enough for them to understand, to help them acquire new words and concepts. You should be teaching them things. And you should of course praise them for learning things. But if you are doing it very effortfully and continuously, you may want to reflect on what you are up to. Are you just filling the silence? Who is your real audience?

What you want to avoid is:

• Creating the impression you are simply displaying your children and/ or your parenting skills for the admiration of others. You will just piss people off. You may not care – that's fair enough too. Here are real-life examples:

'"Oh darling what's your favourite ice-cream?"
Mumble.
"Sorbet? You like SORBET? And which is your favourite? Is it that one we had last week, darling?"
Mumble.
"BASIL AND LIME SORBET? Is that your favourite? BASIL AND LIIIIME?"
Mumble.
"Mmmmm YUMMY Basil and Lime SORRRRBET."
And so on. Forced upon my ears on bus recently.'

(DebiNewberry)

'There was a woman in the library the other day helping her son (who looked barely out of nappies) choose a book. He picked up an early reader which she quickly put back whilst shouting, "Oh no, Jasper, you can read in the 9–12 age range, that is much too easy for you" then takes a smug look around the room to check everyone heard.'

(Kneazle)

And frankly, as we mostly all find, the showing off generally backfires:

'I learnt my lesson many years ago when my son was very young. He could name every plant in my garden and I thought he was nothing short of a genius. One day at a market flower stall, I pointed to a plant and asked him to name it (yes, to my utter shame, I admit I was showing off). He very loudly stated "Fish Finger". Taught me a valuable lesson.'

(LivedinLooks)

'I think the key is to have a little volume control. That's all.'

(Rollergirl1)

- Monologising at your child endlessly. We've all been there. It can be lonely being alone with a very small child. But sometimes they too just want to think their own thoughts or poke at an ant. It's about balance, innit. Or there is really desperate loud parenting where the child doesn't even get a chance to reply before the Loud Parent is calling the child's attention to another natural phenomenon or telling them what sub-genus the dandelion they are chewing is from. If your child says, 'Could you please be quiet, Mummy?', she probably needs some peace.
- Competitive disciplining. This usually happens when your child has bitten off another child's ear at soft play. To dissipate the understandable social tension created, you loudly discipline your child in a possibly inappropriate and baffling way. This can sometimes be necessary to stop another parent from hitting you but may not serve any useful purposes vis-à-vis your own child.

But there is a possibly not wholly contradictory sub-rule here – don't rush to judge other people's loud parenting. You don't know whether what they are doing works with their child and you cannot really know their circumstances:

'I parent loudly, I think. I have a son with special needs and a one-year-old daughter so they both need lots of organising and back-and-forth interaction.'

(ApassionateWoman)

'I do this all the time with my daughter, but she is profoundly deaf with significant speech delay. I'm not sure if you could tell the difference; colours, numbers and nouns are all emphasised in my speech to make sure that she understands, from physical appearances we're just a mother and daughter sitting on a park bench loudly discussing bananas, do I need to wear a badge?'

(hatchypom)

The woman you may think is looking round to garner the applause of other supermarket shoppers as she loudly trills the 'Wheels on the Bus' to the red-faced toddler sitting like an unexploded bomb in her trolley may in fact be peering round fearfully to see if she is pissing everyone else off. The woman chattering away to a newborn who is frankly asleep is post-natal and nuts. Be kind to her. The dad sub-variant of loud parenting is often done to reassure women in the vicinity that yes, he does know what he is doing. Pity is often the humane response here. And the sprightly witterings of a trying-too-hard parent are clearly better than the 'shut the f*** ups' of a parent who isn't trying at all.

And of course, some small children themselves are loud and loquacious in public places and given to boring on in the supermarket about how they threw up that time in the swimming pool and everyone had to get out and there were bits of sausage in it . . . And what is a parent to do but join them?

Do not be frightened of public tantrums

So, you start with these things:

Your toddler: an unsocialised animal whose brain is apparently fast developing neural connections which will tame those gusts of rage and winds of appetite into some kind of rational and orderly and socially acceptable behaviour.

Society: which (in much of the UK at least) is unsympathetic, even antipathetic to the toddler and which seems to consist in some sections of people who believe that if your two-year-old had been slapped enough, he wouldn't be face down and heaving next to the Choco-Crud cereal.

You bring these ingredients together on a bus, in a supermarket, possibly best of all on a longhaul flight and you achieve:

A public tantrum: the arena in which your unsocialised child is exposed to public scrutiny and your skills as a parent are laid bare like entrails in the hot sun. Particularly crucifying is the tantrum of the older child or the child who just looks much older than his age:

'Babies and toddlers are one thing, but last night in the supermarket I bumped into a wild-eyed twelve- or thirteen-year-old boy screaming: "Put it back right now, I hate the one with stuffing, put it back now, I'm warning you". Followed by (as mum walks away): "How DARE you ignore me, don't you dare ever ignore me again."'

(*ViktoriaMac*)

And possibly the worst thing of all about public tantrums is the way they divide you against yourself. So one bit of you is struggling to think what is the best parenting strategy for dealing with the tantrum (ignore? reason? remove? administer sedatives?), another part of you is trying to think how best to actually do the task you need to get done (give her the Peppa Pig lolly, would it really matter that much, just on this one occasion, so you can buy the dinner?). A third part is swivelling its eyes madly round the audience of appalled shoppers thinking how best to placate the tutters/ prove that you are not a really shite parent. This often does not lead to the best and most rational solution to the problem.

So all we can say is: be not afraid. Or be not so afraid that you do not leave the house and exist only on internet deliveries. Pretty much every child in the world will have a public tantrum at some time. However hard you have worked at pre-emptive techniques and however optimal a time you select for getting on the bus or going to the playgroup. Probably everyone will get tssked or tutted at at some stage. Or have some actually offensive remark made about their dealing with their child. And quite likely there will be a moment, or more than one, when it all seems too horrible, when you are staggering through the shop heavily pregnant with a howling toddler clamped to your ankle and sweeping all the detritus up with his body and possibly his mouth and someone assaults you with some surreally inapposite advice.

For some reason we are a wildly toddler-intolerant society, particularly in supermarkets, where supermarket designers have worked hard to make sure the Thomas the Tank Engine confectionery is arrayed at exactly toddler height and that the whole experience is one of perpetually excited and then frustrated desire for the under-fives. Anecdotally, people suggest that in, for example, Mediterranean countries folk will try to distract or entertain your tantrumming toddler rather than suggesting you beat it senseless. But knowing this doesn't make life in the Croydon Asda any easier.

So don't panic. Find some mental space in which you can look on and imagine yourself laughing at the whole scene, reduced by time and distance to a jolly anecdote.

'You get used to the tantrums after a while. One of my twins used to rampage upstairs making a noise like Godzilla devastating Tokyo. She also used to lie on the floor and flip herself along on her back under the cat bed or a cushion a bit like a catfish going for shelter. Once when we were extremely jetlagged, one twin and I were lying on a bed while the other twin was tantrumming UNDER the bed. We were too exhausted to do anything about it and just lay there rolling our eyes at each other.'

(*MadamDeathStare*)

And here are some thoughts for dealing with public tantrums. These may or may not work for you and your child. Some days nothing will work for you.

Coping with public tantrums

Heading off

It sounds trite but is easy to forget – try to head tantrums off by identifying times of day (before lunch, after lunch, getting on for naptime . . .), bodily conditions (when tired, when underexercised . . .), weather conditions etc. which are likely to trigger tantrums. Don't take your child out in public at those times. Unless they are all the time.

Distraction

'Oh look, is that Dora the Explorer who has just walked into the shop? I wonder what she is doing here? Oh look, it wasn't her at all, but let me just snatch up these frozen peas in passing . . . Hey, can you help me find the fish fingers? Do fish have fingers, I wonder . . . ?'

Choices

Again, these can head off a possible tantrum in a child who feels he is being forced to do something he doesn't like. If there are different ways of doing that which has to be done, let him be the one to choose the method: 'Shall we get the cheese first or the cornflakes, what do you think?'

Time out

At a playgroup or other activity, where the child has been tantrumming:
- Tell him what you expect from him before you go somewhere and what will happen if he misbehaves.
- If the behaviour happens, remove him from the situation.
- Calmly explain to him why his behaviour is wrong and that there will be a few minutes' time out.
- Discuss what went wrong and have a hug.

Obviously this only works with a toddler old enough to have reasonable language skills and an understanding of consequences.

Firm removal

If you need to, threaten to leave the place where the tantrum is happening if the behaviour does not change. This assumes that the place is somewhere the child wants to be and not somewhere you need to be to get some practical chore accomplished. If you say you are going to leave, you have to leave.

'Rugby ball hold, remove from area with brittle toothy grin.'

(*coldtits*)

Firm removal may have to happen without warning with a very young toddler with whom you cannot reason. In that case the object is not so much to train him but to stop him annoying others.

Temporary firm removal

For a really bad supermarket paddy:

'Leave the supermarket. Plonk your trolley by customer care and ask them to look after it and go outside until the child stops. A friend did that with hers and it worked very well.'

(*Nekabu*)

Containment

When you have to do what you have to do, you sometimes have to strap a screeching child into a big strong buggy and just get on with it. Sometimes a passerby will help you with the pindown.

Ignore

Some toddlers do seem to need to just work through their rage about the *broken biscuit*, particularly very young toddlers who do not have the ability to understand consequences and so are unsusceptible to discussion and negotiation. And sometimes they will work through it in public. You will probably feel ashamed. We have all stood experiencing the calm at the heart of despair as a child writhes and gnashes at our feet. Do remember to hug the child once she calms down.

Include the onlookers

'Try to maintain a sense of humour. I usually try to remove offending offspring from the audience, but if that's not possible, I play to them. "I understand that you are having a terrible day, and that being two is a truly trying experience. Feel free to have a good shout about it – I'll be here with a hug when you're finished. Oooh, look at all these people staring at you, they probably think we are both stark-raving mad. Never mind – I'm sure MOST mums of two-year-olds have this experience from time to time, we surely can't be THAT strange." (By this time most people have shuffled past, trying not to catch your eye.)

Alternatively, I have picked said child up under my arm and carried on with whatever I was doing. Anyone who gapes open-mouthed at me with screaming writhing dervish under my arm gets an overly bright smile and a "It's a *lovely magical* age, isn't it?"'

(*Joolyjoolyjoo*)

And so far as the tutters and tsskers go, you may find yourself on occasion tempted by one Mumsnetter's approach:

'I was in the supermarket with my son (who has special needs) who was struggling and upset so crying.

Old lady: "That child needs a slap."

End of tether Pagwatch : <<excited>> "You're right! I know, I'll hold him – you beat the shit out of him. Come on . . ."

Old lady exits stage left.

Other shoppers edge away from Pag nervously.'

(*pagwatch*)

But it is probably better to meet criticism and complaint with politeness where at all possible – you model civility to your children and you probably wrongfoot the gripers. Try asking yourself, "What would Audrey Hepburn do?" And try to be nice yourself to parents of tantrumming children. A wry smile and help if help is at all possible might rescue someone else's day.

If you prefer his brother, take it to your grave

But before you decide you do have a favourite child, consider whether what you are actually experiencing is just a temporary fluctuation in feeling. There are lots of reasons why one child may seem more likeable at a particular time:

- A child who had an easy birth and/or who was an easy baby may have been easier to bond with than a child born by ECS who had severe colic for five months.
- A second child whose helpless infant self you feel more relaxed with may inspire a grateful affection which is different in kind from your anxious hovering over his elder sister.
- A child who happens to be at an easier and more appealing stage of childhood may make you happier day-to-day than a four-year-old boy in the grip of a testosterone storm.
- And everyone prefers: 'The one that isn't screaming at that particular moment.' (KerryMum)

Anyone's emotional life with their children is a complex and changing one and many parents find that, actually, were anyone to do the accounting, the bottom line would work out the same as between children – the intensity of the relationship with a first baby is different from but not somehow better than the relative ease of a second. The youngest is the cuddly baby but the eldest is a pioneer and rapidly becoming a real companion. The feelings are different but not different in *size* or importance. And can you really measure feelings?

'Tsunami hits – which one do you save? See: you don't really have favourites.'

(*PosieParker*)

It's worth trying to accept those emotional vicissitudes as just that, because thinking, 'Oh dear, I prefer X to Y,' can entrench as a guilty emotional secret something that actually was no more than the daily shifting that occurs in any human relationship. Imagine if you had two or three husbands/partners/wives and every day you were assessing which one you liked best. You need to let it be, for 'There is nothing either good or bad, but thinking makes it so.'

Sometimes there are longer-term differences in feeling which are to do with how well your temperament fits together with that of your child. Many parents say that they do not experience that difference as a difference in *love* – the child who is more difficult is not less loved than the child they find easy.

'My younger son is still "my baby" (youngest); looks like me; was an easier birth; and is just generally an easier-going, loving child. By comparison my first son was a traumatic birth, PND afterwards, VV bright child, but incredibly demanding, moody, high-maintenance.

I guess I'd say I LOVE them equally, but like being around my younger son a little more.'

(*Legacy*)

And other parents admit, at least via the strange public anonymity of the internet, that they do experience those feelings as a preference:

'I was only thinking of this subject yesterday and how we never mention it in real life because even with your closest friends you can't admit loving one of your children more than the others. In answer to the question, yes I do have one of my three who I love more than the others, but try always not to act on the feelings. From the second he was born I have felt it, and it never diminished.

Have felt guilty about it over the years, but as I said I think the other two are unaware of it, and I would never mention it to anyone, ever. I do treat them all equally though, it's just my little secret.'

(*potoftea*)

In some families there is a division of preferences between the parents:

'I do but in a deeply emotional way, not a favoured child way. My first son is my partner's definitely, his personality is most like my partner's and he held our elder son first after traumatic birth and bonded with him while I returned to some semblance of normality. My second son, though a difficult birth, fought his way out and gave me the VBAC I so wanted. Strangely enough I am so thankful to him for that. Then our younger son is physically and emotionally most like me. He is my favourite. But then we are big enough to deal with that and keep that secret from the kids and not let that affect how we treat them.'

(*Kaz23*)

If you do have a preference, we suggest you work very hard indeed to keep it to yourself. And this is not just a case of not saying, 'By the way, Otis, did I ever mention I like Curtis better than you?' It is about your whole way of being with your children and about the difficult art of parenting different children *differently* without giving an impression of favouritism. Because children should not be treated the same (however much they may think so); they need to be treated equitably.

'You know from a completely different perspective: I always hated as a teenager the fact that my mother treated me and my sister exactly the same. I found it offensive and unloving that she couldn't tell how different we are and how different our needs were . . . Now that I am a mother I rest on the fact that whatever I'll do it will be the wrong thing.'

(*VoLuataire*)

Everyone's situation is different, but here are some thoughts for dealing with different children in an even-handed way, which respects their differences but doesn't feel like an uneven distribution of love:

- It may be useful to try to spend some extra one-to-one time with the child you find harder. Look for and talk up their good points to yourself and to the child. Show that you understand the child's character and interests.
- Find a way to be affectionate with a prickly child – a child who is as huggable as a bicycle may enjoy having her hair brushed. Or maybe playing a board game is as close to physical intimacy as she wants to get.

- Wait and see how the child changes over time. Some relationships flower much later than others.
- Don't impose your own aspirations on any of your children. Try not to be disappointed if they don't want the things you want for them.
- But don't overcompensate – sometimes children form the impression that the more 'difficult' child is favoured because he or she gets more attention.

No one said this was easy. But it has to be worth it, because the long-term effects of feeling like a less-loved child can be profound:

'When I was growing up my brother was *always* my mum's favourite and I was always in his shadow. He was chatty, straightforward, practical, funny, outgoing, with a huge appetite (like her!). On the other hand I was shy, secretive, complicated and a terrible eater (all traits she dislikes to this day in anyone she meets). The way she loved us both has continued into adult-hood and her bond with my brother remains stronger than her bond with me. I can't help but wish she'd made a bit more effort to get to know me as I feel as though her attitude did knock my confidence a lot as a child. I always felt "wrong".'

(*imaginaryfriend*)

And whatever the reality is, children often think that there are favour-ites. It is part of the red-in-tooth-and-claw bond of siblingship. Sometimes it is better to drag those feelings out and look at them. For a serious, reflec-tive child that may involve a serious chat about how relationships work and how people have different relationships and one is not better than another, yada blah. Other parents find that they can joke about having a different favourite every day – if you can all laugh about it, it can't be a deep sad secret.

If you do it right, and get a bit lucky:

'I think my parents were and still are marvellous in that they NEVER showed that they had any favourites out of the four of us. I think they must have had times when they "preferred" one of us to the other because of however we were behaving at the time but I can honestly say that even now not one of us would claim that they had or have a favourite. They have always made a point of giving us each equal time and attention. They are loyal in that they never discuss one of us with any of the others . . . As you can see I think my parents are fantastic.

(*Ghosty*)

'I am one of 4 girls. I could not honestly tell you which (if any) of us was/is a favourite.

My dad is so anal about such things that I remember a phone call that I made when I lived in Vietnam.

"Hi," said I.

"Hello?" said he.

"It's me," I said.

"Who?" he said.

"Your favourite daughter," I said.

"I don't have any favourites," he said.

"Can I be your favourite daughter in Vietnam?" I asked.

"No, I don't have any favourites," he said.'

(*Buda*)

You are not too big to apologise/you are too big not to apologise

Look at what we did with that rule title, it's almost the chorus of a pop song inordinately favoured by *X Factor* contestants. Almost. Anyway.

There is a often a considerable bit of repression of your natural but worse instincts here. Because what has usually happened is that your children have been utterly foul over a prolonged period of time and you have finally been gripped by a fiery wind of anger and found the words 'RIGHT YOU CAN ALL GO TO BOARDING SCHOOL AND BE BEATEN WITH CANES', emerging from your mouth. And were one to conduct a whole war crimes trial of the wrongs done on either side, treating all the parties as adults, it would not be you doing time.

However. You *are* the adult. And you sometimes are ill-tempered and overreact. And by apologising intelligently to your children, you teach them a great deal about learning to take responsibility for their behaviour. And understanding why it happens. So if you say, 'I am sorry I shouted. I was grumpy because I am tired and you lot have been fighting all day,' you teach them:

- That it is right to apologise when you have done something wrong.
- That it is useful to look at the causes of one's ill-temper/bad behaviour.
- That grown-ups are human and have feelings but they are not irrational all-powerful autocrats. This can be a very valuable lesson to convey to a child who is oppressed by the unfairness of the parent/child power balance.

The apology will often be about an overreaction to their behaviour. You are of course entitled to remain critical of the behaviour which provoked the overreaction:

'I think you should apologise for shouting but not necessarily for the sentiment. So you can say, "I'm sorry I screamed at you, but I am really very angry with the way you just ran across the road."'

(swanriver)

If you find it hard to apologise, have a think about why that might be and the message which not apologising is sending:

'My parents were of the never apologise, never explain "old school" and despite the fact they were and are great in so many other ways, I have found that hard to deal with. I do lose my temper with my children and do apologise when I am in the wrong. And then we have a quick chat about why I got cross and how I ought to have handled it. If my son gets cross the same applies to him and will do in due course with my daughter, but she tends to explain with her teeth and fists, being less than two . . .'

(Marina)

Beware of empty apologies though. If you habitually scream at your children and then toss apologies about, you are likely to find they lose faith in the sincerity of the apology. The lesson is that if we are sorry about behaviour, we try to amend it. And the very best result of a family culture where you all take responsibility for your behaviour is that you are all kinder to one another and can be a bit light-hearted about your quarrels. And have the odd cackle about it all too.

'I shouted at my third son to take something upstairs and he turned around and said he was doing it.
   "WELL SORRY I SHOUTED THEN," I shouted. We laughed.'

(ocd)

'Whilst in bed, I heard my husband and my son (seven) having a squabble; when I came down I said to my son, "Did I hear you fall out with your Daddy?? He loves you very much and that makes me sad . . ."
   "Well Mummy, it is like this, it was like those arguments you and Daddy have . . . you have a little moan and then it is all over and done with."
   Personally, I think that is rather healthy . . .'

(BreevandercampLGJ)

There is a little side-rule here about admitting you are wrong about factual matters. Argumentative know-all children are often the products of argumentative know-all parents (nature and nurture conspiring together in these matters). It can be hard to admit you are wrong about factual stuff like the cube of 214 and the start date of the Second World War (some grown-ups of course find it almost impossible to lose at board games too, particularly Trivial Pursuit). But again it is useful to model a little humility. Unless you don't mind breeding up a litter of lawyers. In which case, you just go for it:

'I tend to veer my son (twelve) off on to topics he knows sod all about, like the origins of Israel or Shakespeare, Russian language and literature. This is how I get my kicks [tragic emoticon] and to be honest he is so clever at other things, he could make me look like a noggin very easily. Which is to be avoided at ALL costs.'

(*Piffle*)

Don't overdo the praise/ tell your children every scribble is a masterpiece

In the sort of middlingish bit of the Western world, the bit occupied by people who read parenting books or at least see them regurgitated in newspapers, there was a major shift in thinking about the question of bigging up your children some time after the middle of the last century, very roughly speaking. So some of us will have grown up with the kind of parents who were as likely to dispense a compliment as to they were to sit down to Sunday lunch stark naked. Parsimony with praise will have been in the interests of not making us big-headed and of building our characters. Some of the characters thus built are rather bitter and judgemental ones. Others of us, possibly of the same age, will already have been swept up in the corrective to this approach, which involved lots of self-esteem-building praise and behaviour-modifying positive reinforcement. Some of us didn't like this either (see below). But it probably remains the dominant model, despite some recent doom-saying in the press about how it is producing a generation of arrogant praise junkies who can't take criticism (no doubt inducing some contented chin stroking amongst the fully-clothed brigade).

Which gets us back to our central theme again. That there are no very simple tools you can apply to the black boxes that are your children. There are *ideas* and *approaches* which require constant subtle modification and re-examination and adjustment. Sometimes you will do all this almost without thinking. And at other times you will consciously get out and manipulate your ideas and approaches with all the finesse of Bob the Builder handling his wrench.

What we are advocating is the use of *judicious praise*. We can all do injudicious praise; that is the kind you do when your child presents you with another scruffy abstract picture done in five minutes with a biro and you say, 'Oh, lovely, darling.'

The problems with injudicious praise:

- It stops working:

'Children are not idiots and know when they are being flattered (once they are over about four).'

(*chegirl*)

- Or if it doesn't stop working, the results may be worse – and you will turn out children like those TV talent show contestants who are astonished to be told they cannot hold a tune. Because no bugger in their family had the decency to tell them any earlier.
- Indiscriminate praise eventually renders all effort redundant and all actual achievement meaningless. Some of us fondly remember the occasional nugget of genuine praise doled out by miserly parents – you certainly knew it meant something.

'Everything I used to show to my folks got a "That's smashing love" or "That's brilliant". I got so cynical I used to deliberately show them something that was utter crap – and still got the same response. I gave up showing them anything in the end.'

(*Iklboo*)

So we say:

- Don't put your children down. Don't ever do that knee-jerk English thing where someone says, 'Oooh what beautiful hair/lovely manners/a great goal'. And you say, 'Oh but he's a little terror at home/wets the bed/has smelly feet etc. etc.' . . . Or if you fall by the wayside and do do it, try not to do it again.
- Be specific and (well mostly) sincere in what you are admiring:

'I think the advice is that praise should be specific – so not "you are great" or "good girl" but "I really like the way you used blue in that painting" or "I could see you were trying really hard to find your balance".'

(*edam*)

- Don't be comparing them with other children all the time.
- Some constructive criticism is good as they get older:

'And I lavish praise on my daughters but I also let them know when things need doing better. My elder daughter made a thank you card for friends of ours who bought her a present recently. She'd coloured it in messily and crossed words out. I know she's good at art and writing so I told her it wasn't good enough, as in "You're so good at drawing and colouring usually – what's gone wrong here? Can you do a nicer one now, like you normally do?" Honesty – but with a positive spin, is an excellent idea.'

(itchyandscratchy)

And then of course there is that relatively new chestnut about praising effort and not necessarily going on too much about inherent ability. And mostly we can all agree with that one. But it is artificial not to acknowledge inherent talent and achievement which just comes from that talent as well. It's all about how you do it. Too much emphasis on 'how clever you are' or how gifted a child is at piano will put pressure on some children and make them frightened to try lest they fail, but their talents are part of them and do deserve some measured appreciation:

'I acknowledge both effort and achievement. I tell my son that I *love* that he's good at maths – it'll come in very handy and it's a pretty fab talent to have. I do nag him because he puts no effort into rote-learning his tables. But we did a little victory dance together when he was (finally, in year three) allowed to try cursive handwriting because he could actually form his letters. Now *that* takes some effort for him.'

(TheFallenMadonna)

Apart from praising achievements and the effort which has gone into them, many of us also do positive reinforcement as a way of socialising our children/bending them to our wills. We probably hardly notice we are doing it; it is part of the endless blah of life with a toddler or small child: 'Oh thank you, Ivor, for putting your cup back. How nice of you to share your ball with Timmy. What a clever boy you are to put on those socks all by yourself . . .'

But some children penetrate quickly to the heart of the endeavour and resent being manipulated in this way:

'I don't like being praised, especially not by my dad or other authority figures (doesn't include my mum, bizarrely).

I don't know why. But I get a feeling of suffocation when I get praised for something I *wanted* to do, and fury that me doing something "good" must be so unusual in the praiser's eyes that it's noteworthy. E.g. My dad used to say, "Well done for brushing your teeth without being asked." And I would then refuse to brush my teeth for a week because it was up to ME, and I could either brush my teeth or not brush my teeth as I chose . . . it felt controlling, that he was commenting on every tiny aspect of my existence.'

(*coldtits*)

'I always felt baffled by it. Like you say, I did something I wanted to do (e.g. doing my homework as soon as I came home from school) and my mum would go on about how great I was and it just seemed silly and I never wanted to accept the praise because it felt undeserved (I did my homework promptly because I didn't like it hanging over me, not to be "good"). I still hate it when my mother praises me, and she's very effusive with praise.'

(*skidoodly*)

Other children are like dogs and will lap it up. But for the non-dog-like brigade (maybe they are more like cats), you may need to be more subtle. We suggest you consider these techniques:
• Be a bit casual, dispense praise in passing and don't gush too much.

'My daughter was resistant to praise. But recently it has improved. I know she likes to be praised but I try to praise her after the event to make it easier for her. I often list all the things my children have done well when they are in bed at the end of the day. And say thanks. It's a good way to close the day.'

(*OrmRenewed*)

'Try praising her to someone else. Mention on the phone (there needn't be anyone on the other end) the amazing thing she did and pretend you don't think she can hear you. Some children find it difficult to deal with direct praise, and find it far easier if the praise *about* them is directed at a third party e.g. you could tell the waiter how well she's eaten her food when he comes over.'

(*tethersend*)

• And actually maybe some children just don't want to be soft-soaped, so consider this:

'Instead of praising lavishing adoration for compliance, try a regime of gentle criticism and reasoning: "If you don't brush your teeth, the bacteria in the cracks of your teeth will breed and make your mouth smell bad."'

(coldtits)

Although it would be quite a tough nut of a child who didn't want the brutal advice about oral hygiene at least tucked into a praise sandwich. We would probably mutter something about not wanting their lovely teeth to fall out . . .

You can't choose their friends

(AND YOU SHOULDN'T TRY)

'Last night my daughter said to me, "Nobody says hello to me in the morning, nobody says goodbye to me in the afternoon, nobody wants to sit by me in the classroom, nobody lets me play with them at playtime." How would you feel if that were your child? Just one friend would make all the difference.'

(*belgo*)

And that's what claws at your heart and raises the ghost of your own childhood unhappinesses. And makes you think you can wade in and sort it all out and redesign all the other little buggers at the school. Or perhaps tear out their wicked hearts and grind their bones to make your bread. But for the most part, friendship and its pleasures and pitfalls are things your children will have to figure out for themselves. Including the facts that still cause us little shocks as grizzled old parents when experience makes us learn them afresh – the fact that sometimes even real friends do not behave kindly to you, that people grow away from one another and friendships wither, that friendships need work, that other human beings are ultimately imperfectly knowable and frequently contradictory. Nothing much is as complicated as operating in the social arena and some of us start off with good instincts and skills and some of us have to learn those skills like we might learn Mandarin. Children have to be allowed to make their own mistakes and suffer their own hurts. But you are allowed to hover around on the edges trying to make sure they don't come out too psychologically gnarled.

You cannot engineer your children's friendships but you can help them acquire social skills, retain some self-esteem and grow some social toughness. And in the early days you may need to take a facilitative role and do a little fluffing and fixing and wrangling in relation to teachers and other parents and the cruel little animals who are their peers. As they get older you need to back off a bit and generally help only when help is asked for.

Babies and toddlers

Here is a little world in which you really can orchestrate their social lives entirely as long as (for your own sanity) you recognise that this dream of control cannot last. You can vigorously cultivate the parents of other under-twos and you can arrange squads of 'friends' parallel-playing around your child and occasionally hitting him. We are not entirely cynical about these arrangings – a parent or carer who organises a simulacrum of a social scene for a preschooler can often create a kind of social buoyancy which floats the child more easily into nursery, and the choppier seas beyond, but much depends on the personality of the child.

Early school days

Very young ones who say no one is playing with them

It is very common for a reception child to report that he is miserably lonely. Crowds of small self-absorbed egotists ricochet around early-years units leaving each other out of games and causing largely inadvertent hurt to each other. Hesitate very significantly before becoming excessively vexed about this. If the concern is repeated daily or the child is really upset, it is worth asking the teacher about what he or she perceives to be happening. Small children often remember vividly the five minutes they felt lonely and forget the six hours they were running about:

'My son is always telling us that he has no friends, no one plays with him etc. So I took a walk up to the playground, and he was charging round playing with people. He is a bit depressed and anxious though and everything is a huge drama when he is telling us things and he gets very upset and clingy.'

(*saltire*)

With small children, a teacher who is alerted to a concern can often do a bit of social engineering. Or, often as not, the problem simply disappears.

Problem 'friends' of small children

These are mostly different from the problem friends of later life – the friend who never has a wallet, the friend who tells you home truths and makes you feel crap about yourself, the interminable anecdotalist . . . The typical problem friend of the under-fives is usually a problem because he is apt to bite you or snatch your toys. But there is also a common type who may remind a parent of some of her own friends – the bossy, domineering friend. Some of us have cheerfully endured a lifetime of these or indeed been the bossy friend ourselves, but they can be a bit flattening for a recessive four-year-old who has been elected as the favoured lieutenant of some junior socialite. Sometimes it is the child and sometimes it is some other parent who decides your unassertive four-year-old would be a good friend for her commanding offspring. The bossy friend, who often displays many good qualities such as energy, confidence and physical strength, may demand exclusivity and may alternate possessiveness with meanness and rejection.

Before you panic, bear in mind that sometimes the annexed child is quite pleased to be swept up by the domineering child/juvenile Svengali. A new reception starter may just be happy to have a friend, even a manipulative/borderline evil friend – in which case you just need to help support her as time goes on in branching out and playing with other people.

But if your child is being made unhappy, you can help from the sidelines: some assertiveness training may be in order. Do a role play where your child is the bossy child and you are your child. She can learn to say things like: 'I'd like to go and play with someone else now.' Or: 'I need some space, man.'

Invite some other kids over after school to cement other friendships. A rational parent will be well aware of what her child is like and may be willing to help:

'My daughter has been the domineering child, she tries to be like it at home but we don't let her get away with it. We were told by a teacher in year one that she was being a bit bossy with one child in particular. So we had a long talk with our daughter, who really didn't think about how the other girl might feel. We have to keep her in check and try to praise her lots when she's being good and I hope it's working. So, as the parent of a bossy child I wouldn't be in the least upset if another parent told me that my daughter was being too pushy with another girl. I'd want to know and attempt to deal with it.'

(*HousewifofOrangeCounty*)

Talk to your child's teacher who may be able to give your child space at school by artificially separating him from his domineering friend.

Older primary school children

So you have weathered the settling-in period and your beloved has acquired a group of friends and suddenly the politics commence, particularly amongst triangles of 'best friends'. If nothing too terrible is happening (spats, fallings out, changes of loyalty etc.), listen to your child's concerns but don't get overexcited yourself.

'I have a seven-year-old daughter. I am exhausted with the "A is not my friend any more, M is my friend, and I have told C that if she is friends with A then she is not my friend, L is friends with A and C but she does not want to be my friend . . ." I have come to the conclusion that I should just nod and look sympathetic and stay well out of it.'

(*MmeLindt*)

A child who has got a bit older and is concerned about a lack of school friendship (or has friends who regularly exclude her) may benefit from some carefully calibrated intervention.

You could try targeted playdates and you are likely to find you can actually buy a little love in the early years Try inviting some children over and showing them a really good time:

'How about working out who might be a possible friend within the group and ask a few of them round a couple of times. Doesn't need to be a big deal, and after all, your daughter only needs one person. We all only need one person!'

(*ahundredtimes*)

Some out-of-school clubs or activities can help a child build social confidence and make friends outside of a difficult friendship group.

You can do much to build your child's confidence too. Help your child to react calmly to slights, treat others as he would like to be treated and try to get some perspective on how things change from day to day. Some optimistic stories from your own childhood can help here (if you have any).

'I have lost sleep over my children's friendship issues. Without trying to brush the children's concerns under the carpet, I do think you need to reassure them this is NORMAL behaviour in life. It is not very nice but it WILL happen and they will have to find a way of coping. And the best way to do so is to be brave and cheerful and find other friends and above all not become a victim.'

(*bibbitybobbityhat*)

'And then kill the other children when nobody's looking.'

(*hullygully*)

Try to get your child to formulate possible strategies for dealing with issues so he feels in control of the situation:

'Some parenting experts suggest that instead of saying "don't worry" or suggesting solutions, it can be helpful to reflect the child's emotions back at them so they know they are being heard e.g., "Oh, I'm sorry that happened. It must have been upsetting/that made you feel left out/sad, I expect." Let her talk about her worries and fears and then encourage her to find her own solutions e.g., "What do you think you will do tomorrow/can you think of anything that would help?" And if she can't think of anything, you could say, "Do you want me to make some suggestions?" and then ask your daughter to add some of her own. It's all bit psycho-speak, but I thought it was an interesting approach.'

(*aloha*)

And don't forget to shower her with love. Make sure she knows how truly great and loveable you think she is. Remind her of all the people who think she is interesting and fun and who care for her.

Finally, if a child is being excluded at break times:

'Could the school give the child a role during break times (which I imagine are the worst), perhaps organising a playground game for another year group?'

(*pointydog*)

You can't edit out the undesirables

All this being said, you must let your children select their own friends. You cannot, for example, force a friendship with some child you feel is worthy, or whose mother you'd like to hang out with, or for whom you feel sorry. You can and should emphasise that it is important to be kind to others and not exclude people but your children are not obliged to have endless play-dates with children they have no spark with:

'After all how many of us would force ourselves to invite mothers we don't want to be friends with for coffee? So why should we encourage our children into fake relationships?'

(*Thediaryofanobody*)

'My son (four) started school this year and a couple of weeks later he was invited to a party. The children are from very different backgrounds and the friend had a very aggressive sibling, and then I thought back to my own childhood. I am sure I had friends my parents would rather I did not have, but they were pretty open to at least trying to get on with my friends and in getting to know their parents.

The way I see it, is there is nothing I can do when mine is at school to influence his choice of friends, he has to learn about friendships/relationships and I trust that he is able to make his own judgments and learn from his experiences as we all do. Six months ago he pulled the plug on a friend a year younger whom he no longer wanted to be around due to her aggression. I had always told him if he didn't want to play with her he didn't have to, but he was very forgiving of her until the day came when he stopped putting up with it. They have to learn. You can talk to them etc. but they need to learn some lessons about relationships themselves.'

(*Martha200*)

And we would say this too – there will always be some children with whom you personally have bad chemistry, children whom you just don't like, sometimes for no rational reason – whose skinny necks and rabbity front teeth and relentless silliness just get on your tits. You are the adult. Be extra nice to these children – they sense your hostility and they remember it:

'My best friend's mum hated me. It made me feel like complete shit because I could not work out *why*. She ignored me whenever I was there or would interrupt or speak over me. I was *always* polite – I was a nice kid ffs. My friend's dad could not have been more different (thankfully) but he worked away a lot. Her brother liked me too and I got on with the neighbours. Nothing ever happened that would give her a reason to dislike me, she just did anyway.

Over a ten year period I was surprised at how it impacted on my friendship and now I am an adult I feel quite bitter, she should have known better than to treat a child like that.'

(*StellaWasADiver*)

Older children and teens

Ah, brave new world of increased touchiness and independence requiring you to be more hands-off as the friends become yearly more horrific. Here is our guide to some common issues:

Friendless teens 1: Teens who want friends

This is a big age for friendships breaking down – everyone is changing in unpredictable ways and folk are changing school. You can help a teenager who is a bit lost and lonely. Much of the advice above in relation to lonely smaller children applies, suitably and tactfully adapted, especially the advice about reminding them how great you think they are and helping them to take the long view.

Out-of-school interests can salvage the self-esteem of a teenager in an unhappy school situation:

'My daughter, who is fourteen now, had a bad time for about six months at school. She was left out of things, very lonely, and ended up being bullied. We had to move schools in the end. Anyway, her self-esteem was at rock bottom. I was advised that the local air/army cadets are really good with kids who have esteem issues. She started with Air Cadets in October.

I cannot praise it highly enough. This kind of thing would emphatically not have been my first choice of activity for a teenage daughter, however, the people who run it couldn't be kinder, and she loves the whole thing. It has also been wonderful for her socially, she meets her air cadet friends out of cadets (not one of them goes to the same school as her) and is has paid dividends as her confidence has grown and she has made good friends at her new school.'

(GetOrfMoiLand)

Remember when dealing with this Greta Garbo-ish age group that you must try not to pester your child too much about her social life whilst at the same time being preternaturally sensitive to signs that she might want to discuss it.

Friendless teens 2: Teens who are not bothered

Some teenagers (and anecdotally there seem to be more boys in this category than girls) don't form any very intense friendships or seem to have many social engagements but furtle along quite happily pursuing lone interests. And these teenagers may or may not turn into the forty-year-old men most of us know who partake perfectly contentedly in the family social life and see one old mate once a year for a beer:

'My husband doesn't seem to have many friends at the age of almost forty, rarely goes out with any of them and never has any of them over to ours. He's very sociable and likeable, but is also very happy just spending time with me and his children. I think that men and boys are much more likely to have loose/passing friendships, rather than close ones like women and girls have.'

(Mumpbump)

Some teenagers have patches of unsociability or discover at this age that they are not naturally extrovert. Others have outgrown their existing friends and will acquire some new ones later on in life. As long as the child is happy, don't obsess over it and don't nag him to make social arrangements.

'The wrong crowd'

Ah, the wrong crowd. By which we mean teenagers who are up to no good in some way and likely to draw your child into their bad doings – drugs, crime, reckless endangerment of themselves. Before you condemn the friends, always try to assess them on their own merits and not on the basis of difficult family circumstances.

As for the genuinely dodgy friends, the consensus of experienced parents is that:

- You shouldn't ban contact with the undesirable crony. The friend you try to edge out gains added lustre from your opposition (although we think there must be limits – certainly the fifty-year-old crack addict they met on Facebook is not someone you have to have to tea).
- You keep the undesirable friend close so you can see what she is up to – you invite her over. With a tween or younger teen, it may be sensible to say that the friend is welcome to come to your house (subject to him behaving properly) but not allow your child to go out and about with the dodgy mate (or to the mate's house if you have reason to believe there will be inadequate supervision).
- You try to keep communicating with your child so she does not hide too much from you or feel unable to speak to you if she is getting into trouble. This makes it sound like it might not be too hard but it is no doubt often unbearably difficult and stressful to hold back from making a clumsy or precipitate move when you are frightened for your child's safety.
- Encourage any other friendships, even if it means being a taxi driver for a while.

Bullying

Bullying, sustained unkindness that goes beyond the falling out and politics of ordinary friendship groups, generally requires firm handling, usually by the child's school. The following are good sources of advice:
www.kidscape.org.uk
www.bullying.co.uk
www.childline.org.uk

Don't call it a twinkle

'Then there was the (probably apocryphal) little boy who said: "Men have penises and women have Volvos".'

(probablyaslytherin)

This issue arises because there is no universally acceptable friendly non-porno colloquial term for female genitalia akin to willy for penis. In some communities, fanny is fine and in others you might as well say c*nt. Pussy and twat are obviously no good – they are a bit like dick and cock and prick.

'I started a thread once asking if cock was so wrong . . . to me it sounds cheerful and a bit, well, cocky (for an older boy), but sixty million Mumsnetters disagreed with me. I'm clearly out of step – I just don't hear the vulgarity in "fanny".'

(onebatmother)

So a plethora of friendlier regional and familial variations have grown up – tuppence, flower, twinkle, minnie, wendy, ladybits, mouse, tinkle, fairy, mary, lulu, penny, foof. The all-purpose anodyne 'front bottom' annoys some people the most:

'I loathe "front bottom" it seems so sad for boys to get a nickname and girls to just get an extra bottom.'

(hellymelly)

'I've said it before, but calling a vulva a front bottom is like calling an ear a side nose.'

(FrannyandZooey)

'No to front bottom. You poo out of your bottom, it's a totally different thing. That reminds me of those ladies with the strange water retention thing so that they have what looks like bottoms at the front. Neither of my daughters have that problem, and neither do I.'

(*Boco*)

Some parents invent their own name for female genitalia on the perfectly sound principle that if boys have a friendly colloquial name why should girls have a 'clinical' one, but there is a problem in our current state of linguistic inventiveness around the female genitalia. And it is a communication problem. We are supposed to be helping our children improve their ability to communicate, not handicapping them with private coinages which no one else understands.

And so, on to the curiously offensive clinical words for the womanly parts. The male apparatus is relatively simple as a collection of pieces – there are basically three bits of which two are the same. Penis and testicles – many quite young children know those words and most people don't come over all queer when they are trotted out, or even lisped sweetly by a toddler (peanut and tentacles, anyone?). The weird fact is that there is not only a generally acceptable and well-understood colloquialism for penis, but the word penis itself is more widely used and accepted from the mouths of babes than any of the words for the female parts.

The female genitalia are more multiform, there are more and mostly more modestly-sized bits and their functions to the child mind are likely to be somewhat obscure (apart from the urination function). So it is easy to attach the wrong word to the wrong part. Quite a few of us grew up thinking of the whole kit and caboodle as a vagina – which is of course just wrong. The external flappy thing is a vulva, of course.

'FWIW someone once pointed out that calling it the "vagina" is like calling your face an oesophagus. Anatomically incorrect.'

(*curiouscat*)

And yet many many people never ever say the word vulva and get all wibbly if they hear it from a child's lips.

So we say, the advantages of teaching your children the proper name for the external female genitalia (i.e. vulva) are these:

- To give things their proper names is to bring them into the daylight (so to speak):

'I prefer to use the correct anatomical terms because I think it goes hand-in-hand with an open, unembarrassed approach to sex (not saying I'm unembarrassable by any means, but I'm trying to take this approach with my boys in the hope that they'll grow up to be responsible sexual adults who won't impregnate the local girls before they've done their GCSEs). Using euphemisms seems to me to be on a continuum with treating sexual parts as dirty/shameful/embarrassing, and from there a general reluctance to say, "well, when a boy has sexual thoughts his penis becomes erect . . ." etc. etc.'

(*policywonk*)

- To give things their real name is to improve communication and remove ambiguity:

'One of the reasons I feel quite strongly about this is because I did some work a few years ago in the area of child sex abuse. I remember one small girl who reported it to her teacher by saying that her "uncle" has been touching her "weeble" – the teacher had absolutely no idea what she was talking about, so the child went unhelped for quite a bit longer.'

(*harpsichordcarrion*)

- Children taught the right name don't end up being grown-ups who don't have or are unable to use a proper word for their genitalia:

'A fifty-six-year-old lady came into my consulting room the other week and asked a question about her "noo noo". I thought that was really tragic.'

(*Tipex*)

'If even medically trained staff can't bear to use the real words – I mean any word at all, either medical or vernacular, how can we feel it's acceptable to talk about that part of our body? I was once nearly in tears (of laughter) when a doctor said "I understand you're having a little trouble in the ladies department." Made me sound like Debenhams!'

(*frannyf*)

- Perfectly ordinary words in the English language don't end up being co-opted to do the job of other perfectly good words:

'I was told as a child to call it my flower. It was years before I could say the word flower (in its proper context) without blushing. So I taught my daughter to say vulva.'

(*thediaryofanobody*)

Have your own colloquialism, if you like, as well – because, yes, there should be language in families which is more relaxed and personal, as long as you make sure that your children know the real word and know to use it outside the family. Many children make up their own terminology anyway:

'You will be pleased to know that daughter one (five) has solved all the hat-house dilemmas. Prancing around naked at bedtime she announced to my husband that her "bottom" looked like a "chicken's mouth". "Look, daddy, that bit right in there." Daughters one and two then proceeded to continue prancing around, now shouting out "chicken bottom, chicken bottom". So there you have it. Chicken bottom it is.'

(*hatstand*)

You will get used to vulva and you will get used to your two-year-old talking about her vulva (or her chicken bottom). We just need to wear the edges off the word. Practise saying it. In private. Then in public. VULVA VULVA VULVA. It is not some uniquely ugly word, it's not long, it's not difficult to say. It's a perfectly nice word with its jaunty matching 'v's and its slightly disconcerting, slightly Germanic deep but short 'u'.

'Is it the apparently contradictory associations of vulgar and Volvo that is freaking all you vulva-haters out?'

(*onebatmother*)

'When choosing names for our daughter, my husband and I would get to the end of our inspiration and then fall about childishly suggesting things like "vulva", "vagina" and "labia' as possible names. But they are quite pretty words, I think. "Oi, Labia, put that down and come back here now!"'

(*aloha*)

Tell them they are beautiful (but that beautiful is the least of what they are)

SOME THOUGHTS ON LOVE, APPEARANCES AND SELF-ESTEEM

The flower of beauty, fleece of beauty, too too apt to, ah! to fleet,
Never fleets more, fastened with the tenderest truth
To its own best being and its loveliness of youth: it is an everlastingness of,
  O it is an all youth! . . .
See; not a hair is, not an eyelash, not the least lash lost; every hair
Is, hair of the head, numbered.

Gerard Manley Hopkins, 'The Leaden Echo and the Golden Echo'

What do we mean when we talk about the beauty of our children? It is of course to do with their physical selves, the lustre of their skin, the fine reddish fuzz on a newborn's back or the damp wrinkles in his neck, the newness of all his parts. And it also includes the awkward evidence of growth and change – the too-large grown-up front teeth, suddenly-grown pipecleaner legs, the scar on an eyebrow. But it is not only or even mainly about their physical selves. What we feel to be their beauty we tend to feel as the external expression of an internal truth and that truth does not have a great deal to do with the beauty of fashion models or film stars. When we are moved by the beauty of our children what we are feeling is love for their physical selves as the outward evidence of their actual selves, whatever that means to us. Every hair of their heads is numbered.

Ahem. So, you know, what we are saying is that telling your children they are beautiful is on the whole a good thing, it is a way of expressing love. But you probably need to be sending other messages about appearance at the same time. And like many, many things in the world of bringing up children, this is a subtle art. And it is easy to overthink it and get all unnatural so that you find yourself saying in a stagey parenting-expert-approved way to your child: 'You look really beautiful because, er, your hair looks so healthy but you are also clever and kind, which is of course much more important. Blah, blahety-blah.' (Child wanders off.)

So here are some things to think about. Make sure, especially with girls, that you lavish praise on the things they do as well as the things they are, (although not all the time – 'Hello, gorgeous,' is fine too). Everyone needs a wider basis for their self-esteem than the way they look:

'Telling her that you love her, praising her, noticing the special things she does, making her feel that she matters are all just as important to self-esteem as being told she's beautiful – probably more so.'

(*WigWamBam*)

'Shift the praise to very specific things that she has done, "That is such a beautiful painting. I really like the way you chose the colours for the sky and painted the clouds", and save the beautiful comments for more casual comments like, "OK, beautiful"?'

(*aloha*)

It's good to lay off in public with bigger children or indeed in private if there is eye-rolling. But not completely. And in general, try to keep appearance in perspective. What they should probably understand is that they are beautiful to those who love them:

'I'll always remember what a year three child wrote when doing a "tell me about yourself" piece at the beginning of a new school year. She said, "My mum thinks I'm beautiful, I'm not sure, but I like it when she says it", which was good enough evidence for me!'

(*bee3*)

Remember you may need to help children to handle compliments about appearance and other things, especially if your own tendency when admired is to mumble and kick the floor:

'You shouldn't stop saying how beautiful she is, but could you also talk about how people give compliments, and how it can make you feel embarrassed, but explain that all she has to do is feel good about it, no ties, nothing in return, except perhaps to say "thank you".'

(*bee3*)

More generally, you want to help your children to grow up happy in the bodies they have. Partly this is about helping them to keep those bodies healthy and well – making sure they get lots of exercise and that they eat a reasonably balanced diet. But you need to use a light touch – don't obsess about these things:

It's important not to be commenting, positively or negatively, on the way people look, especially about fatness, thinness and body shape generally.

'Ban women's magazines, especially celebrity mags, which go on and on about weight.'

(*fivecandles*)

Don't forget that fathers have an important role to play:

'I think dads' point of view is important too – my dad made jokey negative comments about my body when I was a teenager and it always stayed with me.'

(*jennifersofia*)

'My dad constantly told me how strong, healthy and good I looked (and I was a plump child). He used to make a really big deal out of it and although he never used the word pretty or beautiful, as a child I used to feel really proud of myself when he said I was strong and healthy.'

(*InARut*)

And of course, everybody should focus on positives:

'My daughter is quite chubby at the moment – but we are doing the exercise and healthy eating thing – but anyway, she has incredibly slim shapely legs so my psychiatrist friend told me to praise her legs every time she moans. So we have bought some really cool shorts for the summer and that's what I'm doing. She says, "I'm so fat – look at my tummy" and I say, "Yes, but it's only puppy fat – and look at your gorgeous legs, you are so lucky – people would kill to have legs like those!" etc. etc.'

(*scatterbrain*)

If necessary, discourage friends and family members from making negative comments:

'Family members, usually men, used to say things referring to my daughter's weight – and I always had to say, "She's only six" or "She's only nine and she's perfect". I think it's about letting other people know to shut the fuck up.'

(*custardo*)

Eating disorders seem to thrive in circumstances where there is generally a lot of anxiety and pressure to perform. Try to get over your own issues (especially in relation to weight/body shape) or at least stuff them in a cupboard. Shut up about your own diet already. Never underestimate your children's capacity and willingness to imitate you. Try to preen around being pleased with your own body shape or at least insouciant about it. Do not stand about lamenting your fat thighs and your bristly chin. Children need to see adults being happy in the bodies they are in to counteract the messages they will be getting from everyone else about body shape.

'I have a very positive body image which I'm convinced is all down to my mother. I always thought she was incredibly attractive but I think the thing that sticks in my mind even now is that she was (and still is) simply very comfortable in her own skin. She knows her "flaws" but embraces them instead of trying to hide them or worry about them. I have never heard her be negative about her appearance or weight or for that matter mine (she thinks I'm gorgeous).'

(*buttercreamfrosting*)

Don't get too hysterical if they start talking about fat people but do deal with their concerns about weight

Small children who suddenly start tittering about fat bottoms are generally not on the road to an eating disorder. It is usually just that they have started noticing such things:

'I remember when I was nannying for girls of about six or seven, they were definitely obsessed with big bottoms. I was bigger then, but I have never, ever had a big bottom yet they used to laugh and tease me often about my "big bottom", and played a game called Big Bottoms which they told their mother I had taught them.

It was all done in a humourous way, the same way a five-year-old will say poo or whatever for a joke. I think big bottoms are just the rudest and funniest thing they can think of at this age – long may it last!'

(*FrannyandZooey*)

If it is no more than that, you can just avert your eyes until they move on to something else they find hilarious. But what if your not-obese child starts to think he is fat?

- Look up BMI measures on the internet to demonstrate to your child that he is within the normal rate for his age and height:

'I found a good online BMI calculator for children. We measured her height and weight and she entered them, and found that she was exactly in the middle of the healthy band. Never heard another word on the subject from her.'

(*Blandmum*)

- Find out if other children have been commenting and help your child formulate some good retorts.
- As above, be positive about your child's shape and your own:

'I have had this with my daughter (eight).

We have been working on a scrap book with lots of positive role models. Could you get pictures of young sports people? You can cut out silhouettes and get your son to pose in the same stance and cut his picture out – if you get the scale right you can compare the shapes.'

(*Katymac*)

- Sometimes even three- to four-year-olds begin to think they are fat. You can explain to a child this age that her abdomen is still a bit small for all of her organs, which is why her tummy sticks out.

Being ginger/being very tall/being different

Those who have a ginger child of course know that there is nothing lovelier than red hair. But not every schoolchild knows that. And the same is true of height and many another physical feature. Finding role models for your child can be helpful. For example, for those lucky enough to have a red-haired child, here are some ideas.

For boys, some lovely ginger men:

Boris Becker
Daniel Craig
James Spader
Little Cook from *Big Cook, Little Cook* (well, we like him)
Eric Stoltz
Damian Lewis

For girls, some flame-haired women:

Various Pre-Raphaelite muses
Gillian Anderson
Nicole Kidman
Elizabeth I
Lily Cole
Judi Trott
Karen Gillan
Katharine Hepburn

Other distinctive features like being very tall also lend themselves to the role model approach, although if you can pick out athletes rather than supermodels for your daughter, you will probably be encouraging a more realistic idea about body shape.

There will often be a dissonance between what you at home are trying to tell your child about how he should feel about his appearance and what the other uncivilised animals he goes to school with are saying. This kind of thing makes you feel like popping down to his school with heavy weaponry. But actually making him feel loved at home is the best thing you can do for him. And the second best is to provide some training in badinage and help him develop a toughened hide. Point out to your child that people will always find something to tease and arm him with some repartee. A fast tongue, if you can help him back it with some genuine confidence, will stand any child in good stead.

Be proud of your geeky child because life isn't, after all, an American high school movie

This Mumsnetter's story says a lot about why we sometimes feel simultaneously charmed by and fearful for our geekish children:

'My elder son was telling us at tea the other night how a boy had called him a geek, and his brother put his hand up and said, very sincerely, "Hang on, I don't understand. I thought it was a GOOD thing to be a geek." Elder son then said, "Technically speaking, it is used as a term of insult, yes," in response to his brother's question.

Now just how GEEKY is that as an answer?'

(ahundredtimes)

And it is difficult to know how much if at all to fret about your geek, because they come in a spectrum of geekish subgenres. Mostly you can recognise a geek by a cluster of geekish interests (computers, maths, science, gaming, some esoteric musical genres, chess, fantasy gaming, science fiction etc.), an intense involvement in those interests and oftentimes a lack of involvement in or ability at team sports ('At rugby last week I watched him standing, engrossed in the Velcro part of his "tag belt" examining the "mechanics" of it, while the ball and the game passed him by!'). A certain verbosity, pedantry and a ponderous style of speaking may or may not be a feature. But geekish children may or may not excel academically (many do; some don't, they just grow up to start microbreweries). And critically, whilst some struggle socially, others do not.

If your geek is happily ensconced with a flock of like-minded Trekkies (or even one; somehow one friend is plenty in primary school) or if he is in fact perfectly adept socially, then you need not trouble yourself with this rule.

'I have a couple of lovely geeks and I don't mind the term. My older son was bought some fantabulous new clothes and whilst preening said, "I will be the coolest kid in geeksville." Geek is used at his school in the same way as jock – a general but rather genial stereotype.'

(pagwatch)

'I have a wonderful thirteen-year-old geek! He has always been a geek since a very young age, and proud of it (although no glasses but now six ft with size eleven feet). He laughs in the face of sporting endeavours and plays all the usual Runescape suspect type games. He is also now really into his guitar. Like all true geeks he is really not that bothered about what others think and follows his own path, but actually has plenty of friends (mostly geeks . . .). The girls at his school adore him and follow him around, although typical for a geek I think he is a little behind in that department and not interested yet. He is as happy now as he was when he was 7. Would that all teenage boys were like him!'

(Greengirlforever)

But if your child is teased, ostracised or just lonely, then you probably need to help him out. What he needs depends on his own personal characteristics and the social milieu and there are no very simple answers. But there are things you can teach him which might ease his passage through the long tunnel which is school.

A child who struggles with social skills can learn some. An intelligent child with no instinct for social interactions can be taught to read social situations like a kind of code (sadly the game of football is not crackable by the intellect unassisted by some muscular coordination).

'I recommend a book called *The Unwritten Rules of Friendship*. There is a chapter in it about the Little Adult. It comes with some exercises to help them realise why speaking the "language" of their peers may help them to fit in.'

(MeMySonAndI)

The truth is that almost no one really wants to listen to the plot of all the Young Bond books and actually most people won't welcome a lecture on the fact they are eating a non-Fair Trade banana. Teaching your child some social skills is not about trying to change her or forcing her to conform but about helping her survive some of the tougher times at school and make it through to the world beyond school (where life can be very good for geeks) as little crushed as possible:

'For what it's worth, I also grew up as a bit of a geeky outsider at school, and based on that I would say that it is absolutely fine and right for your son to do his own thing and not change to fit in *but* skills on how to fit in will stand him in good stead throughout his life, and if he can see it as learning a useful skill like being able to drive a car, he'll feel the benefit even if he doesn't actually feel drawn to any of the people he'll be interacting better with. I always floundered and couldn't work out what to say or how and even now I still feel I get it wrong, but what I wish I'd learned much younger was that I could have used the very "braininess" that made me feel (and probably also seem) weird to learn the "rules" of how to carry out peer-group social interactions when I was a young teenager. It's not a skill you have or don't have, you can actually work at it and improve, *not* with a view to becoming best mates with people you're just not interested in, but with a view to smoothing the path of daily life generally. You could try to get your son to see learning some of these things as a bit like being able to drive or speak a language – not changing himself to fit in, but having a useful skill?'

(busierthannormal)

But there may well be no quick fix. Sometimes a parent just has to keep valuing a child for what he is and telling him that some day other people will do as well. That it is great to have enthusiasms and talents and to be an individual and actually it's OK sometimes to be a loner. And that other children in groups can be barbaric and cruel.

Here are some thoughts on 'geeks':

Many a child who finds no kindred spirits at primary school will find friends at secondary school or at university. Talk to your child about how the situation they are in now is not permanent. Children, unsurprisingly, have little sense of perspective but you can tell them hopeful stories:

'I work in an engineering company stuffed to the gunnels with chaps like this. They're still geeky, and some are a bit weird. But they design the coolest stuff in the world and they are almost all brilliant in their own field. Most of them are now happily married, breeding geeks of their own.'

(Smamfa)

'I know this is for the long term but all my dearest friends were misfits at school and grew into themselves. It's the way to grow up interesting and humble and observational and great to be with. The popular kids at school do much less well in later life, I think.'

(margoandjerry)

Finding an activity outside of school – drama, chess, scouts, vintage comics, musical instruments – can help a child find friends who are more like himself. Similarly, finding a physical activity your child is good at can help. There may not be one, as some of us who remember always being the last one picked for team sports (with the fat boy and the very thin speccy boy) will know. But martial arts are often masterable by a child who is no good at football and can be a source of great pride (and indeed useful for self-defence). Kickboxing? Archery?

Tell lots of stories about great/successful geeks. After all, they are busy inheriting the earth (and all the money in it): Bill Gates, Steve Jobs, Stephen Hawking, Steve Wozniak, Marie Curie, MegWhitman . . .

'I must say that the ability to play football well is not one that is a reliable indicator of future success and happiness.'

(harpsichordcarrion)

It is worth helping a child who is dealing with a bit of teasing (not amounting to sustained bullying – that needs adult intervention) to develop some snappy retorts:

'Teach him some comebacks? "Yep, I'm a geek, like that loser Bill Gates with his multi-billion pound fortune." Or "I'd rather be a geek than a shelf-stacker, you motherfucking imbecile."'

'You have to make sure your child has good self-esteem really, that's all you can do, because then the shrugging is convincing and they're no longer a target.'

(morningpaper)

Sometimes you can find a teacher or other adult whom your geeky child bonds with:

'Any good role models at school? My son's ICT teacher is funny and inspirational and they just get on well socially too. My son went from furious denial of boffin tendencies at six/seven to a realisation that it was a useful thing to be at eight.'

(*Marina*)

For many children who feel like outsiders in childhood, reading is a whole world of consolation. And not a few such children grow up to be writers.

It is important also to remember that your child is not you and won't have exactly your experiences of having large fuzzy hair like the hair in *Hair* when everyone else was coiffed like a *Charlie's Angel* and being tormented accordingly. Don't be too afraid for your child and too quick to cast her in a rerun of your own childhood. Which you cringingly endure alongside her.

'The one thing you do not want to do is to encourage a victim mentality. I think this is particularly important for those of us who were bullied at school for our own geekish/nerdishness. It's so easy to transfer those feelings to our children. Yes, I hated it! Yes, I cried! But fgs it's 30 years ago!!! I don't have to meet those people ever again and what they said then is of no interest to me now. On the other hand, my parents who taught me to love reading are still around – and still sending me books.

I have also got to accept that my daughter is not me. Just because my geek-ishness led to me being bullied, it does not mean that she gets to live my life. She manifestly doesn't. My experiences are not hers. She's a different person.'

(*cory*)

Don't get cross with your dreamy child, learn to manage him

The dreamy child is the child who walks along the street with her face obscured by a book or comic and then looks up with the fuddled expression of someone waking from a long sleep when she realises you have arrived at her school. You hand a dreamy child his clothes and say, 'Please get dressed' then you return ten minutes later to find a sock still drooping from the child's hand, one leg in his pants and one leg out, as he reads, builds Lego, wonders what it would be like if Indiana Jones turned up at his school. The dreamy child may have perfect recall of every Match Attax card ever produced and no recall whatsoever of what you just asked him to do.

'The charmingness of the all-out kind of dreamers is (thank goodness) a constant – they are *always* lovely.'

(*Bink*)

One mother speculated that her son's internal dialogue probably went something like this:

'Me: "Son, will you please get out 4 place mats?"
Son: says, "Yes, mum." Thinks, "Which mats shall I choose today? Which mats would Luke Skywalker choose? If I had to have a lightsaber would I like a red one or a blue one? Which colour lightsaber would Jack/James/Edward like best? Is Jack really going to bring his guinea pig into school on Monday? What was his guinea pig's name again? Ooh look is my sister playing with my Thunderbirds 1?"
Me: "Son – what are you supposed to be doing?"
Son: "I've forgotten."'

(*Anchovy*)

Dreaminess seems to set in around age six or seven and may never let up. At about the age the child has gained the competence to perform tasks reliably for himself (dressing, packing a schoolbag, some household chores), he seems to lose any ability whatsoever to focus on an instruction long enough to follow it. However beguiling the dreamy child can be with her esoteric questions and wonderings about the world, she can also be a source of wild parental frustration. Because no one wants to be the banshee who wanders the halls of their own house keening 'Please get ready for school, oh, please get ready for school.' No one wants to have to replace the sixth winter coat swallowed up by the school cloakroom that year. Much as we love our children, it can be hard as Hell to love what they turn us into.

So here are some techniques parents of dreamy children recommend, not necessarily for dissipating the dreaminess, but for getting by in a practical way until it lifts or the child leaves home and becomes responsible for shepherding his own socks. Don't get cross with the child for being the way he is, find ways of working with him until he becomes more alert and attentive.

For day-to-day practical instructions:

- Make the child boil the instructions you have just given him down to two words and repeat them to you, e.g. 'socks on' 'schoolbag packed'. A child who just says 'OK' or 'mumble mumble' is quite likely not to have processed the instruction at all. The fact of the instruction has simply triggered the OK or the mumble without the instruction itself having passed through the child's brain.
- In urgent situations, reduce your own instructions to a simple phrase which you repeat rather than engaging in a verbose rant (so 'socks on' rather than 'I don't understand what you do with your socks. Why do I have to tell you fourteen times to get your socks on every morning? It's driving me mad . . .')
- Touch the child on the shoulder and look into his eyes whilst giving important instructions rather than bellowing across the room.
- Break tasks down into smaller constituent parts to be accomplished one by one: so 'brush your hair' followed by 'get your schoolbag' etc. rather than 'please get ready for school, pleeeease'.

If you are a hugely organised achieving-type parent, it can be tempting to take over the child's life administration for her. Or indeed if you are just so time-starved and fed up that it's easier to do everything yourself. Insist they look after their possessions, do some chores. They need to develop some competence and learn to look after themselves:

- Practise setting practical goals for the child to accomplish – things the child wants to have happen and can feel pleased about having achieved. Some parents find an out-of-school activity which encourages organisation and responsibility, like Brownies, can help.
- Try giving the child a little notebook in which you and she make a list of things she needs to remember or tasks she needs to complete. Keep it somewhere safe and readily visible in your house and tell the child to cross off tasks which she has completed. If nothing else, this can reduce the stream of parental exhortation to a simple 'Have you done the things in your notebook?' Some children will happily devise a tickchart for themselves to tick off the things they need to accomplish each morning.
- With children (many) who have no sense of time, try getting a timer and getting them to perform certain tasks to time.

As for the long game, some children seem to outgrow their dreaminess by the time they are nine or ten. Some do not. Many adults who were themselves dreamy children say that at some point during adolescence they shook off their dreaminess. Others say they never did but it doesn't necessarily matter:

'I was a terribly dreamy, drifting child. Lived permanently in my own imagination and can hardly remember primary school, except the rare occasions I woke up, and found myself doing maths or something equally alarming. Finally started living in the real world around the time of A levels – could do the subjects I liked and understood – and have hung on by my fingertips ever since. Am now a writer – and my husband, another dreamy child, is a writer too – so obviously all that internal life has led on to something (almost) worthwhile. Am now plagued by a dreamy son who is funny and imaginative, which I love about him, but he also drives me mad as he can't remember to put on socks, or where his schoolbag is. I think I might be a strong advocate for NOT waking dreamy children up – they're storing up a rich bank of thoughts and ideas – and you need to play the long game and hope they'll swim into focus by the time they leave school.'

(MrsMaple)

YOU'RE THE BOSS

You don't have to have a naughty step but the odd star chart never killed anybody

MODERN DISCIPLINARY SYSTEMS
AND WHAT TO DO WITH THEM

Our generation has seen the rise and rise of disciplinary methods which sound like they ought to be trademarked. So we have, inter alia:

- Supernanny and her 'naughty step'
- Dr Christopher Green and his 'time outs'
- Star charts and other reward charts (you can download them, you can buy books of them with stickers)
- Pasta jars and marble trays for rewards
- Etc.

What does it all mean?

Well, naughty steps, naughty mats and time outs are really gussied up and perhaps better thought out versions of what our parents might have called 'go to your room'.

A child aged about two onwards who persistently infringes a disciplinary rule (in the Supernanny scenario a clearly set out 'house rule') is sent to the step/mat/corner, often for a minute for each year of the child's age. The child is repeatedly replaced on the step if she leaves it. Naughty steps can be seen as a punishment or simply as an opportunity for a child to calm down and reflect on her misdemeanours. Much depends on the way in which the whole thing is presented by the parent.

Systems which have time outs generally also have a positive reinforcement side (the star chart or other reward system) or the reward system may be stand-alone. The child gets a star or marble or piece of pasta when she has successfully done the activity which you are hoping to reinforce, be that tidying up toys or refraining from biting a sibling. When she completes a chart/fills the jar a treat follows. In some systems, marbles or pasta are removed or placed in a different container when prohibited behaviour occurs.

The other end of the spectrum

But we also have, partly in reaction to all of this and some authoritarian parenting methods of yesteryear, a host of parenting experts who reject these approaches as being akin to dog-training. These parenting philosophies (which include Alfie Kohn's *Unconditional Parenting*) are not easy to summarise in a few sentences and differ one from another. They tend to include a combination of some of the following ideas:

- Arbitrary punishments are not teaching the child to develop a sense of why it is wrong to behave in certain ways (empathy, morality) but simply not to do certain things for fear of being punished.
- It is important to model good behaviour to children – treat them and other adults with respect and kindness and guide them towards socially acceptable behaviour.
- There are no quick fixes or one-size-fits-all solutions; you have to develop a good relationship with a child.
- You should explain to children why you want them to behave in certain ways and reason with them.
- You should help children develop tools for dealing with conflict and other problems in their lives and find their own solutions.

Kohn suggests that punishment is experienced by the child as a withdrawal of love and that rewards may be seen by a child as suggesting that the parent's love is conditional on him behaving in certain ways. Others towards this end of the parenting spectrum see a place for rewards and positive reinforcement.

As with all methods and philosophies, there are likely to be aspects of these ones you find useful and others which seem to you to be codswallop:

'The "withdrawal of love" thing is nonsense in my opinion. Love isn't like that. Love isn't something I consciously choose to feel towards my daughter. I love her, I love my partner, and however much both of them can sometimes test my patience that doesn't change. However, I can consciously choose to care for her in such a way that she grows up to be aware of her own feelings, the feelings of others and the functioning of the society around her. That may sometimes include telling her off, in an age-appropriate fashion, but mostly means an awful lot of explaining.'

(*Anna888*)

Achieving a workable synthesis (*aka mucking along*)

The variety of approaches can make you feel, once again, like your brain is going to explode within your head as you grapple with utterly divergent advice all presented with great conviction. So the point of this rule is really to say: get the advice in perspective, look at it critically, see what genuinely works for you and be yourself.

Because many of us potter along in a roughly adequate way. And then watch an episode of *Supernanny* or pick up a copy of *Unconditional Parenting* because our four-year-old has started biting us and are struck by that vertiginous sense that we have been getting it Fundamentally Wrong. Once upon a time, family and community (and religion) would have provided us with rules – some of us now try to fill the vacuum with experts. But we need to be critical and nuanced readers and interpreters, of the books and of our own children.

So look – not having a naughty step does not mean your children will be out-of-control horrors and your family life a scene of constant anger and screaming. But, conversely, having the odd star chart isn't going to shake your otherwise secure child's sense that you love her.

For many parents the whole 'naughty step' approach is too confrontational, too punitive, too formulaic or simply doesn't work for their child. There are children who think the whole concept is amusing and go and smirk on the naughty step. Dragging a child repeatedly to a naughty step may be a deeply stressful solution to a problem for both parent and child, a problem which could actually be solved in some other and much easier way. What is particularly ugly and inappropriate is watching a parent constantly dragging a screaming toddler to a naughty step for every piece of mildly annoying behaviour. A lot of what toddlers do which is danger- ous or damaging to property is simply born of curiosity – you often just need to take them away from situations, put things which are delicate or dangerous out of reach etc. A toddler who is unable to reason often just needs to be told 'no' and taken away from the cat he is abusing or the friend he is hurting.

There are often ways to avoid getting into a situation in which any kind of discipline is necessary – distracting a small child from an activity which is going wrong, being alert to warning signs that things are deteriorating between friends, simply being aware of the fact that a child may be hungry, tired, developing a cold.

'My daughters *asked* to have a Simmer Down Chair last week after watching an episode of *Charlie and Lola*. If things are getting all het up I say: "Do you want to go and sit on your Simmer Down Chairs?" "Oh yes please" they say, and scuttle off to sit on them. They think it's hilarious. I don't think the novelty will last.'

(*Slubberdegullion*)

'I tried the naughty step/time out approach with son and it *never* worked. What it did for us is to put even more distance between us as I am sure that he saw it as a way for me to take away my love for him. The impact is such that even two years after I stopped ever using the time out area (he is nearly five years old), he still goes there if something doesn't quite go his way and has a scream. This is not what I wanted to teach him, to be honest.

I found that the best way to teach them how to behave is say what they should be doing in a very calm quiet voice. Anything else, especially with my son, transforms itself in a battle of will. I know I can win at that game, I am miles too stubborn, but it does not achieve anything (my son would still do the "naughty" thing he is not supposed to do) and would leave our relationship in tatters.'

(*Pitchounette*)

To be fair to Supernanny, she herself only recommends the naughty step for very challenging behaviour. But one of the problems with adopt- ing disciplinary systems which don't come naturally to you is that it can be easy to get them wrong.

'I know someone who uses and uses and uses the naughty step and threat of same, so much so that the phrase sets my teeth on edge. Her daughter's not even "naughty" – her mother just doesn't want her to behave like a child, just a mini adult. "Do you want to go on the naughty step? I'll put you on the naughty step if you don't eat your lunch/play nicely/share your toys/read this book properly/sit on my lap beautifully/etc., etc., etc. . . . You know where you're going if you don't x, y or z, that's right, the naughty step . . . This is the naughty step and you will stay on it until I say you can get up again. Stay on the naughty step. Don't get off the naughty step." Oh, yes, had forgotten "Now say you're sorry and you can come off the naughty step."

I want to say, "Now you never say naughty step again and I'll take my foot off your throat."'

(hunkermunker)

On the other hand, some parents do successfully use time outs and reward systems *in extremis* or for special situations. Sometimes an angry toddler or older child does benefit from some time to calm down and recover himself. Sometimes some 'time out' is what a parent needs to take stock and figure out what to do next – send yourself to the naughty step or lock yourself in the loo if that's what you need. If you don't see it or want it to be seen as a punishment, don't call it a naughty step, call it a time out or call it something else altogether – 'the chair of calm and relaxation', the 'corner of deep and reflective thinking'.

Reward systems can also have a place in the overall messy big picture of your relationship with your children, particularly with quite young children, to tackle specific issues. But at some stage people need to start behaving well because they understand it's the right thing to do and not because it might lead to a trip to Legoland. As children get older, many parents find they have more success with techniques which help children find solutions to their own problems and in which parents try to figure out why the child is misbehaving. And that modelling good behaviour really does work. A lot of Mumsnetters like Adele Faber and Elaine Mazlish's *How to Talk so Kids will Listen and Listen so Kids will Talk*. It is American so you have to adapt it with some care or your children will ask you why you are talking to them in that weird way.

And many parents find that once they are old enough to understand about cause and effect, their children better understand natural rather than arbitrary consequences of misbehaviour, so:

- If you hit your friend, you get taken away from your friend.
- If you use your PlayStation when you said you would do your home-work, it gets confiscated.
- If you make a gratuitous mess, you clean it up.

'I do this:
1. Distraction
2. Positive instruction about behaviour
3. Warning with immediate NATURAL consequence (e.g. if you hit me again, I will put you over there so you can't hit me)
4. Follow through on consequence.'

(*Adair*)

And 'no' should always mean 'no' and not turn to 'yes' after a barrage of nagging and screaming.

'I think the naughty step is a bit mystifying for some children and I don't like the way it's not connected to what they've done. Now he's older (three) I try to make consequences for my son linked to what he's done, e.g. if he torments the cat he has to come and stroke her nicely and say sorry, if he throws food he has to help to clear it up etc. Usually has a similar calming-down effect too.'

(*snowleopard*)

Do remember that all children are different and there are a range of things that work in terms of guiding them towards socially acceptable behaviour and which are not likely to damage them. Children with strong tempers may benefit most from being removed from situations and given time to calm down. Some children will take years of boundary setting and discussion before they grow out of certain behaviours – you have to be patient and persistent. Other children will behave well with a minimum of intervention and with a mostly explanatory approach. Similarly, for some parents, a relatively clear system is one they can cope with and feel comfort-able implementing. For others such a system would feel unnatural and authoritarian. What doesn't work is probably the extremes – corporal punishment or complete laissez-faire.

'Really I think if you avoid either of the extremes (i.e. smothering/neglect) most kids will be just fine and we all overthink things *waaaay* too much now.'

(*Morloth*)

'It's about balance. Somewhere between aggressive, overbearing parents and weak, passive parents is an effective balance that works for each individual family. Most people I know wobble back and forth trying to find the balance, not getting it right all the time but trying to be the best parents they can be.'

(*piprabbit*)

'I can't bring myself to use stickers/pasta jars/naughty steps/all that jazz. Partly because I think it's short-termist, soulless, clinical, does nothing to teach children the moral and ethical foundations of behaviour and is essentially rubbish. A robot could apply rules like that. Partly also because I baulk at the idea of shelving my own instincts and original ideas in favour of the latest TV craze. I use a melee of measures with my son (three) including predictable consequences, distraction where possible, humour where appropriate, clear explanations of what I want him to do and why, asking him why *he* thinks I want him to do what I've asked him to do, an icily calm voice (reserved for really foul behaviour), constant babbling about how much I love being with him because he is such a good and helpful and kind boy . . . I have no idea whether it is any good in "media guru" terms, but we seem to be muddling through and he hasn't killed anyone yet. I think parenting is a creative and subtle, not entirely logic-driven process, like playing the violin.'

(*Greensleeves*)

Manners matter

MAKE THEM MIND THEIR PS AND QS

There are, we would like to think, a few discernible themes in these rules, scattered about like the bits of Crunchie in a McFlurry. Themes apart from the overall general ethos of 'get over yourselfness' (which could usefully be visualised as the whippy ice cream element). One of them is an emphasis on the importance of civility as the binding agent between you, your children and society. Because civility lightens and eases all social relations and kind or at least polite behaviour makes everyone happier and better and makes the purveyor of the politeness better liked.

This rule is primarily about manners in the limited sense of rules of comportment but it is also a little bit about the relationship between those rules and what one hopes is developing underneath – kind and empathetic and sensitive behaviour towards others. Manners of the kind we mean are formal expressions of a concern and respect for the feelings of others which a very young child may not yet feel but which we think are more likely to grow in the context of formal politeness.

Because a child who behaves in a well-mannered way will get a better response from society at large than one who doesn't. This tends to create a virtuous circle. A child who behaves in a mannerly way, even if the pleases and thank yous are not backed by any great thought or feeling, will receive greater kindness and civility back. And will hopefully be more likely to grow virtues such as tolerance and kindness. And less likely as a teen to jostle old people and throw greasy chicken boxes around in his neighbourhood.

'The point of manners is that they make EVERYONE FEEL LOVED UP AND APPRECIATED.'

(morningpaper)

Some parents are uncomfortable with what they see as the imposition of formal manners on the natural raw material of the child. But we say that some manners should be rote-learned in the sense that the child learns to use the words without necessarily thinking deeply about what they mean. Because whilst most people would agree that:

'Being thoughtful and considerate is far more important than remembering to stick a "magic word" into a sentence.'

(pagwatch)

We think this is also self-evident:

'Basic manners are learnt by rote – it is the feelings (enthusiasm, kindness etc.) that cannot be taught by rote (more is the pity) which is how you end up with a surly boy saying thank you but his face and body language saying something entirely different. But better the surly boy with the hunched shoulders saying thanks than the surly boy with the hunched shoulders saying piss off losers which is what he might like to say.'

(Caroline1852)

And the notion that the formal expressions are always empty when employed by a child who has been schooled to use them is, on analysis, an erroneous one:

'Just because a 2-year-old does not say thank you does not mean they are not grateful, we have to teach them to *express* that gratitude. We are not forcing them to say something they do not mean we are teaching them to say something they *do* mean.

Please? Yes, it is a social convention but it is also a way of communicating "I am a pleasant and friendly person who would like your help/item/information" all in one word, hopefully your child *is* a pleasant, friendly person so, again, teaching something they *do* mean.'

(KingCanuteIAm)

Some of the anti-rote-learning brigade seem to be offended by the aesthetics of the learning process. We have all heard parents harping on at children to say please and harried children eventually shouting sorry who are not remotely sorry and it is not a very edifying sight.

'To spend all your time loudly nagging your child about manners when in the presence of others is not imho . . . Good Manners.'

(*cory*)

But education is not a tidy process and we all make mistakes and look like arses sometimes.

'My daughter is four and if she refuses to say thank you, then so be it. I will say it on her behalf. She will pick it up that it is the right thing to do, once her social conscience kicks in.'

(*blueshoes*)

And a very great deal of the process of instilling manners can and should be done by modelling rather than by hectoring. Adults should (try to) treat children with the good manners they would like to see, e.g.:

- Thanking the child for nice and kind behaviour
- Not interrupting the child unnecessarily (and practising good phone manners too – so not telephoning/texting when the child is telling you something)
- Listening whilst the child is speaking

The sorts of feelings and thoughts you would like to be underlying the manners can also be taught to some extent, partly by modelling and partly by conscious imaginative effort:

'Actually you can reinforce natural empathy by asking "and how do you think you would feel if that happened to you?", "how do you think they feel when you say/do that?", tailored to age.'

(*Twig or Treat*)

Really very small newly talking children can start learning basic politenesses before they are old enough to argue with you about them. Manners are a bit like language – if they hear politeness all around them, they will tend to soak it up.

'How much easier and probably natural it is for a three-year-old to say please and thank you than it is for say a six-year-old. Children get more difficult as they get older not easier.'

(*Twigor Treat*)

Mumsnetters' essential manners

We all have our own idiosyncrasies but here are some we can mostly agree on:

- Please
- Thank you
- Covering mouth and nose when sneezing or coughing
- Not barging in front of other people but holding doors open e.g. for lift and letting adults and small children in first
- Saying excuse me when passing (except for scooters on pavements, which should not be racing past and alarming pedestrians)
- Thanking adults for hospitality
- Closing mouth when eating
- Greeting people you know, adult or child
- Saying sorry – although many children won't feel real regret possibly until adulthood
- And that frequent source of parental mortification: Coping with an unwanted/horrifying food item which has been offered. We think the acceptable response is to at least appear to give it a go and then thank the provider. An appearance of sincerity should be cultivated. Those of us who have been known to conceal lovingly homecooked tripe in our handbags don't ask for more than that. And this is a first step on the road to behaving diplomatically, a great and important life skill.

Special category: expressing disagreement politely

With freedom comes responsibility. Modern children are encouraged to express their opinions much more freely than were their forebears and this can lead to angry and rude disagreement and bolshiness.

With some children, the art of differing politely may take until adulthood to learn. And the behaviour of their peers can undo any good example you are setting at home. As can some TV shows, in particular those which depict children being rude to adults and adults being a shower of despicable fools. There is much to be said for not exposing children who are too young not to consider those programmes as a template for their own behaviour to the likes of Tracy Beaker:

'We have BANNED Disney Channel (I blame Hannah Montana etc. and all those shows where kids talk to their parents and other grown-ups like they're pieces of shite).'

(mrshibbins)

'Our daughter is banned from Tracy attitude Beaker, Horrid Henry and Junie B Jones. We found that her whole demeanour changed when she read or watched these (fictional) characters. It seemed to us that she felt the need to adopt the phrases they used. On the whole she is now a very loving and lovely little girl, it is evident, however, that when she becomes nasty and sarky she's either been illicitly viewing or reading La Beaker. We have pointed out that TB isn't a terribly nice girl and Horrid Henry is called that for a reason. We have suggested that she will lose her friends if she insults them.'

(kreecherlivesupstairs)

We are not suggesting that TV is the source of all rudeness. All children tend to go through phases of kicking against authority. A certain degree of firmness goes a long way:

'"My children are allowed to question me. They are not allowed to be rude to me while they do so, and they aren't allowed to disobey me."
   I go by this too – if you start when they are really young it is much easier and they don't even think of it. You have to perfect a certain look and an air of authority.'

(piscesmoon)

You can explain to an older, more rational child how much more efficacious polite and reasoned discussion is than unpleasantness and 'attitude':

'Even if your son is not being downright naughty – insulting words, general silliness, dumb insolence etc. can be very upsetting. This behaviour could also lose him friends and invites back to other people's houses later on when he starts school. If my son does any of the above, I say I won't have "attitude" from him, and he can go to his room until he can be nice again. If he professes ignorance or says it is not fair, I don't go into lengthy explanations or justifications. He certainly knows what he is doing. This is one situation when I don't embark on lots of one-to-one talking. He will not be receptive to reason right then – too bolshie.

When he eventually comes down, he is a changed boy. If I need to reinforce the message, I do so when he is being nice again, but keep the words brief.'

(*tigermoth*)

Other people's children

In our culture there seems to be a general uncertainty about how far it is acceptable to discipline or at least reprove other people's children. There is often a fear that another parent may be offended or set his dogs on you.

If you have no reason to fear an outbreak of violence, we would suggest it is acceptable to correct a child who is behaving rudely to you or to your child, if the rude child's parent is not in the vicinity or is not doing the job himself. Sometimes this is relatively simple – giving a friendly prompt to a child about 'please' and 'thank you' or asking a friend's child not to interrupt you. It is not appropriate to hector other people's children in a bad-tempered way.

'This isn't at all about me trying to teach someone else's child good manners. (Too late for that!) I do think that's the mum's business. But when it's between me and my children, I don't want to be spoken to rudely, and what I also find difficult is when I'm working quite hard to consistently remind my son to be polite, to share the playground equipment etc., and then right in front of him he sees me taking orders from another child – that seems wrong to me. So it is more about me and my son than trying to "intervene" in my friend's parenting, as it were.'

(*snowleopard*)

But don't be the manners police. Be conscious of whether the parent is struggling to deal with the situation or there are special circumstances calling for special handling. Bring your own manners and tact and diplomacy to bear on the situation.

Any child who says, 'What's this slop?' when presented with supper or otherwise behaves in a grossly and unrepentantly vile way on a playdate should be sent home:

'You ring them up and you say e.g. "Hi, just ringing to ask you to collect Timmy as soon as you can, he doesn't seem to be very happy at all."

"Oh dear, what's wrong with him?"

"I don't think there's anything seriously wrong, but he called his dinner slop, kicked the cat and made a hole in my wallpaper, which I'm *sure* is out of character for him, so I thought you'd better handle it. Everyone's the expert on their own child."

"Um, ok, er, when shall I collect him?"

"Now would be fine, we'll wait on the front porch for you. I think he's eager to be home."'

(coldtits)

But have a sense of humour and some pity too:

'Just spare a thought for those with less malleable children – who despite regular exhortations and reminders fail to do many of the polite things unbidden.

I always have a slight frisson of trepidation and fear when my daughter goes for a playdate after school that they will think she has been raised by wolves.'

(handlemecarefully)

And remember that sometimes it is going to be your child who is being unmannerly and foul. Unless you live in France, where all children are mannerly and tidy at all times. Sadly we haven't yet figured out how this is achieved but we are working on a theory which links it to a) the fact that there are more varieties of yoghurt and custardy pudding than there are cheeses, b) the smoking of Gauloises, c) the wearing of quality babygros with envelope necklines.

You don't have to have family meals

"'Family meals", whose frigging idea was that? Because I pretend that they are fun but they are awful. My husband shovels food in as fast as he can to stop the agony. Kids eat either super fast or slowly. And oh it's vile. No doubt you lot all sit there talking about madrigals. Oh God you all LOVE it don't you? I am a scruffer. Pass the kebab in the polystyrene tray.'

(NotCod)

Family meals are one of those seemingly small things which have bloated wildly in importance until you can feel like you have single-handedly *broken society* by not stuffing fish fingers with your toddlers. Because, we are told, lovely family meals lead to:

- Socialisation and good table manners
- Good nutrition and lack of obesity: apparently your children see you enjoying some parsnips and calves' brains and stop living off mini cheddars
- Intimate and supportive family relationships: 'Pass the rutabaga, JohnBoy.' 'How was your day, Mary-Ellen?' etc. etc.

And then sometimes you feel a tiny little sceptical backlash happening in your breast:

'We do this every fricking day. At some point the children will just turn into well-bred individuals merely by eating chilli in front of us while we talk about work and shout at them.'

(Cappuccino)

So look, some people can't do that many family meals together for a variety of practical reasons. It's not their fault and it's not the end of the world either:

'The only reason I can manage to eat all together as a family is 1. because I work at home and 2. there's no daddy coming back from the office at 8 o'clock! Otherwise, I don't see how people manage it either unless Daddy/Mummy happens to be a builder or in a job like that which finishes early. Unless children are older, of course.'

(*Caligula*)

'The decline of family meals is an effect of our long-hours work culture, but no politician lecturing us about parenting practices is honest enough to make the link.'

(*oldieMum*)

'We do our best with the hand we've been dealt (presumably the children of shift workers have such appalling table manners that they can never eat outside of the house).'

(*Zog*)

But we are here to tell you, there is no need to fret. If you are fretting about your children missing out, try casting your mind back to the family meals of your childhood. Even if your family wasn't entirely dysfunctional, you probably weren't the Waltons either. Many seventies dads, for example, were, under the sideburns and the porno moustache, just retreads of fifties dads and many family meals were arenas for control-freakery of various kinds.

'We did all eat together as children, it was awful. Mainly because our stepfather was (and is) a control freak and we weren't allowed to start eating until he sat down. He'd be sitting on his arse reading the paper until the food was ready and *then* he'd faff about for ages while three hungry children and their mother (my mother) stared ravenously at the food on the table and watched it get cold. We were only allowed to eat once *he* sat down. And we got what we were given, no choices. I think my mother was very wrong to let this happen and he was a tosser for doing it so no, no happy memories of eating en famille here!'

(*wickedwaterwitch*)

And even if no one is being forced to sit for hours in front of some congealing liver, there is so much that is underscintillating about endless family meals. Refereeing the badinage about who is a plopper. Enduring the symposium on the best attributes of Pokémon cards. Parrying the whining about the lovely tasty handmade food you have placed in front of them. As you sit, keening your own threnody: 'Eat up that broccoli, don't fill yourself up on drink, use your fork . . .'

Sometimes reinforcing other people's good behaviour is just incompatible with enjoying your own food. Or it is simply too stressful waiting and waiting for a child who eats very slowly and bursts into tears when confronted with everyone else's waiting . . .

The actualité and the, er, non-actualité

Fantasy family meal

'Would like:
    Calm conversation – "How was school today?" "Really great mummy and I learned so much. Did you know that the Elizabethans wore stockings?"
    Ravenous all-consuming children.
    Praise – "Mummy that was delicious, I love your cooking! Can I have some more?"'

(*pushchair*)

Real family meal

'I keep thinking, "must eat with kids in manner of someone in a magazine" and then do it and it's horrific. Got a fantastic expensive free-range chicken, did nice roasted veg la la la and the kids whined and bickered and *cried* ffs. Husband went into a decline and I ate in record time due to stress and nobody really tasted their food. Disaster.'

(*mabanana*)

So go ahead, have some meals without your kids. Have all your suppers without your kids if that's what works for you.

'We eat together at the weekend (lunches) and we always have breakfast together. We often go out for Sunday lunch en famille which is lovely and both girls have fantastic "restaurant manners".'

(HeyEnidYou'veLostWeight)

Meals without kids mean different things for different people. Some people whose lives are a bit more like chicklit than the rest of ours might be chopping herbs whilst their husband or partner does something clever and marvellous with a fish before having intelligent conversation and/or an erotic interlude with some good wine. Others of us might just want to eat a jacket potato with the TV. Or crisps in the bath.

If your children eat before you do, you can always sit with them and drink a cup of tea or pick at some salad and chat. But don't scrutinise – some family meals go bad because one person is not eating but is just policing all the bad doings. Don't be the meal enforcer. And it's not terrible for children to eat sandwiches or pizza in front of a DVD from time to time.

Here are some tips for family meals which are more funnerer:

- Do not comment on eating/drinking habits unless absolutely necessary.
- Keep them pacey: eat, chat as much as you want, leave when you're done.
- 'Cook together, take it to the kitchen table . . . all have own jobs, eat quickly, listen to music, get kids to clear table, don't do it too often.'

(Twiglett)

- 'Basic rules that go without saying, although obv they have to be said here.
    1. Make quick simple meal favoured mostly by children.
    2. No frills – no nice table setting, just water, no heated plates, no condiments.
    3. Anyone who has finished can go straight on to afters without asking as long as they help themselves. If they can't help themselves they wait till adult ready. If they can't wait till adult ready they can leave the table and come back later for afters.'

(pointydog)

'That's not a MEAL that's IKEA cafe!'

(NotCod)

Food options for family meals: same or different?

Obviously when children are tiny, dinners are going to have to differ. Unless you are all sitting down to carrot purée. Although if you do baby-led weaning, babies can simply have a subset of the adult meal. As children get older and different kinds of fussiness set in, some families become entrenched in different dinners:

The extreme segregation option:

Adults: Curried quails' eggs and sea urchins in a coulis of mongoose followed by an avocado en croute lightly bathed in a seasnail cappuccino.

Children: Recovered, reconstituted and breaded ears and arses with chips and peas.

The all for one option:

Adults and children: Spag bol, garlic bread, salad.

Or, flippancy aside, many families find they can adapt the dinners so everyone is happy.

For some families this means erring on the nursery food side and having a lot of fish fingers and beans and chips. We suggest unless you are a huge school dinner fan that you start from the other end of the food spectrum and work your way in. Like this, for example:

'I would do a basic tomato pasta sauce with salad and garlic bread, chilli flakes and parmesan on the table, adults could have theirs spicy, children too if they wanted or they could have it plain, anyone looking forlorn would get asked quietly if they wanted a cheese sandwich.'

(*Oliveoil*)

Let them fight amongst themselves

The only good thing about the boring, vicious, pointless, interminable, epic fighting your children will engage in for part or all of their mutual childhoods is that it holds not a mirror but maybe a prism up to your own childhood and makes you look at your parents in a slightly transfigured way, possibly with some little rainbows at the edges. Because:

- You realise how utterly boring and awful you and your siblings must have been when you were clawing at each other's faces in defence of the borders between the seats in your no-rear-seatbelts car.
- You possibly begin to see how much wiser your parents were than you have hitherto given them credit for. When they let you and your siblings just get on with devising ways to cause as much pain as possible without making marks, they were, maybe, helping you get to a stage where you could sort out your own differences. When they went away to sit in a quiet room with a packet of Rothmans King Size and a bottle of Blue Nun, they were gathering the shreds of their own mental health and regrouping them so they too could live to fight another day.

'I think fighting is pretty much inevitable – or it was when I was growing up. Actually, it's a skill I'm quite proud of. Sometimes I look at people in meetings who are annoying me and think "I just bet I could sort you out if needs be, mate!"'

(*Anchovy*)

If things your parents said to you have not already started emerging like frogs or pearls from your mouth, they will probably start to pop out once your children are old enough to start fighting with each other. And they will be rapidly and dispiritingly recycled. It is hard to feel you are at the top of your parenting game when your three-year-old is bellowing, 'I've just had enough of the lot of you.'

So we suggest that this is an area of parenting where (slightly tweaked) retro is the way to go and that means, in general, letting your children fight their own fights and not getting involved.

But there are, inevitably, exceptions to this rule: you must obviously have regard to age. Toddlers are notoriously riven by homicidal urges in relation to new baby siblings, sometimes papered over by a willingness to provide practical assistance. That practical assistance may provide opportunities to drop, bash or drown the sibling and must be closely supervised.

Two or more toddlers together will also require parental intervention. If you are at home, you should probably separate them and set them up with different activities. You have an advantage because they are small enough to lift and separate, unlike older children.

If one child is actually physically harming another (e.g. there is blood or bite marks), you will obviously have to physically separate them.

The truth about older fighting children

Older children tend to be passionately obsessed with fairness (in relation to themselves) and convinced that parents are actively and constantly looking for ways to treat them unfairly. Rather than occasionally and ineffectually trying to stand up for the notion of civility in a world of wanton violence.

You can never satisfy their desire for fairness in relation to their internecine struggles because, and we cannot stress this enough, it is impossible to tell in any child disagreement who is in the right and who is in the wrong. Even if you had CCTV all over your house and could look at actual footage of the dispute. And each child will present you with a version of events which differs in almost every material particular from that provided by any other child or children. And it would take you all day to try to get to the bottom of it and by the time you were even halfway there, they would have made it up and wandered off to play together.

So if there is a lot of arguing and whining and tattling going on, generally speaking you should say: 'Sort it out amongst yourselves.' You can, if the wrangling is really relentless and unceasing, wade in and throw them the odd negotiation technique to try: 'I simply cannot tell whose baby doll owns this bottle from your stories so can we agree to flip a coin?' Usually the technique is angrily rejected but you may find them adopting it at some later date. Try flattering them a bit: 'I know you can sort this out amongst yourselves.' It's not so much a lie as an optimistic forecast . . .

Again, where actual violence occurs in front of you, you may have to intervene and dispense some injustice, by separating the combatants at the very least. Backed up with whatever punishment you may feel is appropriate.

Laissez-faire is more

Some Mumsnetters take a hardline approach:

'Don't wear yourself out with it all! Just learn to ignore it. I have spent months trying to mediate, behaviour modify etc. etc. etc. my two children's behaviour towards each other. All to no avail. So a change of tactics had to come before my sanity went! I thought a lot about other species and this type of behaviour and have come to the conclusion that it is entirely normal and just a part of being children. I was certainly like it with my sisters and I know most of my friends were too.

I now refuse to get involved *at all* with any disputes, horseplay, rough and tumble – anything – that happens between them. If one of them gets hurt, upset or whatever because of something the other has done, I don't listen – not even for a second. They are bluntly told that by engaging in this constant bickering and fighting they are accepting of the consequences so don't bother telling me when it all goes wrong!

It hasn't improved their behaviour at all, but it has improved mine and my husband's! With time I have to confess to barely noticing it these days!!!'

(*soapbox*)

Others think an occasional wading-in is appropriate:

'I often think these situations offend our sense of justice in that it is logical to think one started it and the other retaliated. I'm afraid that even a European Court of Law could probably not decide who the aggressor was so I always think it is best to separate them. I normally end up screeching, "If you can't play nicely then one of you go in here and one go to play in your room", or if I'm feeling generous, I'll create some tasks that need doing and ask my daughter to do one of them and my son to do the other.'

(foxinsocks)

Some favour laissez-faire interlaced with some more vigourous wading-in where there is serious violence occurring:

'I agree about not intervening too much, separating them when it gets too heated. Also, and I can't quite remember when I started doing this, but I think it was around when my second son was four, I sometimes catch them before it's got too hysterical, go in, and say, "I *know* you can sort this out without fighting. I will give you five minutes to sort it out WITHOUT shouting, or I'll come in and sort it out myself/take the toy away that you are arguing about." The first time I tried this, I didn't hold out much hope, but it worked a treat.

Another thing. If there has been a big blowup and one or both are very upset/angry. I separate, give them five mins to calm down, and then do a family discussion. Basically, each of us gets a turn to say how we feel, without shouting, and we hold a wooden spoon to show it's our turn to talk. No one can interrupt while someone else has the spoon. Again, sounds unlikely, but this really works to get them to feel that they are able to have their say. I have used this since my second son was about four as well. Obviously, you can't use this all the time, as it's a bit time-consuming, but it's useful if the same arguments keep recurring.

Also, praise them for negotiating with each other or playing nicely.

I was forced to these interventionist strategies because real violence was happening a lot – biting, scratching etc. The first time we did the wooden spoon thing, my older son had a serious deeply felt rant about the injustices meted out by my younger son, I had my say, then my younger son (age four) got hold of the spoon, put on a funny voice, and said, "Hello, I'm Mr Spoon." Certainly diffused the tension.'

(Jamieandhismagictorch)

When fighting is particularly chronic (we're thinking of half-term here), here are a few potential preventives.

Separation: if circumstances allow, try to arrange for children to spend time apart, if possible including some one-to-one time with a parent. They like each other better when they see a little less of each other and you like them better when you have only one chatting sweetly to you rather than three snarling around your ankles. And that goodwill carries over a bit into times when you are all together.

Separate bedtimes: a variation on the above. Bedtimes can be bad times, not least because you yourself may be feeling tired, hungry and desirous of being tucked up with a story. With children who are fighting unabatingly at bedtime, try the staged bedtime approach. The older child gets the privilege of staying up a further half-hour, say, and they both get some quality time with parents uninterrupted by clandestine kicking under the duvet. You can also achieve the same effect with children being read stories by two parents in separate rooms. More complicated arrangements have to be made with three-plus children.

Try to spot boredom fights developing: not always possible we know, but if you see that a child is kicking about looking for trouble as a way of alleviating ennui, stepping in, even if only to dragoon the child into helping with an unattractive chore, can prevent a whole afternoon of disputation from igniting.

Get out of the house: a panacea for almost everything. Exercise and fresh air improve the tempers of everyone.

Some of those futile fights in full

'My daughter is a prima donna and cries at the drop of a hat – I have quite often rushed upstairs thinking my son had thrown her off the top bunk to find that he was in fact "sitting on my fairy outfit" or some other minor faux pas.'

(*puddle*)

'Offences I had to mediate yesterday evening include "talking to me in a really nasty voice" and "looking at my felt tip pens". My favourite fight is the exaggerated showing of some forgotten – and usually fairly pointless – object, creating an immense and insatiable need for it, and then whisking it away with a "you can't have it".'

(*Anchovy*)

'And/or the uncovering (usually by the smaller child, for once faintly less in the wrong) of a long unloved and really quite pointless toy . . . which is then grabbed with a heartrending plea of "It's MIIIIIIIIIIIIIIIIINE!"'

(motherinferior)

'Current favourites are: "My sister did a pumpkin face at me" and:
  "Daughter 2, think of a name for a horse."
  "Rosie."
  "No that's not a horse name, call it Thunder."
  "No I want to call it Rosie."
  "OK Thunder, come on."
  "MUMMEEEEEEEEEEE I want to call my horse Rosie and Daughter One won't let me." [immense amount of tears and wailing].'

(IHeartEnid)

Don't shame your children up about fiddling but do make them to do it in the bedroom

Some small children fiddle with their genitals and some don't or not so as you'd notice. It can be most disconcerting if you've had a first child who sleeps with her hands crossed chastely outside her clothes to be faced with a second child whose hands are firmly lodged in her pants. It's kind of funny but not so funny on the bus and sometimes, when it's relentless, you can find yourself repressing some disgust. And feeling bad about the disgust . . .

Just so you know you're not alone, here are some variations and permutations. Some just like to take the air:

'My son is two and loves pulling down his pull-up pants so that his willy sort of sits on the top, hanging over the edge. It's not always immediately noticeable until he does a wee . . .'

(*Wordsmith*)

Other children seem to be conducting rigorous tensile strength testing:

'Makes my eyes water when my son pulls his . . . he really stretches it. Doesn't seem to bother him, though, merely amuses him.'

(*edam*)

This may lead to a career in engineering in some instances:

'O god, my son made his bleed once he fiddled so much. Even when he came to tell me it hurt he was still fiddling. The funniest was when I found him naked,

sat crosslegged and playing with his cars. He had it stretched out and was holding it down on his ankle, using it as a bridge!'

(gigglingoblin)

Some children seem to be the dog/toddler evolutionary 'missing link':

'My daughter (eighteen months) has recently taken to humping her cuddly toys,
and grunting.'

(frogs)

'My son was humping away madly the other night while I was cooking dinner
and I shouted through from the kitchen for him to stop. He yelled back, "Just
adore [ignore] me, Mummy!"'

(marthamoo)

'Willy guitar', there are no words:

'Mine had a hideous game called the "willy guitar". Years later they can still bring
me out in hives just singing the twangy soundtrack they used to accompany it
with.'

(turquoise)

Very young fiddlers

With babies and young toddlers, you can just ignore the fiddling and if it
seems to be going on too much, try some gentle distraction. There's nothing wrong with investigating a part of your body you may not see very
much because it's usually in a nappy. Many babies are just initially rather
surprised to see their genitals. A bit of nappy-free time, maybe before or
after bathtime, can be an opportunity to get to know their bits a little
better. So they don't have to greet them with quite such vigourous delight
every time a nappy change occurs.

If you can't curtail the joy, you may face some hygiene issues, i.e. hand
goes to bits before poo has been wiped off, poo goes on hand, face, hair
etc. . . .

There are a few techniques you can try:

- Provide an exciting toy before the nappy comes off to keep the hands busy, whilst you swoop in with a wipe and deal with the genital area first.
- 'I ended up changing them on my knee, so I could sort of block their access to it with my arm/body. I am the queen of lightning nappy changes.'

  (*mankyscotslass*)
- 'I've found a solution to the dirty nappy one. As you remove the nappy start singing "the little green frog". By the time you get the pooey nappy off you will have got to the "tra la la la la" bit, which means that any self-respecting toddler must wave their arms about frantically. You then quickly clean the poo off the penis before the verse finishes and they dive in!'

  (*fisil*)

Obviously small girls should be deterred from poking things into their vaginas and toddlers generally should wash their hands after a fiddle.

Older fiddlers

As children get to the more sentient bit of toddlerhood, some lose interest in their genitals and some do not. This is when you can start suggesting that whilst it's perfectly fine to play with your bits, it's not something to do in company. The almost inevitable result of your sensitive handling is that your two-year-old will announce to his grandparents that 'I'm just going to my room to play with my willy.' This can be a good parenting moment in excruciating parenting moment clothing, depending on the grandparents.

You may find you have to keep reminding some children as they get older.

'Was at a sports relief thing yesterday and looked across the line of kids, there were about sixteen kids there, nine of whom were boys, six of those standing playing with their willies, one of whom had both hands down the front of his trousers having a right good rummage. Is there a code or something to say, "Give it a grab NOW"?'

(*dizzydixies*)

'My seven-year-old son still does this, as do many of the men I've known <sigh> so I think the answer may be that men never grow out of that absent-mindedly fondling their willy when they think no one's looking thing.'

(*wickedwaterwitch*)

Many parents find a cue word such as 'fingers' will remind a child who is distractedly fiddling to take his hands from his pants. Or just yank the hand out. In a sensitive and caring way.

Turn the computer games off

One of the things you struggle with time and again once you have your own children is turning into the person you resented when you were yourself a child, i.e. the person who wantonly spoiled the fun of others, the fun you knew in your child heart was perfectly harmless. And sometimes you do it out of suspicion of things which are different from the things you grew up with. And then you feel a bit uneasy because maybe there is nothing wrong with the new thing, just as there was nothing wrong in times past with, say, BMX bikes or pogo sticks or ghetto blasters or making small fires at the bottom of the garden or playing naked games.

But we say stand firm in relation to computer games and social networking sites and internet use generally. This is not like the olden days when someone had Pong at their house – no one ever got dangerously addicted to Pong. No one frittered away his childhood playing Pong. No one was ever 'groomed' on Pong.

Now this rule is not mainly about restricting access to inappropriate content. Of course you must have an internet filter such as Net Nanny (and you must educate your children properly about internet safety – see the websites listed below for advice and guidance) and no, *Grand Theft Auto* is not a good game for a six-year-old.

This rule is largely about time and the way a person's life can simply be inhaled by the world wide web. Many of us would like to believe that children who are not subject to restrictions and bans will eventually come to self-regulate, perhaps after an initial wallowing in excess and eighteen straight hours on the Playbox Z or whatever. And in our hearts we cannot face being the enforcers of seemingly arbitrary rules about 'screen time'. It offends our *amour propre* to be the petty tyrant unplugging the laptop or locking away the games console.

But many children are unable to self-regulate in relation to computer games (or indeed to hunting for Pokémon cards on eBay). Yes, the odd child does cast the games aside like children of yore chucked aside Furbies or Transformers or whatever was the toy of Christmas. But the games are like cigarettes: they have been designed to be addictive. We are not saying that all games are intrinsically evil or that some are not interesting, interactive, stimulating. But they are not all that any child should be doing with his free time. Or even the bulk of it.

A young child or even a teenager is not necessarily in a position to gauge the effect playing the games is having on his moods or the extent to which excessive playing may be limiting his time and energy for other activities, including physical exercise and non-computer-based social interaction. Call us luddites, but we say sometimes it is better for a child to be doing something imaginative with Lego. Or a stick. Or reading a book. Yes, we are going to say it, READING IS BETTER FOR YOU THAN PLAYING COMPUTER GAMES:

'Books require you to conjure up the picture of what's being described. They require you to empathise with characters.'

(*Litchick*)

'You don't need to MAKE a child be sociable but I can't BELIEVE that anyone seriously thinks it isn't harmful to allow a seven-year-old child complete access to computer games in all their free time. You may as well fry their brain TBH. Do you HONESTLY think this is OK for their physical and mental well-being? Children need to be CHILDREN. That means playing and developing imaginative games and fantasising and finding things to DO and learning skills for life and that includes learning to be BORED tbh.'

(*morningpaper*)

'As a teacher it's sooo easy to spot the boys (and it does always seem to be boys) who veg out for hours in front of a screen. They tend to be fairly unmotivated and uninterested in most things (as they obv like computer-generated stuff and graphics and noise). They also tend to have low-level skills in empathy or imagination.'

(*MaloryDon'tDiveIt'sShallow*)

'The gaming industry is a multi-billion dollar industry who know full well how to get people hooked.

Games generally are fast-moving and deliver hits of dopamine regularly by collecting points, eliminating a target etc. Then it's on to the next level where you have to try that bit harder to get your dopamine hit. At no point do you have to develop any social or empathetic skills.'

(Litchick)

Rational limits

So we say unplug, switch off, confiscate as needs be. Here are the rudiments of our plan:

- No computer time before school. And no TV either.
- Keep the computer/console out of the child's bedroom. And the TV.
- Supervise what they are up to. Be in the room if they are playing internet-based games.
- With younger children, don't rush to purchase dedicated consoles. See if you can restrict usage to children's games available on the internet.
- Resist peer pressure on their behalf in a judicious way. It may be hard on a child to be the only person is his class who is never allowed on *Club Dinosaur*. But the fact that Ralph's dad lets him stay up all night on fifteen-certified *Zombie Massacre* is no reason why your kid should.
- Many parents set limits on amounts of time allowed on the computer – so much time at the weekend and so much time on (selected) weekdays. Exclude weekdays when they would otherwise be at swimming or martial arts or whatnot. Some parents find that for some children allowing any time on weekdays leads to frustration and misery for all concerned.

'My sister found her ten-year-old was wanting to do nothing else except play video games so her husband put it into his car on a Monday and took it to work and brought it home again on Fridays for a while. Now it is just banned during the week and he is fine with it.'

(Buda)

'I had to ban all computer time during the week because just thirty minutes was actually making them worse. I think the games were so exciting that nothing else was interesting enough to do when they had finished playing.'

(*LadyPeterWimsey*)

- Try to find games which are not just about eviscerating zombies. Parents who have allowed first-person shooter games and other violence-fests past the threshold often report a deterioration in behaviour – lack of empathy, rudeness, ill temper.

'If you choose carefully they are either acquiring useful skills (like planning and budgeting), it is sociable (as in swapping Pokémon on the DS) or the game has a natural ending (like *Legend of Zelda*) so they won't play forever.'

(*tatt*)

- It can be helpful to think about 'total screen time' so if you are allowing an hour, it is an hour of telly/console/surfing the internet.

'We eventually ended up with an agreement like the Conservative/Lib Dem coalition pinned up on the fridge which limits each child to a specific time slot each day.'

(*tatt*)

- Screen time should generally take place after homework or instrument practice or mucking out the pigs or whatever else the children have to get done.
- One way of avoiding the horrible howling that you set off if you come and turn the game off yourself is to have some sort of timer system – if the game is on the internet, the computer can be set to log off the internet. Or you can put a timer device on a socket or only charge a console battery to a limited extent. Some consoles have built-in timers.

'When they were younger and had Game Boys I had little digital timers which were set for one hour a day. They could choose to use it all at once or in bits and that worked really well for years. The Xbox has a built-in timer you can set to limit game play. That didn't work for us because of the sharing issues. We eventually ended up with an agreement like the Treaty of Versailles pinned up which limits each child to a specific time slot each day.

One day a week it's off all day and never before school.'

(inthesticks)

If you have to, you can despotically remove controllers, headsets etc.
- Another way of coping with the child who does a less green impersonation of the Hulk when unplugged is to institute sanctions for computer-game-related misbehaviour. Call us Pol Pot if you will. For parents not philosophically opposed to reward/sanction based disciplinary systems, the threat of computer time removal or the possibility of extra time being rewarded can be very effective behaviour modification techniques.

Social networking sites

'Kids need a life not a Facebook account.'

(NotAnOtter)

There are insaniacs who join up their newborn babies or fetuses to Facebook. There are those who think it's a good way for children to keep up with faraway relatives. To which we say fah! Just fah! Send an email, skype the grandparents, send a postcard. For thousands of years human beings have found ways to keep in touch with each other which did not involve status updates.

And think of Facebook as a portal through which the rest of the internet might stream into your house in the manner of those blackish smoke-like things in the Harry Potter films. Even if you carefully restrict who your child 'friends', quite probably some old mate or sister-in-law will post an inappropriate status update or have some nonsense on her wall. This is why people get sacked for posting 'I hate my boss' – because people incontinently friend everyone and then forget what they've done.

'I have an eleven-year-old stepdaughter with a FB account and both her father and I hugely disapprove. None of our other children (two of whom are older than the stepdaughter) have accounts. She has in excess of 170 FB friends!!! There is no way an eleven-year-old knows that many people and many of them are over eighteen. Her profile pic is a full-face shot of herself. From the pictures and chat on her page (and those of her friends) you can clearly work out where they go to school, how they get there etc. etc. There is also the issue of her being exposed to conversations, pictures etc. that it's not necessary for an eleven-year-old to be part of (drunken pictures, foul language, racist and other suspect video postings etc.) which will turn up in her news feed when the "friends" post or comment on the activity of others.'

(lemonadesparkle)

So just don't do it. We say social networking sites are not for the under-thirteens and should be subject to time-limited and policed use thereafter, which means:

- High privacy settings
- Minimal personal information
- Profile picture of a cartoon character or a doughnut, not child in make-up/swimming costume

'My son turned 13 last week and that is when I allowed him to have an account. He survived perfectly well up until then. And OMG at some of his friends' pages. No privacy settings with full name, HOME ADDRESS, msn address, mobile number, school and photos on! His will be policed heavily, I have his password and he is on my friends. Not so I can snoop, but so I can make sure he is playing by the rules we have agreed.'

(mumto3boys)

If it's already gone wrong

This advice may come late for you, and your child may already be a drivelling console-based room-slinking, etiolated, wasted-of-muscle spectre. In which case you must do a forceful addiction-stylee tough love intervention and forcibly re-engineer her leisure activities:

'If he won't be pro-active, you need to be. Get children round for tea. Enrol him in Scouts. Or Cadets. Or judo. Drag him along kicking and screaming if you have to; as you say, once he's there he will love it. Play board games with him. Get him out in the garden. Get him to read a book. He sounds as if he has gotten into the habit of being lazy, and it will take you putting a rocket up his backside to shift him off it.'

(WigWamBam)

'Pull the plug. To be honest, I would rather my daughters hated me for a while than to exhaust all their creativity and passion on the internet.'

(Enid)

Why must I be a teenager in love with Call of Duty?

With teenagers obviously you need to approach the whole arena with considerably more tact and allow much for individual circumstances. Clearly it is better for your sixteen-year-old to be safely at home on Facebook than out and about taking drugs and stealing cars. But he may need your help to figure out what the sensible limits to his activity are. Teenagers have exams to take and social lives to be pursuing. They have post-teen lives to think about. Try to discuss the whole thing and involve your teenager in the decision making. You may need to agree a proper contract about what is acceptable use if you have a teen who is badly addicted.

'When my son was doing GCSEs we cut off the wireless connection. He still had the laptop for school work but without the distraction of MSN, Facebook and football blogs. He (reluctantly) agreed it was a sensible move and we agreed he could use the computer downstairs whenever he needed to.'

(Buda)

Internet safety

There are various sites where you can obtain detailed advice on internet safety, including: www.mumsnet.com/internet-safety
www.thinkuknow.org/
www.childnet.com/
www.chatdanger.com/
www.beatbullying.org/
www.kidsmart.org.uk/

Make them do chores and start them young

It is very easy when you are a parent to get into a sort of dreamy coping state in which you carry on doing the things you started doing when your child was a newborn. So you continue dressing it and wiping it and spooning food into it. And you get better at doing those things and feel more confident and generally happier. And then you notice it is an eleven-year-old boy who can't make a piece of toast. And you have forgotten to teach him to ride a bike or swim (those, incidentally, are the things you must teach any child capable of learning them – riding a bike and swimming. And reading. The rest is optional). And he is about as capable of keeping himself alive in your house full of food as a tomato plant at the North Pole.

There is no clearly signposted temporal dividing line between the helpless frog you take home from hospital and the competent child you should be turning it into. The road to self-sufficiency is a long one and progress is slow. And for a very long time it is going to be easier to do the tasks yourself because you are better and quicker at them and don't make a big fat mess doing them.

But start young and start small. Toddlers can start helping to tidy toys away before they are two. And at around two or three, children can usually start putting their cups and bowls in the sink and putting their dirty clothes into the laundry basket. Uriah Heep-ish levels of parental gratitude and admiration are appropriate here. Many children will be charmed to help with small tasks like packing their own juice and wipes into a backpack. Laying a table or helping with a cooking task can confer an enormous sense of accomplishment. In relation to more complex housework, there is often a smaller constituent task a toddler can perform – passing clothes pegs, stirring something. Or they can be copying what you are doing with their own duster or brush and pan. Relax your standards to reflect the age of the helper – a three-year-old who swabs a wet cloth around a table is doing well. An eight-year-old can be expected to actually get it clean.

Learning to cook is also an incremental process with modest beginnings – pouring a bowl of cereal successfully, making toast, making a sandwich, making a cup of tea, heating a tin of beans. There is no reason why, with a little luck and some careful grooming, you can't be the mother of an eight-year-old who can rustle you up a full English breakfast and make his own packed lunch.

The point is not so much the quality of the output as the fact that they are learning to perform the tasks, for themselves and for the family in general And the great thing about having children who help, even a bit, is that you feel less like an angry drudge. And you don't feel you are bringing up children whose spouses and partners will eventually spend their lives railing at them about their slatternly ways. And, yes, chores are a feminist issue:

'It's vital that boys don't get the impression that girls were put on the earth to be their slaves. I am regularly horrified at the uselessness of some people's husbands or partners – one would die of thirst before making a cup of coffee, for example.

I'm not a great believer in huge lists of chores just for the sake of it but simple tasks done as a team is a great basis for the independent men you'll hope to turn out into the world.'

(*Pikelit*)

Some children are more eager to help than others and some are better at it. Some bustling eighteen-month-olds follow you round waiting to put your wrappers in the bin. Other small children bemoan the unfairness of being asked to do anything at all. You may have to impose some consequences on the very reluctant ones (toys that don't get tidied up are made at least temporarily unavailable for playing with). Having a routine helps as they get bigger – so that they know what jobs are expected and when they are expected to be done. You do need to break large tasks down into constituent parts for reluctant or distracted children – so not 'tidy your room' but 'put the Lego in the Lego box'.

'The biggest mistake people make is they wait until the kids are teenagers and then suddenly expect them to take on chores. Start young and make it fun. If it's something they've always done it won't be a problem. If you ask for more help when they are older they won't see it as a battle rather it will be an extension of something they do anyway.'

(freename)

There are different views on the issue of whether there should be any linkage between pocket money and chores (older children) or star charts and other reward-delivery systems for younger children. We suggest very limited usage. Some jobs should always just be part of family life and unremunerated – especially cleaning-up-after-yourself-type jobs. But there is nothing wrong, we would venture to suggest, in offering extra pocket money for special jobs or the odd twenty pence to make mummy a cup of tea . . .

Don't worry about the imaginary friends

(BUT DON'T GIVE THEM EXTRA CAKE EITHER)

'Oh yes, imaginary friends can be quite weird I think, and you do want to say, "Look you know this isn't real, right? You do know that?" because it can be freaky. But don't worry, it's not really freaky and I think quite normal. My son had two, one of them was vile and rude and wasn't allowed out a lot and met a dreadful death in a place where "he shouldn't have been in the first place", the other one just grew up and left. My daughter had a whole world of babies and it was a very complicated kingdom with different coloured rooms and a Queen who ordered them to do jobs, and when they'd done them they could re-paint their rooms, and there was a taxation system, and it was all very weird and very constant.'

(*ahundredtimes*)

The world of children is dense with imaginary friends. If one could render them all visible the streets would be teeming, a city of ghosts. Anecdotally, they seem to occur a lot amongst only children or in families with big age gaps between siblings. Although it should be said that sibling groups do sometimes produce elaborate joint ventures, multiverses crawling with imaginary beings. In very large families, of course, orphan fantasies may predominate. Imaginary friends seem to arrive when a child is around two or three and often peter out (or die violently) somewhere between five and seven, although some stay longer or at least continue to visit occasionally. Don't fret too much about them when they are resident. Otherwise happy and sociable children may have imaginary friends and they often seem to run in families.

Imaginary friends can be anything from peculiar adults to animal species unknown to nature. Some children have imaginary houses or carry imaginary books.

'My son (three years and four months old) has a whole menagerie of animals but no people ... He has been acquiring them over the last six months or so, but definitely knows they are not real. A few days ago my mother offered him a runner bean for his rabbits and he looked at her very scathingly and said, "They are pretend, you know." I get a running commentary of what they are up to all day long and have to hold the boot open when we take the dog for a walk so the rabbits and kangaroos can get in too!'

(Drusilla)

Imaginary friends seem to exist in response to different needs in different children. Imaginary friends who hit and hurt other people are often just expressing anger on behalf of their real-life friends or perhaps just experimenting with what happens when you do express anger or do things which are forbidden. A lot of imaginary friends seem somehow to be a way of orienting the child in relation to a reality which can be confusing or frightening:

'My daughter uses her imaginary play to take things on board or come to terms with things too.'

(EachPeachPearMum)

An imaginary friend can be something as simple as a loo buddy for a newly toilet-trained child who feels a bit lonely in the bathroom by himself. Or the imaginary friend may help a child play out fantasies of power and self-aggrandisement:

'My son has Peter who always does everything before, better and bigger than us. He also has five huskies.'

(fin42)

Or he may just be a useful device for a cunning child:

'My son has an imaginary friend – an older adopted brother called Rupert whose own mummy and daddy threw him out on the street. He is often the reason why unpopular activities must be delayed or cannot possibly be undertaken, or why we "have to" do other things. My son becomes quite incensed if I ignore Rupert's needs or don't speak to him when he is "present".'

(Blu)

It's worth looking at some broad types of imaginary friend and the relationships you might cultivate with them.

The annoying and controlling imaginary friend

Some imaginary friends have rather intense imaginary needs and are underfoot rather a lot:

'I mean yadda yadda fertile imagination blah creative blah just play and all that but flipping heck it's irritating the socks off me. It's like having another child without the sex first. And if my son tells me I can't "sit there because that's where Peter is" one more time I swear I'll throw the imaginary blighter out the door so fast his feet won't touch the ground. Peter has an amazing ability to be just under wherever my backside is about to land.'

(*meowmix*)

Some imaginary friends require not just attention but feeding:

'He told everyone that he had a little brother called Daniel. I had to set a place at breakfast for Daniel, give him a bowl of cereal and a slice of toast. I wasn't allowed to throw the food away before we left the house. But when we came back later, my son would happily polish off the stale toast and cereal on the grounds that Daniel had left it . . .'

(*edam*)

Other invisible playmates need to be swung on swings, have a bed made up for them, get left behind on the bus and cause hysteria. And it can be hard to know with someone who is invisible precisely where he is or how tall . . . This sort of imaginary friend can be somewhat considerably tiresome to have around.

Some parents of children with the more omnipresent type of imaginary friend have hypothesised that imaginary friends are just outlets for very chatty children. When the quotidian is exhausted, the exploits of the imaginary friend can be relentlessly rehearsed:

'My daughter aged four has had an imaginary friend called Chloe since she was two. We tend to go along with the concept – i.e. simply passively echoing my daughter's comments about Chloe, never challenging Chloe's existence but also never actively encouraging my daughter to expand upon Chloe's current adventures, preferences, etc. But . . . I did crack one day with unforeseen consequences: I was tired, driving in heavy traffic and my daughter, sitting behind me in her car seat, was going on and on and on about what Chloe was doing today and what Chloe was going to do today and what Chloe was going to eat (daughter is a fussy eater while Chloe has a dream appetite!) and how Chloe's bedroom is going to be decorated ("sparkly rainbow colours and pink"). I looked up in the mirror and said, "Can we stop talking about Chloe for a while, please? Mummy is a bit tired of hearing about Chloe." There was a pregnant pause and then daughter said, "Chloe's DOG is going to the cinema today. Chloe's DOG said to me that her bedroom is going to be painted sparkly rainbow colours and pink. Chloe's DOG doesn't like peas, she likes broccoli and sausages and fairy castles with princesses. Chloe's DOG has a boyfriend called Luke, who has a horse" etc., etc. After several days of hearing about the Chloe-esque life of Chloe's "dog", I asked my daughter to tell me what Chloe was doing today. And "normality" was resumed.'

(*VodaMum*)

The common-or-garden, somewhat annoying imaginary friend

Generally, we would suggest that you treat imaginary friends as a normal part of your child's life. Some children are secretive about their imaginary friends but many will readily chat about them, although possibly not in general company and parts of the imaginary lives may be off-limits. Whatever you and your child are comfortable with in terms of interaction between imaginary friend and real-life parent is likely to be fine. Some imaginary friends are driven away by too much parental interest so be a bit careful you are not trampling on a small area of the child's life where he has sovereignty with your enthusiasm to be charmed by his imagination and intelligence.

Imaginary friends are a useful outlet for feelings which a child might not want to express. And you don't want to discourage the expression of feelings which stops a reasonable distance short of criminal damage.

However, if the imaginary friend is becoming a scapegoat for real-life dubious doings (loss of or damage to toys or whatnot), you'd best step in. Consider giving the child responsibility for ensuring good behaviour by the imaginary friend. And make sure that the disciplinary arrangements for imaginary friends are the same as those for the real-life child to prevent the imaginary friend being too much of an outlet for mayhem.

'When I accidentally sit on "Amella" and get into trouble I just say something along the lines of "no, I didn't, Amella jumped out of the way before I sat down" and that's that. I think I sort of treat Amella the same way I treat my daughter – I wouldn't be dictated to by my daughter as to where I sit or which bowl I use, so I wouldn't pander to Amella's demands either.'

(*BroccoliSpears*)

You might be able to arrange a sudden demise for a really very awful imaginary friend:

'My son (not so long ago) had an imaginary friend called Bob. "Bob" did a lot of naughty things (although nothing dangerous). If my son wouldn't own up to doing something he blamed "Bob". The last straw came when my son cut down a pair of trousers and a T-shirt to fit "Bob". (Bad mother – sharp scissors!!!) So my son and I took "Bob" to the toilet and flushed him away!!!!!! Not mentioned again.'

(*jampot*)

You can also make sure a very pestersome imaginary friend has to make do with imaginary treats – so an imaginary friend who requires biscuits might have to be fobbed off with imaginary biscuits.

And imaginary friends can grow to be your friends too. Even somewhat annoying imaginary friends can be great distractions for a child who is bored whilst shopping or on a long car trip. And you yourself can 'imagine' what they are up to, in cunning and useful ways:

'Oh I'm sorry, there is no chocolate left, your friend ate it!'

(*whomovedmychocolate*)

'My son only had one for about six weeks, but it was very useful.

Son: I don't NEED to do a wee.

Me: Oh, right. Well, does Spotty Horse need to do a wee?

Son: [after some thought] Yes.

Me: He'd better go to the bathroom, then.

Son: OK . . . I'm going with Spotty Horse [goes and does wee].

It's never been so easy to get him to do stuff, before or afterwards <sigh>.'

(PortandStilton)

The mean imaginary friend

Rather more alarming than the merely voluble or rascally imaginary friend is the mean imaginary friend, the 'friend' who is abusive or hurtful to the child or makes the child hurt other children:

'My five-year-old has an imaginary friend called Sammy, who is (allegedly) the colour blue. She says that he calls her stupid and tells her to hit herself.'

(geraldine1969)

An abusive friend might be a sign of distress on the part of the child. You probably need to investigate with tact and discretion:

'Is your child scared of anything? Has she seen any domestic upset? Could anything be upsetting her at school? Is she being bullied? Any recent upset at home? You need to sit down and think of anything that could be wrong. I would avoid asking her directly and perhaps try to sneak the answer out of her as she may be scared that she is doing something wrong. Imaginary friends are always there for a reason.'

(Helsbels)

Where the imaginary friend is inciting violence in the real child, you need to investigate the reasons why that violence might be occurring whilst maintaining very clear boundaries about what is acceptable.

Do not act scared by the scary imaginary non-friend
and other things which go bump in the night

Some imaginary 'friends' are dead and some are ghosts or monsters with both benign and less benign aspects. This sort can be significant sleep interruptors. Some of these are just a little bit uncanny for an imaginative parent – the ones who sit and talk to the child alone in her room at night or who purport to be 'from history'. It can all be a bit like the scene from *Poltergeist* where the little girl says, 'They're heeere . . .' and it can spook you a bit yourself but for God's sake don't act spooked. It will be hard for a child to conquer an irrational fear which is frightening her parents.

'She is picking up on the feeling that you are scared. Sleep with her for a couple of nights, gradually leave in the middle of the night, reduce to leaving after she falls asleep, leave a night light on.'

(*LaurieScaryCake*)

Generally the spooky imaginary beings are ways a child works through fears of being alone and being in the dark. With the scary entities, you need to give the child tools to drive them away rather than trying to ridicule or minimise the fears.

'My son also went through a stage of thinking something was coming to get him – I told him to just say, "NO – go away and leave me alone" – it gave him the "power" to control his feelings and seemed to help him settle down.'

(*LewisFan*)

Some of the following may help:
- A toy or picture with protective qualities. A teddy bodyguard. A dreamcatcher at the window to catch bad dreams.
- Some kind of bedtime ritual: checking there are no monsters, then using 'monster spray' (a bottle of coloured water, maybe, with an appropriate label) to keep them away.
- Investigate to see whether there is a noise or something else scary which is causing the problem (e.g. a clattering window). Show the child what is causing the noise and see if you can fix it.
- Sometimes there is a doll or toy which the child finds scary or a book;

you can remove the frightening object from the room. Or strange effects of light may be created by the configuration of curtains or blinds.

- Let the child help devise strategies for dealing with the scary friend and be inventive:

'I had something similar when my daughter was small. She woke up screaming one night saying that spiders under the covers were biting her legs. Then for the following several nights, flatly refused under any circumstances to get into her bed. Eventually we rearranged the furniture in her bedroom so that it looked different and was a bit of a novelty, to take her mind off it. That coupled with sitting with her, cuddles, letting her fall asleep on top of the covers and a big stuffed dog called Henry to "chase the bugs away" – after a week or so she gradually forgot about it and things got back to normal.'

(*pjmama*)

'Give her a weapon. We subscribe to the Terry Pratchett school of childrearing and gave our son a sword to take to bed with him (a toy one! though it was wooden and quite heavy as far as toy swords go) when he was scared of the monsters. We told him if they bothered him again to tell them to go away or else. Or to call us and we would give it a whack. Haven't had a problem since. He will now quite happily move around in the dark.'

(*Morloth*)

All the dead dears: how imaginary friends depart

Imaginary friends often meet disturbingly violent (if imaginative) ends. Others just quietly move out or are not mentioned again. Some return from the dead:

'My daughter's imaginary "friend" is called Auntie Pesto. She's "a lovely old lady, with nice grey hair, and red coat and lovely brown socks". She phones us up and comes round to deliver jars of pesto that she's made in her shop.

I asked after Auntie Pesto last week as we hadn't heard from her for a while, only to be informed "she's dead". Apparently she died in a car crash. However, on Sunday my daughter announced to some friends that Auntie Pesto had got better and was celebrating her 100th birthday. Phew!'

(*The Moist World of Septimus Quench*)

Some imaginary friends will rather touchingly return for years to support their fleshly amigos in times of stress.

Imaginary people we love

Some imaginary friends are charming and fascinating, better than the child's real friends. They may have very detailed personalities and appearances and likes and dislikes and languages with their own linguistic oddities. And as you eavesdrop, you may fall prey to a parental fantasy that your children are the Brontës (in the sense of being tremendously creative rather than likely to die of TB).

'My daughter has an imaginary friend called Pierre (yes, even the imaginary friends in my house are poncetastic) who is always sick in bed. He is her brother, although his mother is called Moller. He also takes the embodiment of a small Playmobil figure. He lives in Australia but goes to school in Muddle, and his teacher is called Botus.

We love Pierre. She asked me today if I would phone Moller and ask her if Pierre can come to CenterParcs with us when we go in Feb . . . now where did I put her phone number . . . ?'

(*Bodkin*)

'I probably will, one day, miss Freddie the flying-whale, and Pew, Bella, LittleB and Draffir (rest of the flying-whale pod whose names I remember), the Badlanders (evil but stupid, enemies of the flying-whales), the Igglebongs (evil but with a glimmer of ability), the Hooligs (evil but clever – particularly good at possessing ordinary London pigeons so as to execute their wicked plots), the palipoms (birds with fur instead of feathers & complex genetics – of which charts are drawn – producing corkscrew beaks, & short beaks, & all kinds of different colouration), the Noise Whales, the Space Mice (which breathe helium & therefore move by hovering), the currency (one Rai, two-or-more Rain, complete with forex tables) . . . '

(*Bink*)

'My son (3.7) has a couple of imaginary friends – you may spot a name theme occurring:

Martianty-martianty (an alien – every time DS sees a vapour trail in the sky he says it's MM's spaceship).

Ghostity-ghostity (erm . . . a ghost who hides inside dice. DS throws dice and decided what GG is doing).

Dragonty-Dragonty (a red dragon with green wings).

And Dragonty-Dragonty has an imaginary friend of his own called Mousity-Mousity.'

(Iklboo)

'When my son was two-and-a-half he had two friends, Jim and Jack, who had blue faces. Jack always crashed the car so Jim drove. They often knocked on the door, and I had to shake hands with them. Woe betide me if I picked the wrong height to shake at. Over time, they acquired a mummy, Julia, who abandoned them for weeks just after my daughter was born. My son was cross with me of course, and Julia returned the day before he told me he loved me again. They also had a little brother called Ozlin K Sozlin. They were builders and he did work for them for £7 a day. In the end, quite brilliantly, they ripped him off on a major building project and when they spent all the money they owed him on beer and betting on horses (my dad's hobbies emerging here) he ditched them.'

(MerrySibhmas)

'My four-year-old kind of has one. A long-distance one. It's a girl, her name is Alan. She lives in Iceland with her mother (Alan) her father (Alan) and her baby sibling (Alan). They are often referred to as "all my Alans".

Alan has long messy hair which is all different colours. Sometimes her mother cuts her hair too short. She has lots of playdoh but has mixed the colours up.

The family drives a red car with some marks on it.

Alan invites my son to her parties, and he invites her to his. He gets quite upset when she never turns up. The Christmas present he wrapped for her is still sitting on the staircase waiting to be picked up.

Some interesting things to note: Alan's parents are always referred to as her mother and father (my partner and I are always mummy and daddy).

We have never been to Iceland. We don't know anyone called Alan in real life (I think he got the name from an allen key??). Alan's parents sometimes die and leave her all alone with her baby brother/sister. They normally get not dead after a while though.'

(thisisyesterday)

Do not let your child dress like a ho

PINK, PRINCESSES AND OTHER GENDER-SPECIFIC STUFF

Vast quantities of stuff are created to be sold to and used by our children. Some of that stuff is just aesthetically offensive or crap (especially plastic gizmos which are supposed to make ice cream or cupcakes out of bags of floury chemicals). Some of it is worse – it seems to send dubious messages about the roles we expect girls in particular to play. Is it bad for a three-year-old to wear nothing but a Princess Tiana costume? What about toys which are marketed primarily at girls, like dolls and kitchens? What about high heels and hot pants?

Sometimes in one's head there is a conflict between the sense that, as a matter of theory, the domestic and princess fripperies shoved at girls are likely to give them a very odd and unfortunate view of what being female means and a pragmatic feeling that the odd fairy wand is just a bit of harmless fun. But what about the clothes that are designed for mini-Nuts centrefolds rather than mini-Snow Whites? Our conclusion is that a bit of indulgence in the fairytale froufrou side of life is fine and for some girls (and a few boys) would be futile to resist. But that you need to make sure that there are other, stronger, messages reaching them about what it means to be a woman, to be a man and to be human. And that when it comes to tiny tart clothes, you must just say no.

Make-up

Here is a tale from the 1970s, before the widespread princessification of girls' childhoods:

Three small sisters bought their friend a 'lipstick tree' as a birthday present. This was a pink plastic 'tree' with many different shades of lipstick forming the branches. The friend opened it to great excitement on the part of all of the assembled small girls. Shortly after the birthday party, the father of the recipient summarily disposed of the lipstick tree. There was widespread little girl sadness. And then the small girls found a stash of old cosmetics thrown out by a neighbour and tried those out instead. These were girls who wore camping shorts with small pocket knives and climbed trees and mined for 'coal' in the side of house of the little girl with the lipstick tree until her father came out and shouted at them.

The moral of this story is that little girls (and boys) have long been messing about a bit with make-up and parents have long been grumbling about it. And indulged in judiciously, it's pretty harmless stuff. You need to give your small children credit for the very many interests they are capable of sustaining. And to see that a bit of experimenting with cosmetics is not in itself sinister or sexualising, particularly as most very small girls are indifferent as to whether the Unicorn Fairy Tinkerbell lip gloss is on their lips or their eyebrows:

'It's not as if small girls are going to put it on in a "normal" way. They always look like Coco the clown. Harmless fun.'

(*cocolepew*)

Many parents are happy enough for little girls to play with make-up at home but draw the line at going out in the stuff. Although others feel reasonably relaxed about use of make-up:

'My two (five and two) love playing with my make-up and I let them. I don't see the need to make it an "adult" thing. The other day when we were leaving for the shops, the two-year-old asked for "my lipstick!" before she left. When my older daughter goes to parties, I put glittery eyeshadow and blusher and sparkly gloss on her. She LOVES it. She looks in the mirror and thinks she looks fantastic and amazing and completely different.

I don't see it as a sexual thing. I think make-up is just a fun part of women's lives and they enjoy role playing that. I think what's important is that I try to install healthy body images and tell them that they are great and fantastic EVERY DAY.'

(*morningpaper*)

For many parents, make-up is more of a concern in relation to a girl approaching puberty who wants to wear it to look 'pretty' than it would be in a toddler who happily coats her entire face in purple sparkle goop. A girl who is beginning to look more like a woman is also far more at risk of creating an impression which is sexual, which can be disturbing both for her parents and for her. Even if you don't live next door to Humbert Humbert.

After the pre-teens, there are different views. Pretty much no one would want their teenage daughter to be utterly preoccupied with her looks or to think that she can't go out in the world without a full face of slap but many parents also recognise that experimentation with one's appearance is, if kept in proportion, a harmless part of growing up. Maybe make-up is one of those things which have to be seen as part of a bigger picture of all the messages you are sending about appearance and self-worth and gender roles.

'Covering your face with slap at twelve is one of life's milestones.'

(*FYIAD*)

'I will never forget the conversation my mum and dad had about my full face of make-up when I was twelve and heading out to the library at about dinner time.

Dad: "GET THAT MUCK OFF YOUR FACE YOU ARE NOT LEAVING THE HOUSE LIKE THAT!"

Mum: "Let her. And when everyone laughs cos she looks like a clown, she won't do it again, will she!"'

(*SmugColditz*)

But don't dress your daughter like a ho

'Little girls are being groomed into passively accepting their place as objects in our increasingly pornified culture, and it stinks.'

(*TenaciousG*)

Sexy clothing for small girls is worse than inappropriate:

'The issue of sexualisation of children has been researched, and the findings show that it is damaging for young girls: the American Psychological Association has published research linking early sexualisation to eating disorders, low self-esteem and depression in girls.

The Association said its research found evidence of sexualisation in every form of media, "as well as in goods marketed to children". The effects on society were catastrophic, it said, and included an increase in sexism, increased rates of sexual violence and sexual harassment, and an increased demand for child pornography.'

(MmeLindt)

What are we talking about? Well, the kind of clothes that encourage young girls to think that they should look sexually pleasing to others, sexually available, clothes that encourage the world at large to look at them in that way. Sexualised clothing is easier to recognise than to define, but generally the following are no good:

- Sexy or sexualising slogans ('Future WAG')
- High-heeled shoes (except for clopping about to do dress-up at home)
- Padded bras
- Leather hot pants and fishnets

'My daughter is ten, not a pole-dancer.'

(Yeahbut)

'I will not buy ANYTHING which requires people to read a slogan on my daughter's bum.'

(PeedOffWithNits)

Obviously there will come a time (fairly soon) when they make their own clothing choices; hopefully you will have persuaded them by that stage that there are better and more interesting life choices than being Jordan.

And then there is: pink sparkly princess tat

Now this is another area where there has actually been vast change since the olden days:

'I was born in 1974 and was dressed in purple dresses with orange flowers and yellow tights. In the summer I would be permanently in towelling shorts and a grubby T-shirt. I had one summer dress. It was blue with little flowers on. I don't think I had anything pink.'

(smallorange)

It is not just that there are far more dressing-up clothes now than in yesteryear (when we had to fabricate costumes out of hand-me-down and predominantly brown garments made from by-products of the petroleum industry). It is that there is a positive avalanche of gender-specific pink sparkly dressing-up clothes and pink sparkly ordinary clothes and lots of stories about vapid princesses. And there are distressingly large quantities of toys marketed along a gender divide which basically assumes little girls want to play at nurturing and flouncing about in frocks and boys want to tinker with vehicles and weapons.

'I categorically deny that being a "princess" is a necessary and inevitable developmental and evolutionary phase for a small girl, and am a bit pissed off that we are being "merchandised" this as an idea. It certainly wasn't the case in the sixties when I was growing up. Where and when did this happen?'

(Anchovy)

And the storybook princesses thrust on our daughters are on the whole unedifying role models: preoccupied with their looks, more or less passively awaiting redemption at the hands of a husband on a horse, and part of a fairly unattractive social order:

'I don't want my daughter to grow up thinking life for girls is like in fairytales. I know they're not real life but come on, let's just go through what happens to them:

Snow White. Cleans for a load of men. Killed by stepmother for being too pretty. Brought back to life by kiss of handsome prince.

Sleeping Beauty. Wicked fairy casts spell that says she'll die at sixteen. She falls asleep for 100 yrs instead. Brought back by kiss of handsome prince.

Beauty and the Beast. Well, she's pretty much defined by her looks (the clue's in the title). Trapped by a beast and forced to do housework (!) and then a spell is broken and guess what? He's A HANDSOME PRINCE! Whaddya know!

Rapunzel. Locked in a tower as stupid father promised a witch (again, women are either witches or princesses in these) his first born in return for a cabbage. Has long hair and is eventually rescued by a Handsome Prince!

Cinderella. Beautiful girl forced to do housework. Ugly (and therefore horrible, in fairytales) stepsisters make her do housework. She goes to the ball and is kissed by A HANDSOME PRINCE FFFFFS.'

(wickedwaterwitch)

So, if your daughter catches princess fever, what do you do? Here are some thoughts:

- Make a range of toys available to her – cars and trains and Lego (and not just the wretched pink stuff) and bikes. It's not wrong to play with dolls and nurture things or to enjoy cooking. As long as these aren't the only things you are expected or encouraged to do.

'Another form of sexism is when anything that has traditionally been done by women – sewing, embroidering, knitting – is devalued and traditionally male crafts are valued. So equality becomes a matter of teaching women to enjoy male pursuits, while female pursuits are quietly ditched by everybody.

Personally, I don't particularly see why woodwork is intrinsically more valuable than sewing. Or, on a more serious level, why childrearing is less important than banking.'

(cory)

- Think about the implications of the clothing you buy:

'I think the thing is that if you presented a Martian with a pink, glittery sequinned dress, & a pair of DPM combat pants, & said: "Right, one of these is for parties, & the other's for climbing muddy trees . . . can you tell which is which?" – well, it'd have to be a pretty dim extraterrestrial not to work that one out. Pink is a frivolous, impractical, easily dirtied sort of colour. I think dressing girls in pink all the time sends them a message that they too are expected to be frivolous, impractical & easily dirtied.'

(ravenAK)

So make sure your girls have some clothes they can run around and climb in. And refuse to buy the worst nonsense – shoes which are no good for her feet or for outdoor play. And maybe if your daughter does go through a phase of princess-only dressing, you should be relaxed about dirt and destruction. Some intrepid three-year-olds will stomp through hell and high water in a ragged and disgusting Belle costume and the remains of a tiara.

'Wearing pink does not stop the tomboy play though. When I was a child I would dress in the most girly-princessey-frilly things I could and then run out and dig up worms/make mud pies/climb trees/go fishing.'

(*SalBySea*)

• Offer attractive fantasy alternatives:

'My three daughters aren't very princess-oriented, they love fantasy play, we have lots of pirates and witches and talking animals, and a few fairies. You can have a vivid imagination and still bypass the synthetic passive princesses.'

(*Fennel*)

To that end, try reading more interesting books with them, books which offer more exciting role models than princesses or which reinvent princess stories (see our list below for some suggestions).

• Give them some critical tools with which to approach the princesses:

'I make a few suggestions for Cinderella's predicament while reading the stories . . . "She doesn't have to clean and cook though does she, darling – she could go to college and then get a good job, couldn't she?'

(*Chuffinnora*)

• Show your daughters that there are lots more interesting things to think about than personal appearance. This is really just about offering lots of types of different play – art activities, different kinds of imaginative toys, outdoor stuff. Frankly, if you are interested in the world beyond your face, chances are your daughter will be too:

'Beauty is the main focus of all the princess legends isn't it and that sucks a big one. I have really noticed that all the little girls my son plays with are massively more aware of looks and clothes than he is. (He just isn't, basically, and that isn't biological. No one – except me – cares about his appearance or focuses on it, because he's a boy).

It's easy to sell dreams and fantasies of purchasable beauty, so the Disney princess of today can become the Jordan of tomorrow. (And Jordan, of course, named her daughter Princess, god bless her.)'

(Domesticgodblessyoumerrygentlemen)

Growing out of it . . .

Even toddler girls who have passed their preschool years in a cloud of synthetic pastel hoop skirts and plastic crown jewels tend to put the whole dream of princessitude behind them by about age five. Try reading one of those princess magazines and you can see why – they are full of stultifyingly dull stories about the domestic life of Sleeping Beauty and Prince Charming or what Belle cooked for dinner (which maybe in their own ways subtly subvert the whole happily-ever after account of married life . . .).

'I have a tomboy. She wasn't always like that. When she was first at school she liked pink, fairies and the whole princess paraphernalia. Her first school birthday party was a fairy princess theme – I even made her a fairy castle cake. But she grew out of it – by the age of six. And that is fine. It only becomes corrosive when it carries on into later life – when being pink and feminine becomes a way of getting through life, simpering and being a bit feeble is a way to get what you want. Baby pink and princess crap is OK for a baby. Not for a sensible intelligent child, or, God forbid, for a grown woman.'

(OrmIrian)

Reading list for girls who don't need to wait for 'true love's kiss'

There are of course loads of good children's books: here are a few which subvert the usual messages about princesses and girls generally (for girls at the most princess-vulnerable age).
Babette Cole's *Princess Smartypants*
Robert Munsch and Michael Martchenko's *The Paper Bag Princess*
Catherine Storr's *Clever Polly and the Stupid Wolf*
Shirley Hughes' *Ella's Big Chance*
Julia Donaldson and Lydia Monks *The Princess and the Wizard*
Lauren Child's *Beware of the Storybook Wolves*

It's OK to be a boy princess or a boy with a buggy

Or at least it should be. Because whilst girls may be encouraged to focus on their appearance and domestic skills, no one raises much of an eyebrow if they decide they'd rather play with trains or run around with sticks instead or as well. But a boy who wants to go to nursery school in a dress or acquire a Barbie styling head may well find he gets mean remarks from other kids and the parent of such a boy may get stupid remarks from other parents:

'Really winds me up. I always bought my son whatever he wanted regardless of what it was. He loved kitchens and teas sets. My husband used to know one guy who would always make stupid comments about it, my husband could never understand it — he uses the kitchen, makes tea and pushed my son's pushchair so why are those things seen as girls' toys?

My son's favourite thing ever was a little three-wheeler pushchair that he used to wheel his teddy to nursery in every day, until one day one of the teachers laughed at him and said it was for girls (he was only four, bless him). He still gets stupid comments as he's seven and really good at dancing, tap and ballet in particular, but he's grown a thick enough skin now for it not to bother him. A little boy called him gay the other day (!) and told my son what it meant, which caused my son to piss himself laughing — one of the reasons he loves his dance school is that he is one of the few boys and all the girls love him, he has so many little girlfriends.'

(lolapoppins)

Many parents of boys who like to carry handbags struggle with how to walk the line between making their sons feel OK about looking after their baby dolls and experimenting with lipstick and avoiding exposing them to derision from the outside world. A lot may depend on the character of the boy involved and the character of those he is likely to come across. If you live in a neighbourhood where boys in tutus are common or you have a very confident and charismatic child, you may not really need to fret too much.

'One of my son's friends was more interested in Barbies etc. and when he came round to play, he and my son used to raid my daughter's dressing-up box and her hair clips. He used to say to my son: "Do you want to go for style or fashion?" He is a talented dancer as well and by the time he left primary most of his friends were girls. I never ever heard that he was teased or bullied.'

(christywhisty)

Perhaps the best thing you can do with a child who is old enough to understand is to try to help him work through the issues himself – to recognise that there may well be peer pressure not to wear a princess dress to World Book Day and that he has a choice how to deal with that. He can decide to do his own thing and arm himself with some useful sallies for children who laugh at him or he can decide that he may want to just wear his princess dress at home. Either way, he should know that there is nothing wrong at all in wanting to wear the dress and that it is the conformists who are lacking in imagination.

'It is sad to think that boys who are more in tune with their feminine side have to hide that while girls are allowed to be tomboys, or the boys have to fight to be allowed to just be themselves. I guess it depends on the child, some children are strong enough to confront any negative comments, some children are not. You have to help your son decide how he is going to reconcile his interests with the expectations of society.'

(Mme Tussauds Chamber of Choc Horrors)

With a school-aged child, sometimes it can be useful to have a word with a teacher, who may be happy to have a chat with the class about how it's really OK for people to play with all different kinds of toys and wear all different kinds of clothes.

Be hypocritical
about swearing

Words, words, words. They are all just words. And most adults use them at least some of the time. You may feel very strongly about children swearing, you may feel unfussed about it. Or you may struggle to think why children shouldn't do it when you do it yourself.

Given the fact that children have to live in society and be judged within it, we recommend what you could call hypocrisy or, putting some perfectly fair positive spin on it, age-appropriate language. Swearing, like drink and sex is for adults. This is why:

Aesthetics

Some people do find it funny when a two-year-old struggling to dress a dolly says 'fug it'. Other people purse their mouths up to the point of invisibility. Fine, the world is capacious enough to contain us all and our divergently mature senses of humour.

But almost no one finds it amusing or attractive when a seven-year-old tells his sister to 'fuck off' in anger. So if it is ugly in an older child, it has to be squished in a younger child.

'I love swearing and have a mouth like a navvy when not with my children BUT I hate hearing children swear. I remember cooing over an angelic-looking little lad who was about three or four years old years ago and he turned round and said, "Eff off you fat bitch", which was awful, gawd I was two sizes smaller then as well. It just sounds so wrong.'

(lizzlyLou)

Inability to use appropriately

Words can be weapons. You do not let your children play with sharp knives because they are unable to use them in a safe and socially acceptable way. Swearing in adults can release tension and is potentially expressive/funny if it is not used all the time. Used to express hostility it is generally socially unacceptable. And frankly, adults who swear continuously usually don't have the most interesting and rich vocabularies. It is better and more charming to learn some other words first and then garnish them with the occasional swear word.

These aspects are no doubt at least part of the reason why swearing children are subject to:

Social disapprobation

Swearing is frowned on at nursery and at school and by the public at large in small children. If your children swear in these contexts, they are going to get into trouble with teachers and other parents. They risk socially isolating themselves if they do it a lot – if your child sounds like something out of *Pulp Fiction*, other parents are likely to drag their kids away. But don't stress too much about the occasional lapse, the odd falling by the wayside happens to most of us:

'My son used the word "fukkin" in his written work in year two (aged seven). I can't tell you how proud I was . . .'

(*SoupDragon*)

'Were you embarrassed because he spelled it wrong, Soupy?'

(*Sazisi*)

'Not at all, because they teach them spellings phonetically and it showed initiative. His teacher could barely contain her laughter.'

(*SoupDragon*)

Dealing with swearing

With all of the usual caveats about how different children respond to different approaches, here are some thoughts on how to deal with your own junior Sweary Mary.

With the under-threes, if you can edit yourself you may be able to fend off the problem until they are more out and about in society. If you can bear the tweeness, you can try substituting a range of retro ejaculations for your usual knobjockies and twunts: e.g. 'Bother' not bollocks, 'Oh my word', 'Golly gosh', 'Oh my giddy aunts'. The Batman ones are perhaps marginally less prim. Try 'Holy Guacamole, Batman'. Or 'Suffering succotash' as Sylvester the Cat used to say to Tweety Bird. But no one born in digital times will know what the golly gosh you are talking about if you use these and they are, arguably, so starchy and nauseating that you will begin to long for a volley of really hardcore expletives. Some people just use the toilet-related words children like anyway but you rather reap what you sow if you go around exclaiming 'Oh, poopoo'. You do not have to rewrite your entire personality just because you have become a parent and you may find just keeping a lid on your usual language is less of an assault on your sense of yourself than the use of archaic or saccharine curses. Inventive invective can of course be fun but usually only when there are some actually rude words in the mix. Or at least a double entendre.

Many of us will not manage to edit ourselves at all times (or the builders, teenagers, random people of all sorts our toddlers come across) and are likely to be confronted at some stage by a Swearing Toddler. Like much toddler behaviour, this often holds up an unflattering mirror to your own doings and your automotive etiquette in particular. As you reflect whilst you watch the toy car swerve round the corner and mutter "wanker" at the other toy car . . . With very small cursers, not reacting and not acknowledging early experiments with swearing may be enough. Don't laugh (in front of them), whatever you do. But making a negative fuss can itself be reinforcing. Remember the three Is: Ignore, ignore, ignore.

Sometimes deliberately mishearing what has been said and substituting another word can work: 'Oh sheep.' 'For frog's sake.' And you can offer a toddler some of the simpler substitute exclamations for moments of frustration: 'Pants!' Or invent some: 'Oh poodlebottoms!'

For middling-sized children from about three upwards, depending on level of understanding, you can start to explain that some words are not OK to be used in public/at school/by children and that they will offend people. Children tend to understand about social disapprobation and want to avoid it.

And here's something that works with some slightly older children:

'Ask him if he can explain the real meaning of all these words. The embarrassment sometimes stops them, and being "allowed" to use them for a proper conversation. Whenever mine found out a new word, they were allowed to tell us so we could make sure everyone knew what they meant and why not to be used. Teach them other really "intelligent" words to use. Mine loved halitosis and flatulence as they sound impressive. It's also fun using a thesaurus (try smell!). If your child knows that if you catch him using a word he will have to restate the sentence using its proper meaning he will soon stop.'

(Milliways)

If you have a hopelessly sweary partner or cannot repress yourself in traffic, encourage your children to act as enforcers. Children enjoy being censorious, as exemplified by their habit of enquiring of people smoking in the street whether they realise they are killing themselves. You could let them run a 'swear jar' for the entire family, proceeds to go towards some generally desired treat.

'Pushing my older daughter (then aged nearly three) in the buggy some years ago now, tripped and twisted my ankle, and said what most people would say under the circumstances.

Little voice from the buggy: "Did you just say 'shit', Mummy?"

Mummy (apologetically): "Mm."

Little voice (severely): "That's a very rude word, Mummy, don't say it again."'

(frogs)

School age and beyond

They will hear the words, they will understand their currency. They need to be taught discretion. They can do it when they are grown up. They should not do it at school with other children. Good luck with that.

HEALTH AND SAFETY

Let them eat dirt

Phase 1: Let people touch your baby

There was a long-ago television advert starring a roll of kitchen paper so lusciously soft and tempting that people would be irresistibly drawn to approach and fondle it. The kitchen-roll fondlers would then get told off with the actually very memorable tagline 'Don't squeeze the [insert name of kitchen roll]'.

The advert made no narrative sense (why couldn't you squeeze the kitchen roll, was it actually made of glass? Was it guarded by an army of OCD sufferers?) but the kitchen roll was obviously a kind of metaphor for baby thighs. The ones that are pretty much pyramid-shaped and have serried ranks of creases and dimples. The kind you see passing in a supermarket trolley and find your fingers itching. Also very touchable is ringlety hair. Or see-through, barely-there hair. Translucent cheeks. A fine coating of bodyhair like a bumblebee. Fat feet like small slabs of spam. And baby skin generally.

However, when you have a new baby yourself and are sterilising everything in your house including your partner, strangers who want to touch and squeeze can seem like walking Petri dishes teeming with microbial life which they are waiting to smear all over your infant.

You generally (subject to the exceptions below) need to lighten up.

Exceptions

You have our blessing to beat the stranger off with sticks if one or more of the following applies. You have:
- Very tiny baby (newborn immune systems are not fully developed)
- Asleep baby
- Baby with immune issues/severe allergies

- Baby who is frightened of strangers
- Baby at the height of a major epidemic
- Stranger obviously afflicted with communicable disease, e.g. dripping cold sore/high on drink or drugs/Gary Glitter.

Otherwise, your infant needs to come into contact with some germs and will frankly spend most of her early months with some cold or another. As she gets bigger, she is going to be putting all kinds of germy stuff in her mouth. Germs are going to be sailing through the air to alight on her. Once she is big enough to socialise, she and other babies are going to be sharing a lot of bacteria. And once you have more than one child, her very dirty and germy siblings are going to be all over her. At many parent-and-baby groups, newborns get passed around by mothers and drooled on by toddlers.

'My daughter eats mud in the park. The park that dogs shit in. What can you do, she wants to pick daisies?'

(*Oliveoil*)

Letting people touch your babies is part of accepting that they belong to the wider community and the world. It's part of getting over the understandable and inevitable loony control-freak stage of early parenthood. If you are starting to consider having little T-shirts made up saying 'Hands off' or 'Don't squeeze the [name of kitchen roll]', you need to get a hold of yourself. It would be a sad world where people didn't touch babies and had to order spooky dolls which look exactly like real babies from eBay.

'If drunken tramps wanted to touch my baby I might be a bit worried but so far only lovely old or middle-aged ladies have ever wanted to touch my baby. And I've never had so many smiles from or conversations with strangers as I've had since having a baby and I find it all rather lovely.'

(*Manictigger*)

Remember, in some cultures strangers put coins into babies' hands. In many countries, babies and small children are hugged and kissed and showered with sweeties. If you go to Italy, young men will fall practically off their Vespas rubbernecking an attractive baby. It is like pushing a pram with a tiny celebrity in it. It's nice.

'The lovely Indian granny lady who runs our paper shop came running around the counter when I first brought my daughter in in her pram and, without a moment's hesitation, reached in, squeezed her cheeks and squee-ed "Chaddy chaddy chaddy!" at her (which I assume is Hindi for "big fat baby squidge cheeks" . . . ?) I thought it was really lovely, actually. '

(Lovecat)

If there is a good reason not to allow the touching (or you can't get over yourself), try:
- Stating clearly why your baby can't be touched (severe allergies etc.)
- Indicating with your body language that touching would be unwelcome (clasping your baby firmly to your chest with one hand and making wild flapping gestures with the other can work)
- Carrying and proffering an antiseptic hand gel

'When someone particularly unsavoury has wanted to touch a baby in my care I've usually gently pushed their hand away and said she's afraid of strangers/he's not very well, you don't want to catch it etc.'

(Wandering Trolley)

Phase 2: As they get bigger

Yes, they must eat dirt, even some actually dirty dirt. In the interests of wholesome exposure to microbial life, they probably should be allowed to do the following:
- Eat dropped morsels off the floor (some parents have a ten-second recovery rule – it's a matter for you – but maybe snatch the item from his grasp if your house has recently been invaded by a rat or the floor is in a public loo).
- Ingest some mud (but, if possible, not dogpoo, bird crap or fertiliser):

'I used to eat dirt as a little boy and it did me no harm. My mum tells me I used to sit in the garden with a big lump of dirt in my hand eating it like an apple. I remember licking dried mud off wellington boots.'

(NorbertSmalls)

- Eat some apples with the skin on.
- Snatch and enjoy someone else's dummy.
- Lick the odd dog.

You should not:
- Wipe all the toys at playgroup/in your home with antibacterial wipes.
- Become hysterical if you find them mouthing the bus stop.
- Refuse to go to softplay *because of germs*. It is of course perfectly rational to refuse to go because there is poo in the ball pit, the coffee is bad and big children stomp on your toddler.

In general you should bear this in mind:

'There are scientific studies that show that children who grew up with older siblings and pets have a stronger immune system than those who did not.
It is the hygiene paradox – the cleaner you are, the fewer germs your children get exposed to. The immune system does not get a workout and instead of attacking foreign germs, it starts to attack itself – hence the explosion in auto-immune conditions such as asthma and allergies in modern times.'

(blueshoes)

Let them fall over

AND DO ALL MANNER OF OTHER
DANGEROUS THINGS

'Life is intrinsically, well, boring and dangerous at the same time. At any given moment the floor may open up. Of course, it almost never does; that's what makes it so boring.'

Edward Gorey

This may be one of the hardest things you ever do. Risk assessment is never easy but it's something which, in relation to our own adult selves, we have had decades to master. We face the world with some basic (near) certainties: I can climb those stairs. I can eat those grapes. I can judge how fast that car is travelling and whether I have time to cross the road before it smushes me. But in relation to my child I struggle to assess risks. Can he eat that large slice of apple safely? Will he fall off that slide? Is that old geezer a hovering paedophile (almost certainly not)? The problem is compounded by the fact that a child's competence to deal with the physical world is increasing over time so it is necessary to reassess the risks continuously. And it is not a straightforward upward progression. A toddler is far more physically adept than a baby and therefore capable of putting himself into far riskier situations until his intellectual abilities catch up with his physical ones. Teenagers are exposed to new freedoms and temptations. And risks. And older children and teenagers need to learn how to assess all of those risks for themselves.

All of this is further complicated by the fact that we don't necessarily judge risks altogether logically. A very very small chance of something really bad happening is likely to deter us more than a really quite significant chance of something quite bad happening. And a risk which we could have prevented will haunt us more than one we could not.

Another hard thing about risk assessment is that we often, consciously or unconsciously, take cues from other parents as to how we should be doing particular things. Which can be a useful corrective if you are being overly cautious. But you also need to base your assessment on your own particular child and not just look at what his peers are doing. Just because his friend knows to stop at the kerb when racing down the pavement on his scooter doesn't mean your child is yet roadsafe or even capable of learning to be roadsafe. Some children roam the world looking for sharp, burning, high, drowning things to engage with. You will probably know if you have one of these.

Autres temps autres mœurs

To digress for a moment, sometimes you catch yourself fretting and fussing over your child and have a moment when you reflect on how very different your own childhood was. So many people seem to recall being sent to the shop as toddlers to lay in the parental cigarettes or being one of fourteen children cheerfully packed into the seat of the car before being abandoned with packets of crisps whilst parents enjoyed a night at the pub. We would nonetheless suggest that you engage cautiously with the past – memories of childhood are small windows on to the actualite, windows made of that rather thick bobbly glass. And the anecdotal 'I was fine without a seatbelt' stuff rather neglects the statistical angle and overlooks the fact that those who weren't fine haven't survived to reproduce:

'We have several charming family photos with evidence of stuff I would never do. A couple such examples include a heartwarming photo of two-year-old Wigglesworth with her Mum at Butlin's holiday campsite club, Mum had a John Player Superking in one hand and me on her knee. Another lovely picture included myself (I was probably about two-and-a-half years old), my brother and my three cousins sat outside my Wendy house. I wasn't wearing any drawers with my legs open, tuppence on full display and my youngest cousin (must have been about eighteen months old at most) brandishing a packet of Embassy NO1 and using them as a rattle. Needless to say they never made it into the Wigglesworth Family album.'

(*Wigglesworth*)

'My mum used to get me to light her cigarette when she was driving. I often sat on their knee and steered the car while they worked the pedals. Or I used to like changing gear.'

(lazymumofteenagers)

'In the early seventies (I was about three years old) I was playing outside on the green in front of our house when a couple who we had never met before knocked on our front door. My mum answered and the women said, "Hello, is that your daughter? She is very pretty isn't she? We are keen photographers, would you mind if me and my heavily bearded boyfriend take your daughter away into the woods for a few hours and take lots of autumnal pictures of her?" My mum thought about this (as she didn't want anything to make her late for her perm appointment that afternoon) and then said, "Yes, why not? Have lots of fun."

So off we went and they took lots of photos which were lovely and we still have them to this day and yes, I did indeed look very pretty. I LOVED the seventies.'

(70schild)

But back to . . .

Dealing with risk

Babies and toddlers can't assess risks – you need to be constantly vigilant on their behalf whilst helping them to become more and more physically competent by trying out new things. In other words, your toddler has to be allowed to fall on his arse but not from the top of the climbing frame.

As they get bigger, you need to train them up to deal with water, roads, fire, other people. Because we are not protecting them at all if we don't provide them with the skills to look after themselves.

'Helicopters are the types who are helping their five-year-olds on the jungle gyms designed for toddlers at the park. Or telling them to get down when they are climbing the rope ladders because they *might* fall etc. Or getting involved in even little disputes between kids when really they should be left to sort stuff out a bit. There have been times when watching my son that my heart has jumped into my mouth and my instinct has been to rush over and "save" him, but I think for his sake it is a good idea for me to give it a minute and see what he does (obviously excluding *real* danger). 99.9 per cent of the time he can get himself out of predicaments and as he has gotten older and the predicaments have gotten more complex so have his responses, because he has learned along the way.

He went ice skating for the first time yesterday. I felt every crash, winced at every wobble and my instincts were screaming, "He is too little, he can't manage, he is going to hurt himself." But I kept my mouth shut and let him get on with it. He *learned* from the falls and the wobbles, he learned when they were coming and what to do to avoid them. After an hour he stopped falling over and managed quite a few glides. If I had given in to "helicoptering" I would have taken him off the ice and he wouldn't have accomplished anything, but he would have been "safer".'

(*Morloth*)

So you need to maintain a kind of enlightened vigilance whereby initially you give them controlled opportunities to assess risks for themselves and manage hazards for themselves. And you must teach them the skills they need to deal with water, fire, roads, people. So, for example:

- Teach them to swim as young as you can.
- Teach them to cook things when you judge they are old enough to understand the risks and have the physical coordination to manage them.
- Teach them road safety and gradually get them to decide when it is safe to cross (you can always extend a hasty claw if they get it wrong).
- Get them competent at cycling and think about cycling proficiency tests.

To be physically competent and confident that you can face and manage the challenges the world presents – these are very great joys and gifts you can give your children by not overprotecting them.

We assess some risks for you

Although every child and every context is different, there are some generalisations which can be made. Here are a variety of risks which have troubled Mumsnetters and a consensus view on how you might deal with them. Or at least what factors you ought to be weighing up when assessing them.

Grapes

Yes, grapes. We are not suggesting that your child is likely to fall from a grape, drown in a grape or be abducted by a grape. That would be foolish. It is not foolish, however, to treat grapes with respect and to keep cutting them up for your preschool-aged child. Because of their size, shape and adhesive skin, grapes are particularly cunning bastards in the choking department. Simply chop them up and you eliminate their superpowers.

Leaving child/ren in car whilst you pay for petrol/pop into a shop

Generally this is more sensible than extracting a bunch of babies and toddlers from the vehicle and struggling across the forecourt with them. They are statistically more likely to be hit by a car in the forecourt than the car is likely to spontaneously combust or to be inhaled by an alien spacecraft.

With older kids and non-petrol-station-type shops, you need to assess the situation:

'No good leaving your children alone in the car if they will fight with each other, fiddle with the controls or open the door and escape. For instance, I left my six-year-old in the car outside a greengrocer's. I was gone for five minutes. When I returned he was clutching his finger in agony as he had put it in the cigarette lighter socket.'

(*tigermoth*)

For other bits of shopping you might be tempted to do solo, again there are all sorts of variables to look at, in particular:
- Distance between shop and car/visibility
- Age of child/ren
- Idiocy of child/ren
- How long you are likely to be away from the car

Home alone

The law doesn't lay down an age when it is OK to leave your child alone in the house for ten minutes/an hour/the afternoon, so yet again this is an area where you need to exercise judgment.

The NSPCC gives this pretty useful advice:

'If your child is under the age of about twelve, they may not be mature enough to cope with an emergency. They should not be left alone for more than a very short time. And remember to put all obvious dangers out of reach before you go, such as medicines, matches and sharp objects.

Even when leaving older children alone, make sure that they are happy about the arrangement and that they know how to contact the emergency services. Keep your mobile phone with you and make sure they know your number so they can call you if you're needed.

If your child is under the age of sixteen they shouldn't be left alone overnight.'

Babies and toddlers should never be left alone in the house, even if they are sleeping and you are popping out for ten minutes.

And on the vexed question of what age your child must be before you can go out for fifteen minutes to a local shop, we say this depends very much on the child. Can he be trusted to follow instructions? Will he be frightened on his own? For most children we suspect that nine or ten is the correct age. But we are well aware that in some parts of the world children younger than that are holding down jobs and caring for siblings, so again we say, take a good look at the child you have and how daft he is.

And as the NSPCC guidance suggests, you need to train children, tell them what to do in any emergency which might arise (fire etc.). Make sure they know who to contact if they are worried or you are not back within a reasonable timescale. Do some fire drills. Try very short periods initially and don't go very far away.

Sun exposure

Put them in clothes which cover them up and make sure they don't get too much exposure in the middle of the day. Use sunscreen. Your aim is to never get them burnt.

Unsupervised play (in your house/garden): do distinguish between 'benign neglect' and 'neglect'

Almost everyone of an age to be a parent seems to have childhood memories in which the joy of the thing was unsupervised play with their friends, turning unstructured time into badness in other people's gardens, inappropriate nudity and accidents involving collapsed roofs, fire or auto-asphyxiation. This may in fact be a species of collective false memory syndrome:

'I think the freedom of the seventies is much overhyped. When I was at primary school in said decade, I played out a lot, played on the cotton bales at the local mill, walked a mile to school etc. etc. BUT I also was made to go to Brownies, church choir rehearsals, Sunday school and my single dad's school play rehearsals (the highlight was when the big boys and girls took me to the shop to get sweets). I particularly remember resenting Brownies because it was at the same time as *Charlie's Angels*.

I think all of the above, feral and otherwise, was in the name of getting me out of the house or otherwise occupied.'

(*postername*)

And you do need to bear in mind the limits; there is a balance to be struck between anxious over-supervision and actual danger:

'I had parents who practised this "benign neglect". My sibling or I did the following as small children:
  Fell through old hen house roof
  Jumped out of a tree on to gardening implements (bad scars)
  Broke big old beds by jumping together from the ends to the middle
  Broke mantelpieces by jumping from the wardrobes on to them
  Fell through attic floor
  Collapsed an old greenhouse from the inside
  Sneaked up on sleeping cows to jump on their backs and have a rodeo
  Tied our baby sister on to the dog's back
  Made a sled for sliding down stairs
  Pulled an enormous wardrobe down on ourselves (luckily the door fell open and my brother wound up inside, some kind of miracle).'

(*AvrilH*)

In other words, hours and hours of unsupervised rampaging by children under the age of ten is probably not a good plan, particularly if your house is dangerously decrepit and your garden a theme park of hazards.

'What is indisputable is that "preschoolers need checking on".'

(*tiredemma*)

So a two-year-old can pootle in your pond-free garden whilst you do stuff in the kitchen (but not three floors up, assuming you have three floors to go up) as long as you can hear what he is up to and you have a squiz at him every ten minutes or so . . .

'Playing out'

In the Hovis advert past, really very tiny children were rolling tins down cobbled streets all day. And 'playing out' is such a very great joy and freedom in the otherwise constrained world of childhood. But much, as ever, depends on your child and your environment: what space there is to play in, what the traffic is like, what children are around, what adults are around and what the relationships between the various adults and children are. A small cul-de-sac with parents and carers constantly in and out of houses is a different proposition from a major road in a city where the only adults actually on the scene are necking Woodpecker:

'The more kids that are out the safer it becomes. They learn from the older ones about playing safely in the street. They watch out for each other and more parents are aware of the kids being outside and keep an eye on them.

The reason my two are very road aware is because from a young age they have played out, I would sit on the doorstep whilst they played and when a car came all the older kids shout CAR and move their balls/bike/goals off the road and the younger ones copy.'

(*sherby*)

Many kids in appropriate surroundings can play out from about age six but, on the whole, very small preschool-age children should not be out and about unattended:

'At three they just don't have the awareness of safety and boundaries (as in area) and will go off in search of excitement without really thinking about it until suddenly they realise they are lost.'

(twinkerbell)

A sensible school-age child should be able to go to a local park or shop provided she is road trained and the distances are reasonable. Try to find some possibilities in your neighbourhood for giving your children a bit of freedom, or if you really live in an urban jungle, are there opportunities on holiday to let them roam a bit? Campsites can be great fiestas of children playing out.

'I let mine (who are now ten and eight) go to the park on their own (two roads to cross), the shop (one road to cross), the school bus (one road to cross) and play in the moat behind the house on their own. I've been doing all this for two years. We live in a small village. They also go and call for their friends, and their friends come here.'

(MrsSchadenfreude)

If they do play out, they need some tuition in:

Stranger Danger

This is one of those areas where the risk is very small but the consequences of the risk eventuating are so ghastly that our brains go into panicky mode and we can end up doing this to our kids:

'I was in a public loo in London a few months ago and this woman went into a cubicle telling her son of eight or nine to wait for her outside the cubicle door. He started to panic, telling her not to leave him outside "because someone will take me away". I thought she had probably made too big a deal of stranger danger.'

(LadyGlencoraPalliser)

So we say: there are ways of protecting your children but scaring the bejeezus of out them is not a good one. Statistically the risks to them from strangers are very small indeed. They are more at risk of abuse from people they know. So you need to instil in school-age children who might be away from adult supervision some basic rules without scaremongering about the whole thing.

Talk to children about what to do if they got lost or hurt in particular places and situations – what adults would be appropriate to approach, e.g. uniformed police, people who work in shops, teachers, a woman with a baby in a pushchair and so forth. And they should remember some basics:

- Never accept gifts or food from a stranger.
- Never get in a car with a stranger.
- Never go anywhere with a stranger.
- They should say 'No' loudly and firmly if a stranger suggests any of the above. And they should know that it's OK to make a big fuss if an adult says or does something which makes you uncomfortable.
- They should trust their instincts if a person, place or situation doesn't feel right.
- They should pay attention to their surroundings if they are going somewhere alone.
- They should tell you or a teacher or another trusted adult if a stranger approaches them.

'I think it is good to talk about dangerous situations rather than Stranger Danger. For instance, talking to a strange man in the park when your mother is nearby is fine. Following him out to the car park and getting in his car is not safe. Also how to handle people asking for help finding a kitten or asking for directions – that is when a child could say, "I'll get Mommy or Daddy to help you" instead of going off with them.'

(MadamDeathStare)

'I went to a talk given by the police about protecting children from paedophiles and they emphasised that strangers are not the danger. They said that the best way to protect your child is to be an attentive parent, to encourage your children to be confident, to be visible as a parent. Paedophiles don't just pick a child at random. They look for insecure children, children whose parents would not notice if they were half an hour late home from school/football club/scouts group.'

(MmeLindt)

For more reading, try: www.kidscape.org. And a good book for younger children is Anne Fine's *Stranger Danger?*

There are also non-scary ways to protect a child from the possibility of sexual abuse:

'It is better to, from a very young age, teach your child that nobody has the right to touch them if that makes them feel bad, nobody, not a parent, grandparent, uncle, auntie, friend of the family, *nobody* and that they should always tell someone. They should be taught about good secrets and bad secrets. They should be given the consistent message that they can tell you *anything* (to avoid the 'if you tell your mum she won't love you any more' thing) etc. etc.

In short, educate them about their right to privacy, their right to not be made to feel uncomfortable or afraid, their right to not be touched, the importance of speaking out, that nothing they ever say could ever make you stop loving them, their confidence, and so on and so forth.'

(*HecateQueenofWitches*)

Or, in more graphic terms, for a young child:

'I have told him his body belongs to him, and that if anyone wants to touch it in a way he doesn't like, it is OK for him to shout NO and that he should tell me about it. And that his willy and bottom are private and that other people shouldn't touch them, unless they are helping him in the toilet, and that even if they are helping him they shouldn't "fiddle about" with them (couldn't think of a better way to explain it).'

(*FrannyandZooey*)

And finally

If you find yourself the mother who compulsively says 'be careful', you need to take a hard look at yourself. Don't be this parent:

'The single most astounding thing of this type that I heard in a park was a mother telling her approx eight-year-old son who was waving a piece of string around to "Please be careful darling, string can be quite dangerous." I would be really grateful if anyone could list the inherent dangers of waving string around because I am at a loss. I have often thought about this.'

(*ALMummy*)

You don't have to bathe your children every day

This is another of those things which creeps up on you – you start with the daily bathing and you can't stop dunking them until you realise they are too heavy to carry and have body hair. New parents often wash babies with a kind of superstitious zeal. It is a task you can accomplish and know you are getting it approximately right. There are none of the many grades of failure you feel in relation to eating and sleeping and, as time goes on, all the different facets of education and discipline and raising them up to be functional and pleasant human beings who are reasonably cheerful.

So if hygiene is a small area where you enjoy a sense of control, we would not wish to discourage you from daily indulgence in the soap bubbles and rubber ducks. *Pas du tout.* But if daily bathing is just a chore you have imposed on yourself, there is no need to berate yourself if you drop the reins.

Babies

Some babies hate baths, hate being naked and covered in water and not snuggled up in their own fuggy baby garments. Some parents hate bathing babies – something about dangling that naked screaming helplessness over water with its well-known drowning properties. It is a bit like the fear some people have that they might jump off a tall building, the fear that you might wantonly drop your infant in the bath and fail to fish it out again.

The truth is the majority of small babies do not get that dirty. They don't commute to work on public transport or footle about in mud. They don't do anything much:

'My baby however is either being held, or on a play mat. If he does a poo explosion I do bath him, but apart from his own bodily fluids he doesn't really encounter any dirt and he definitely doesn't smell. He hasn't got enough hair for it to look greasy.'

(BonjourIvresse)

What babies need is for the areas where bodily fluids congregate to be cleaned – i.e. face and nappy area. Any dirt which finds it way on to other parts can be wiped off and their hands should be cleaned. That is the necessary minimum:

'My son had all of three baths by the age of three months! He hated them. At six months, I think we were still only doing it every few days. By about nine months, we'd got into a bedtime routine that included a nightly bath, but look on it more as playtime than getting nice and clean. Of course, if he has a runny stomach or is sick, or rubs his fishcakes into every orifice <glares at angelic-looking, fishy-smelling son>, then we wash as needed.'

(MamaGoblin)

If your baby loves bathing or it is part of a soothing bedtime ritual, bath away:

'Mine have a bath every night but it is not really to clean them . . . it is because:
  1) My husband gets to have his quality time with them whilst they are in the bath while I race around doing washing/starting dinner etc.
  2) They adore the bath.
  3) I am not sure what else I would do with them when they reach that 6pm whingey stage and it is getting dark outside!'

(clemette)

Childhood baths can of course be the start of a lifelong love affair with the porcelain:

'My daughter is three-and-a-half and has a bath every evening, she loves it and I enjoy it too. She then gets into a clean pair of pyjamas, and the whole thing stupidly makes me feel like a good mother just because she is all lovely and clean . . . Easily pleased, I guess. Sometimes if we've been out and having a bath means she will get to bed really late, then we skip the bath and have one the following day.'

(Frenchgirl)

Exception for teeth

Teeth should be cleaned twice a day in general, allowing for the odd slip-up.

Bigger children

With bigger children, much depends on what is actually convenient to you. If frequent baths are troublesome, you can resort to scratch and sniff – is the child visibly dirty in a way that cannot be cured with a bit of wiping? Does the child smell?

'I think if you've one or maybe two kids who can bathe together, and the bath chills them and you've the time, and they can both sit up in the bath and play without killing each other, a bath every night can work. But I have three of very different ages who fight EVERYWHERE, who have to be shepherded into bed at different times and one of whom is only just sitting up. One needs a breastfeed and nappy change also. So we pretty much insist on a weekly bath but other than that it's whenever they smell or have poohed in their pants (the three-year-old, not the nine-year-old, though TBH he still doesn't wipe very well).'

(Monkeybird)

'I have to hose my daughter (two yrs) down every night after nursery – caked in paint and sand. Other non-nursery days I give her a bath every other day.'

(SarfEasticated)

It is sometimes quicker to put, say, three reasonably compliant children into a bath together than to wipe each down individually. For children who really don't like baths, some parents suggest you resort to frequent swimming:

'Can I join the slutty mother support group? My son, gulp, rarely gets a bath. He used to love them and had them three times a week, but refuses point blank now, and screams blue murder when I try to wash his hair. Instead I bring him swimming twice a week and persuade him to shower there. Saves a fortune on heating.'

(eefs)

And some parents find there is an intimate relationship between love and hygiene which makes bathing essential:

'Five kids all bathed every day! Kids need to smell like fresh laundry for me to love them!!!'

(PaulaYatesBiggestFan)

Teenagers

Most should be encouraged to wash their entire bodies on a daily basis.

Numbers

There are definite economies of scale to be had where bathing is concerned and we would encourage you to bathe as many children as possible at the same time. You can chuck in some friends, cousins or neighbours' children for variety and enjoyment from time to time.

When to stop bathing older children with younger children is a matter for some debate:

'The oldest one will inform you, loudly and at length, when they don't want to bathe with the younger one.'

(colditz)

Or you may find the bath becomes an uncomfortable forest of limbs, depending on the numbers and gangliness of your children and that you have to hive the eldest off for a private bath or shower. Which for a child who is so inclined will seem a great pleasure and privilege. Some children also become body conscious earlier than others and might welcome the privacy of a solo bath at a relatively young age, so be sensitive to individual tastes.

Baths plus: multitasking at its best

In summer, may we suggest you consider putting a little bubble bath in your paddling pool (perhaps not dishwashing liquid as used by one mother) and thus avoiding formal bathing altogether?

'It's the only way we can get the youngest bathed at the moment, for some reason he has decided that having a bath in the bath is about the same as being tortured. The kids have never been so clean and neither have half their friends.'

(*babyicebean*)

You could also consider popping in melamine dishware and some laundry. And then water the plants with the contents of the pool – the soap apparently has mild insecticidal properties.

Another strange but true fact is that many children will happily eat fruit in the bath which they wouldn't give the time of day to on dry land. If the fruit is messy fruit, you achieve a nutrition/hygiene double by feeding it to them in the bath.

'My son, four, and daughter, two, are becoming rather difficult eaters, at the table sometimes they eat barely nothing, but, if I give them a small bowl of fruit, say a handful of grapes each, whilst in the bath, they eat the lot, they have polished off a punnet of raspberries between them in the bath tonight. They see it as a real treat.'

(*pepsi*)

Keep your poxy
or vomiting child at home

Who would think to bring their young Typhoid Marys into the social arena, you cry. Well, there are stacks of people who will bring a child who is flushed with fever to a children's party. Or a baby dribbling diarrhoea to a parent and baby group. Or push a child covered in fresh, new chicken pox around the supermarket. (And there are crowds of tutters who will glare at a child with harmless old chicken-pox scabs, but no one said you could win – social disapprobation is an inevitable side effect of reproduction.)

'I have a few friends who do this, their children will always be back at school or nursery straight away after a tummy bug. One mum even cleared up the vomit from her son who had been sick in the car, sprayed him with perfume and took him into nursery.'

(*displayuntiltwelfthnight*)

Do not be these people. Yes, children get a million bugs and yes, many illnesses are contagious before the symptoms come out. But these facts are not excuses for you knowingly smearing your child's contagion over all and sundry, including the pregnant, the elderly, the newborn and the immune-compromised.

We recognise that in many cases, obliviousness to the symptoms is born of desperation – the thought of a toddler raging all afternoon because he is missing a party you have foolishly been trailing all week. OK, he feels a bit hot and has a glazed disoriented look, it's probably nothing . . . And we recognise that the morale-sapping awfulness of being confined to quarters for days and days with your querulous chicken pox sufferer can lead to you re-thinking your obligations to society at large. You must be stern with yourself.

And we are not saying working parents have to stay home every time a child has a cold – some children would rarely be at school if sporting tusks of snot were a bar. If there is no vomiting, no severe cough, no fever and the child is not miserable, the child can go to school or nursery. But for more serious illnesses, the child should not be dosed to the eyeballs with Calpol and dropped off. It's not fair to other children and is miserable for the child herself.

'There gets to be a point where, regardless of whether the child is infectious or not, he/she needs to be at home/grandma's/another quiet spot as they are suffering and yes they might perk up once home but it's because they are at home and not in school that they feel better.'

(*bossybaublesinherbritches*)

'I'm a nursery owner.
Runny noses, minor coughs and bright eyes are welcomed. Hacking coughs, fevers, anything obviously infectious and ill-looking children are not.'

(*Bauble99*)

No one is saying it is always easy to be conscientious, particularly when guidelines for schools and nurseries require, for example, that children be kept home for forty-eight hours after the symptoms of a diarrhoea and vomiting bug have cleared. Some thoughts on forward planning:
• Where there are two parents, emergency childcare should be a shared responsibility – this should mean less of a strain on employment relationships than if one parent is shouldering the whole burden.
• Think abut what emergency childcare you might be able to call upon, if any, before the situation arises – family friends or a paid scheme (we recognise that this is expensive and not possible for many people).

If you have to take a sick child to school or nursery to collect a child who isn't ill, have some common sense. The sick child shouldn't be cuddling other people's babies or chasing her friends round the playground. Get her to keep herself to herself as much as possible. If you can call in a favour from some other parent and get your well child collected, even better.

But a word also about economic duress and judging others. The truth is that some parents find themselves in situations where they cannot afford to take any more time off work to care for a sick child, because their employers won't put up with it. And they don't have any backup to call upon. And in those circumstances, they probably do make choices which are a bit antisocial:

'Sending a child into nursery when they are below par is often done by parents who know that the bills won't get paid unless they go to work.'

(*Reallytired*)

'What they're doing is not right, but let's have some understanding of why they're doing it, eh? And let's direct our anger to where it should go – towards a society which doesn't value childrearing and a workplace which makes it nigh on impossible in some jobs to function fully both as a parent and as a worker. (I speak as one of the very tiny and privileged minority of people who has been lucky enough to have more or less always had a part-time job where I can just take time off and work from home if my children are ill. But most people can't.) It's never very constructive to blame individuals for responding to structural problems. I'm not saying it's OK, it's unfair on everyone, but I think indignation should be directed to where it belongs.'

(*LittleSleighBellasRinging*)

You must not allow your children to be a safe house for parasites

'There ought to be a sash of badges you can earn as a mother. A bit like being in the Brownies but on a gross scale.'

(*TsarChasm*)

'I have my worm badge. And now my nits badge. I also have my "Catching Vomit In My Hands" badge.'

(*ghosty*)

Parasites 1: Headlice

Once upon a time there were nit nurses and a regime of public shaming in schools. Now it feels like every classroom has at least one child whose head is seething with adult lice to the extent that the hair actually writhes about like Medusa's snakes. And schools respond by sending out generic and non-accusatory announcements that there are some headlice about rather than cracking down hard on headlice harbourers. And thus it can feel like treating your own child is an exercise in futility.

But you must fight the good fight and hope that other parents will get sense. Fix with a stern look of reproach any parent who says waftily, 'Oh, they all just have them all the time. There's not much point in doing anything.' Remind that parent of Kant's categorical imperative: 'I ought never to act except in such a way that I could also will that my maxim should become a universal law.' Consider getting this printed on T-shirts under a big picture of a headlouse.

Because unless you are one of those lucky people who seem to be unattractive to headlice, you will get them yourself. And frankly it is hideous having headlice. It itches and you get little burning itchy bumps on your head. Which turn into scabs when you scratch them. And then you are frightened to go the hairdresser. And there is no up side here – remember that headlice don't just love your clean shampoo-advert lovely-smelling hair; it's not a bloody compliment that they have chosen to take up residence in your barnet. They like any old hair with scalp under it. Apart from that of your proudly louse-resistant spouse or partner.

Treatment

You have a couple of options in your battle against headlice. Most people are reluctant these days to use the chemical insecticides of our own childhoods, or paraffin, or headshaving. So we suggest you use that stuff which suffocates the lice and which is readily available from the chemist. It is abominably expensive but you can actually get it on prescription. It is especially to be recommended if you have children with thick impenetrably uncombable hair.

Otherwise the solution is to comb, comb, comb. Use conditioner to slow the insects down and make the hair easier to comb and a really good nit comb (i.e. not the cheap comb they sell you with nit treatments, the fancy metal kind that tends to cost about a tenner). Some people suggest you comb daily during an infestation but at least do it two or three times a week to interrupt the headlouse life cycle. And carry on for at least two weeks – some say don't stop until you have been finding no further evidence of insect life for several combings. In classes where headlice are endemic, some parents comb twice a week for diagnostic and early treatment purposes. You can section and detangle the hair first with an ordinary comb then get to work with the nit comb. Nit comb should go from roots to tips of hair in one sweep. Then wipe on some white tissue to see what booty you have collected. Or dip in a beaker of water and see what sinks to the bottom. Repeat the nit combing on any section where you have found eggs or insects.

Advanced nit tips

Blow-dry hair after combing. Heat seems to kill off some of the louse population. Look behind ears and at the nape of the neck in particular when diagnosing an infestation and hunting down the miscreants. To nit comb yourself, again use loads of conditioner and comb over a sink where you will be able to examine what has emerged.

Now all this combing would be fine and dandy, you say, if it were being carried out on, say, one of those Barbie styling heads. But a real-life child who is apt to scream and hop about can be a whole other kettle of headlice. You may need to look at what bribery and distraction will work best in your house. A very large bowl of popcorn and a good DVD are our best suggestions. And hopefully the hair will be so lovely and tanglefree with all that conditioner and combing that the activity will become less painful for parent and child over time.

Deterrence

To reduce reinfestation rates:

- Tie up the long hair of a long-haired child:

'Tie it up within an inch of its life. Like a tight french plait. I think it's bending over towards other children in groups that causes them to pass between children.'

(*loubyloo*)

- Advise children to keep their hair to themselves:

'What worked with my ten-year-old daughter after four bouts of nits in four months was a long chat about not putting her head close to others in her class and playing responsibly (plus a huge headband – covers half her head and a very tight, short ponytail).'

(*LauriefairycakeseatsCupid*)

- Spray hair with a bit of tea tree or lavender oil in water in a plant sprayer or a ready-made tea tree or lavender oil based product.

And although there is really nothing good about having headlice yourself, there is something that appeals to our primate souls about delousing one's offspring – hunting the critters down, cracking them with your fingernails, watching their little wiggly legs stop wiggling. Some of us are regularly to be found at bus stops or in parks, idly turning a lock of our child's hair to have a look.

'I spent half an hour tonight de-nitting my daughter. (We made it to half term before they appeared.)

I love it. She isn't the most cuddly child with me, so that time with her snuggled onto my lap, just having my undivided attention is a big thing.'

(*FlamethrowersKillZombies*)

Horrible science about headlice

'The lice fart their way out of the egg sacs you know, and a louse can manage without breathing longer than almost any other animal. Female lice often cement themselves to the hair shaft as they are laying their eggs and die there. The one thing that you cannot do is try to drown the little bastards. You can hold a headlouse under water for so long that its body swells and its legs stick out at right angles to its body, and the bastards are *still* alive!'

(*Blandmum*)

Best to crack them in half to be sure of inflicting mortal damage.

Parasites 2: Worms

Threadworms, what are they for? Maybe they are the cunning invention of a headlouse PR agency. You can see the brainstorming session: 'So, hey, how can we improve our image with the general public?' 'I know, we need some guys worse than ourselves, some guys who actually live in people's anuses and, like, itch!' 'Sick, dude!' 'Oh, yeah, they'll hate that. And what if these guys were creepy little white worms . . .' 'Oh, man, we are going to look positively dreamy next to those guys . . .'

So anyway . . .

Detection

Generally you will be alerted to a threadworm infestation by the fact that a child is scratching its bottom. Some children wake up with really fiendish night-time itching:

'I always know because of itchy arsiness. When the kids were babies (LOOK AWAY IF EATING), I noticed because the poo in their nappies was full of wrigglers but once they are kids, it's the itchy bum and sometimes with girls, they get itchy vaginas (without even noticing itchy bum). Some children also suddenly bed wet and get tummy pains.'

(oi)

For more advanced and conclusive diagnostic techniques, some parents suggest creeping around at night with a torch and shining it at child's anus (the worms emerge at night to lay eggs). Or putting a small piece of Sellotape over the anus (or a blob of vaseline) and then gloating over the catch in the morning. Or trapping a poo in a potty and seeing if it waves at you. Those of us with less naturalistic zeal/less compliant children (who are these children who don't mind having sellotape on their arses?) prefer to simply treat a suspected infestation, bypassing close examination of faeces.

'First time I got them (was horrified), I tried to do some very odd manoeuvre with a mirror and a torch and some strange positioning. My husband came home and I looked at him with pleading eyes and he said, "In marriage, with some things, you have to keep the mystery."'

(oi)

Treatment and prevention of reinfestation

Now the first bit of this is relatively easy – you buy the appropriate de-wormer at the chemist and administer to everyone in the household as directed. The prevention bit is harder:

'Worms are also a PITA re the washing of sheets etc. It's like a total household curse! Itchy arse and loads of housework!'

(oi)

- Wetdust all surfaces in house.
- Clean bathroom with bleach.
- Hoover all floors, carpets, soft furnishings.
- Boil wash all sheets daily whilst the problem is being treated. Boil wash favoured cuddly toys. Boil wash towels and nightclothes. Don't waft these soft items around, the eggs fly into the air and can be inhaled.
- Wash pets.
- Change toothbrushes.
- All family members to wear clean tightfitting pants at night (to stop scratching and hence eggs getting into fingernails).
- All family members to wash bottoms in morning.
- Cut all nails short and scrub hands frequently.
- Discourage nailbiting.
- Throw out any playdoh that has been handled by a worm-infested person.

Worm identification for laypersons

'Worms don't have legs. Not ever. It is sort of a defining characteristic of worms, that they are, in fact, legless. Devoid of legs. Threadworms are less than one cm long and about one mm wide, but no legs. They look like thick threads. That wiggle. And wave.'

(Blandmum)

FUN AND GAMES

You don't have to play Sylvanian Families if you don't want to

'When I had children I thought that their childhoods would be like my own – playing out all day and exploring, a bit of TV watching and playing nancy nurse with all my teds and Monopoly with the cat (who always lost). I didn't realise that someone would come along and change the rules and say, "oh mummy you have to play with your children when they are children" or "why on earth did you have children?"'

(IvyKaty44)

Consider this – most people's best memories of childhood involve driving around in a cardboard box customised with felt tip pens, making a small fire in someone's back garden using rocks and those gunpowder caps they don't seem to sell any more, or constructing a spook house in a neighbour's attic. These activities generally happened with your mates, your siblings or with the biddable younger boys next door. Very few people will remember their mother talking into a Star Trek communicator made out of a cunningly folded sheet of A4 paper or indeed anywhere at all when these things were going on.

And here is the hard truth – if you, the parent, sit on the floor and move Star Wars minifigures/Sylvanian Families about whilst doing appropriate voices, you will rapidly become disoriented with boredom. If your eight-year-old child spends twenty minutes talking you through exactly how many and who are the doubles of Wigan and West Ham players he has in his Match Attax folder or telling you a very very long story about a rabbit, a great grey cloud of unknowing will fall across your faculties. There are loons who lie under the baby gym with their three-month-olds batting the dangly things with their oversized grown-up person hands; they know not what they do. The adult brain is simply not wired for these activities.

So this rule is about knowing how much playing with your kids you really need to do, and what sort. Remember, too much parental playing is, arguably, not good for them anyway:

'I used to play with my daughter 24/7, but it caused problems when she got to school as she insisted on having the teacher's attention 24/7, so I have slowly introduced playing on her own. She loves drawing etc. anyway, so is perfectly happy drawing while I clean and tidy and cook, and then we will go out and play football/play pool in the playroom/bake/read, then she will have some more time on her own, then more with me etc., and she is now seeming to prefer being on her own.'

(*Pawslikepaddington*)

'This modern parenting notion of playing with our children constantly is setting us and them up to fail. Children need to be able to occupy themselves, every-one in the family has needs, it shouldn't all be totally focused on the children. Playing with children constantly inhibits their creative development and affects their ability to use their own imaginations, they also need their own "me" time away from adult intrusion/direction.'

(*minxofmancunia*)

'My mum watched me leap up every time my son grizzled and do all sorts of waving, gurning, toy twirling shit and said: "Leave him alone. Children have to learn how to just be."

It was great advice. I have children who play and draw and imagine and sit and watch clouds go by.'

(*pagwatch*)

'I don't entertain children all day. It's very dull as a rule, and I'm not five and I don't see why I should pretend to be five. She is five, I don't expect her to pretend to be thirty-eight and drink coffee and talk a lot on the telephone, so all's fair I think.'

(*ahundredtimes*)

*The section wherein we slightly backtrack on the general
rule in respect of babies and toddlers*

The truth is that people under the age of about two or three do want and
need you to play with them and gradually help them towards being able to
spend some of their time in independent play.

'My son is ten months old and I do play with him – we like playing anticipation
tickling, where I move my hand slowly towards his waiting (and ticklish!) tummy/
neck. And we play "bite your toes" where I pretend to eat his foot and he
laughs hysterically. And we play "Where's Bob?!" where I "search" for him and
he sits stock still and stares at me till I look at him and say, "There he is!" and
then he giggles uproariously!

He has a collection of toys on the floor during the day and he's quite happy
to play with them by himself while I'm in the room doing other things, but I do
also play with him for several extended periods of time a day (although this
varies as we're out and about quite a lot). I have always left him to play for a
certain amount of time each day though – he'd think something was wrong if I
was right next to him the whole time!'

(*Hunkermunker*)

As they get to be toddlers, you should let them lead the play – so you
get to be the Sylvanian rabbit the dog chewed and they get to be all the
other Sylvanians. And they get to make up the plots. And wear the best
costumes.

Sometimes this will be kind of fun for you and sometimes it will be
pretty damn tedious, especially on a winter's day when you are on your
own together and both suffering from cabin fever. Perversely, you will no
doubt miss those times when your four-year-old decides that playing
with you is deeply uncool and shouts at you when you turn up to take
her home from school. Because playing with infants usually features at
least some moments of great joy in what can sometimes be a dirty grey
soup of boredom.

As they get older, do stuff you like with them

You can ditch the imaginative games that do your head in. That doesn't mean you stop spending time with your children when you actually concentrate on what you are doing together, but it does mean you play to your strengths. If you like crafts, do crafts, ditto cooking, biking, football, swimming, nature walks . . . Because the important thing is that sometimes you are focused on the child and the thing you are doing together and that is really so much easier when it is something you both enjoy.

Some folk like board games. Although not many adults can long endure the ones where you simply roll a dice to get a plastic figure to the end of a path thingy, the unfathomable pointlessness of the activity lightly disguised by a theme about pirates or ponies. Or the plastic ones where some plastic bits balance on some other plastic bits until something crucial breaks and the entire assembled company becomes hysterical. Bear in mind that you can teach children to play poker for poker chips/sweets/hard cash from the time they are borderline numerate and able to distinguish between the different playing cards.

'Uno is good, also Jenga (esp when it crashes down) (and there is a Uno version of Jenga where you have to pull a particular colour/number). I like Mastermind too, and Monopoly as long as it gets going evenly before some bastard gets all the money and the rest of you have to limp round on the verge of bankruptcy for the rest of your lives.'

(*JanH*)

'I can do Top Trumps except it NEVER ends.
    I can do ludo, Cluedo, playdoh that kind of thing.
    I can do reading lots of books.
    I can do watching a film.
    I can do a walk.
    I can do chatting.'

(*wickedwaterwitch*)

Other parents find that Top Trumps can be soul-destroying. A good wheeze with a child who is nagging to play is to suggest he makes his own Top

Trumps of family members or schoolmates or teachers. Try suggesting some categories. ('How does Daddy score on "obesity"?') Hours of fun.

'I spent half an hour this evening sat at the table with my son (age four) looking at UK Atlas – he was looking at all the symbols and asking what they were – he can find golf courses, caravan parks, railway stations, airports and motorways on it now – OK perhaps not the most useful thing in the world at four years old – but I love maps, and he enjoyed it.'

(*Gwenick*)

And you can also:

Do useful stuff with them

Even toddlers can actually join in things you are doing if you are able to slow the pace – cooking or cleaning or sorting socks, although probably not taking work-related phone calls or any DIY activity performed at height. You can also open your post whilst she opens hers (consisting of pizza flyers and large 'cheques' from Reader's Digest).

'But interaction is the main thing in my opinion. I've just been unblocking my dishwasher by dismantling the pipework and getting in there with the plunger; my son (thirteen months) loved watching and "helping" by holding bits of plastic for me while I got on with it!'

(*Stilltrue*)

'We talk all the time, go for walks, swings, feed the ducks, go shopping etc. – ordinary day-to-day stuff he can get involved in. I think it's just as good for him to help me load the washing machine so we can have a chat about it as it is to have structured "down on the floor" playtimes.'

(*Moomina*)

It's OK to 'parallel play' with your children

It's a good thing for children, at least by the time they get to school age, to know you are an actual person with your own actual interests and pursuits.

'I'm not great at playing *with* my children. And I wasn't when I didn't work either. I have no problem finding time to read a book and drink coffee at weekends, while the children get on with whatever they're doing. And I take my five-year-old especially out with me, and we have a coffee and I read the paper and she colours or something like that. My children like me being there, and I mostly like them being there. I just don't really do children's games.'

(*TheFallenMadonna*)

More free-range parallel play shades into what some call benign neglect. Even if you don't live in a safe suburban paradise or a Sunday supplement-style rambling old farmhouse, you can allow children some freedom round the house. Making a big camp out of all the furniture in the house, some sheets and some umbrellas is the most fun you can have with your clothes on and no imminent danger of death.

'I am a stay-at-home mother with three children and I have to say I am not the get-on-the-floor-and-play type at all. It bores me to tears. I practise benign neglect – my kids are told that through boredom comes creativity.

So I let them make a mess (paint themselves blue, build an adventure play-ground in the sitting room, whatever . . .) as long as they leave me to get on with things. So sit down with a book and a coffee and tell children they will have to amuse themselves. Give them the tools to do that and don't complain when they make a mess.'

(*smallorange*)

Guilty secrets of the toy nerds

There is another side to all of this, of course. There is no shame at all in enjoying children's games. Or their toys. There are parents whose ears prick up as the Lego catalogue flops through the letterflap, whose hands tremble a little with anticipation as they tear off the plastic wrap. There are indeed parents who lie in bed at night devising new ideas for Playmobil sets:

'I would start with Greek gods and goddesses including Playmobil Pegasus and minotaur. Legends would be fab too so you could have Robin Hood, a cute little Playmobil Friar Tuck with removable bald pate.'

(*postername*)

'I have recently felt there needs to be a pregnant woman. I have said before that I want a lighthouse (not the old-fashioned one in the pirate range, a red and white one with a lighthouse keeper's cat). Henry VIII and all the wives, with beheading equipment. In fact the Tudors, with Shakespeare, Eliz I, Gwyneth Paltrow, etc. The English Civil War, with witches, roundheads and cavaliers. And I think a great plague Playmobil would be good.'

(*wickerman*)

'Palaeontologist/archaeologist set, with trucks, tools, microscope, sample boxes and fossils to fit together – my partner and I were wishing for this for our son the other day.'

(*MadameDuBain*)

'When I was young my big brother and I wound up our little brother by telling him he was going to get a Playmobil cemetery for Xmas. We got carried away imagining it and describing in detail the coffin with bones in it, gravedigger, hearse etc. When Xmas day arrived and he opened his lovely Playmobil inn the poor boy was disappointed it wasn't the cemetery. So I think it's about time they made one.'

(*Kathyistwelvefeethighandbites*)

'Playmobil Ikea would be cute . . . lots of teeny tiny Spunka chairs and Krappe beds and hordes of little people in queues pushing little trolleys.'

(*mwahahahamwahahahallyroge*)

Drink wine and hide

THE ART OF 'PLAYDATES'

Let's get the nomenclature issue out of the way first. Yes, we all feel a little queasy the first time we utter the word 'playdate' and no, nobody ever had such a thing in our day. We all just 'played out' variously with cricket bats and ponies, nuts and berries or broken bottles, depending on inclination and locale. But nowadays when children mostly seem to get shepherded around by parents from one venue to another and consequently hide together in the furthest bush in any park you take them to, so desperate are they to be alone with their own kind, it is convenient to have some name for the thing people do when they take their children to other people's houses. We could call it a srpuyshged or we could call it a playdate. A playdate is a playdate is a playdate. As Gertrude Stein didn't say.

It helps when approaching this subject to think about what your underlying purpose is in entertaining other people's children in your home. Are you trying to socialise your children and foster their friendships? Probably you are. Maybe you are trying to foster friendships with other parents too and maybe you are trying to build up some credit in case you need someone else to take your kids. That is why you are having the things. But your anterior purpose, the purpose behind all of your parenting is to avoid death and despair (parent or child).

Don't start too young if you want an easy life

The younger the child, the more work a playdate will entail. Babies and toddlers obviously require constant supervision. Probably any preschool child will come accompanied by a parent or carer so you will have help with the supervision but you will also have the proffering of refreshments to the parent and the chat to be a-doing. At the good end of the spectrum, this can be a pleasant encounter with someone you like or could get to like, at the other end it can be glacially slow death by biscuits and small talk.

'My son (two years and six months) is happier, better occupied etc. when he has a friend over, I get a bit of a break from playing with him, he uses up a lot of energy, and I get to chat to my friends at the same time.'

(*naturopath*)

'By some horrid quirk of fate, this is my third afternoon in a row. My jaws are aching with smiling (though my eyes are dead, like a shark's).'

(*onebatmother*)

As children get to school age and parents get less twitchy with each other, unaccompanied playdates start to occur. Probably you will find yourself grimacing over a cup of tea at least once with each parent of a new playdatee in reception before that child is left with you solo. With reception age children, you will generally find that you need to stay involved if you want to reduce biting and screaming:

'Don't just leave them to their own devices. Do something with them – get some pizza bases and let them put their own toppings on for example. You are there to keep the peace, they are absorbed in an activity and the sharing of a fun experience will help forge some sort of relationship.'

(*fortyplus*)

But you are moving towards the Nirvana of . . .

The unaccompanied playdate of the older child

Some parents find this kind of playdate to be great (in the specialist sense of not actively unpleasant) and others utterly infernal. There is much to be learned from studying the accounts of the two camps:

Hell is other people's children

'Am I being unreasonable to hate playdates? And to really struggle with other people's kids and their bizarre food fads, and tale telling and sometimes bad manners, and demands for attention? And to find my own kids much harder when they are running round the house screaming in a mad frenzy of excitement? And to hate the mess that results from a child coming to a new house and having to discover all the new toys? Would I be unreasonable to join some kind of sect where children are not allowed to socialise with other children in their own homes? Would I?'

(themildmanneredjanitor)

'Has anyone ever had that horrible end-of-playdate nightmare? The whole thing goes well enough until the other mother arrives to pick up her child/children and in the spirit of warmth and hospitality, you offer her a cup of tea/glass of wine (even though you had enough at about five to four and would really like to shove her children, holding their shoes, out on to the pavement) and the two of you sit politely in the wreckage of the tea table . . . Whereupon all hell breaks loose upstairs.

With both mothers present there's an odd hiatus in authority, which the children seem to sense and take full advantage of. Loud thuds are heard as missiles and bodies are hurled off bunkbeds, duvets come flying downstairs, and the unmistakable sound of *your* bedroom being ransacked is heard. And you know that *your* children aren't the ringleaders because they know they're not allowed to do all that, and are probably waiting for you to come up and read the riot act, but you can't bring yourself to shout at someone else's children while their mother is there, and are hoping that she will take her own children in hand, but she's obviously sitting there looking at the toy-strewn ruin of your house and thinking, "blimey, what a liberal household this is . . ." So nobody does anything, and you wrack your brains for ways to bring the whole thing to an end.'

(3PRINCESSES)

Heaven is a playdate on earth

'Love 'em. Don't see my kids for dust; disputes get short shrift; too much running round shouting gets TV on; difficult children don't come back too often; eat what you're given or have a sandwich; parents come around five or six, wine opened about ten mins after, no work at all <hic>.'

(Twiglett)

'When my daughter (four) has friends over I just hide – sit in the front room on the computer, with a nice cup of coffee and some biscuits. Foodwise – they get what we are eating. Usually pasta. They can eat it or leave it – there's always fruit and bread and butter instead. If they argue, I shout "Stop it" in their direction. If they expect me to play *for* them (in that annoying way some kids do) I say I'm too busy. If all else fails I do popcorn and video. In fact I have come to the conclusion that the best way to get an afternoon without being pestered by my daughter is to borrow someone else's daughter.'

(StripeyMamaSpanx)

'Invite child/ren. Bring them home with you along with your own (refusing to carry anyone's bags, naturally, as this will make you feel put upon). Give them a biscuit. Let them loose. Produce pasta at teatime, bellowing to them in enough time to get them to do some tidying up. It's not particularly complicated or difficult.'

(motherinferior)

From these accounts we can distil . . .

The elements of a successful playdate

Hide but keep an ear cocked

If you work from home you can tap away at your computer and have important telephone calls whilst your children announce in loud whispers outside the door that you are WORKING. Some parents with no work to be doing, however, find they hover about uneasily combating their own sense of sudden redundancy. Others find it no trouble at all to fritter away the time with a newspaper or *Come Dine with Me*. If going suddenly from being overburdened with your child's attention to being *de trop* makes you feel weird, some parents recommend that you find a useful activity to busy yourself with. Such as gardening or batchcooking if that's the kind of thing you do.

Keep interventions to a minimum

Do not get involved in listening to everyone's account of why a fight took place. Say this: 'If you can't all get along, I will have to call X's mother and X will go home.' Rarely will the children call your bluff.

Make uncontroversial and easy food

See Sub-rule: Serve pizza.

Consider doing an outdoor activity for the first twenty minutes or so

It's worth supervising some bike riding or trampolining or park activity if they all burn off some energy that would otherwise be directed at deconstructing your furniture.

Ban certain areas of the house

Your bedroom and study are the obvious ones. Although 'upstairs' in its entirety is also a possibility. We can't be the only people who remember a prepubescent friend showing us her parents' condoms . . .

'A couple of years ago my daughter went on a playdate with a lovely girl from a lovely family and when she come home I asked her what she had done and she said, "We went in XXX mum's bedroom and XXX showed me the stockings and suspenders and A BLACK BASQUE mummy, and then we put her wrinkle cream on." I still don't know whether my friend knows they did this.'

(*nametaken*)

Also bathrooms have razors and pills and things which your own child may know not to mess with but a visiting child might get into.

Only one child in lavatory at a time

Enough said.

Have some backup activity to whip out if times get hard

This could be the time to trot out all the presents you carefully squirrelled away after your child's birthday party.

That which is not acceptable when done by your own child is not acceptable when done by a guest

But you need to be flexible with this one. Abusing a dog or baby or destroying property should be dealt with firmly. But you may feel that more minor rules (sit down at the table and don't waggle about during tea) need to relaxed for both host and visitors due to the excitement of the occasion. This is easier on you frankly than being the Enforcer.

Put on a DVD to sedate children

If they are all just past it and revolting. Or you really need to get some work done. Or just because.

Have group tidy-up time

Make your children and their friends tidy up before the friends go. Some people wonder whether this is akin to asking your own guests to stack and unstack your dishwasher after a dinner party. It isn't. It might be the equivalent of asking a friend who happened to tip all your clothes out of your drawers and throw your duvets down the stair to please put the things back. And it is no bad thing to get a reputation amongst the younger set for being a bit *farouche*. If you wait until the friends have left you will be faced with the old unfairness accusation and assertions that all of the untidiness was the idea of and/or single-handedly perpetrated by the guest(s). Whilst the guests are there, energy levels and spirits will still be high. Once the guests leave, your child will lie limp as a plaice on the seabed murmuring feebly about how tired he is. At best.

Sometimes the guest leaves unexpectedly early. In these circumstances, it probably makes sense to help with the tidy-up yourself.

'Sometimes I just want them to go home and not prolong the agony, depends on child actually.'

(ggirl)

If you are very untidy yourself and really don't care about the mess, feel free to leave it.

The little wine poem

'Wine
wine
wine.
Substitute wine for coffee, you will be fine.'

(niceglasses)

If you are a bibulous sort *and* you aren't just desperate to get everyone out of your house *and* the parent in question isn't the sort of person who is going to haunt your nightmares, you may want to offer wine to a) the parent who has stayed with her child (maybe wait until 5 p.m.) b) the parent who turns up to collect her child. This can help you all shuck off your grown-up parent skin just a bit and grease the wheels of future social interactions. Or you might get horribly pissed on half a bottle and talk about your husband's erectile dysfunction. Social occasions involving alcohol being something of a crapshoot.

Reciprocation

Some people feel that something is going wrong if they invite children over frequently and their children receive few invitations in return. It is worth offering this one up frankly. There are a million reasons why some parents don't have playdates which are neither mean-spirited nor any reflection on you or your children:

'There have been many reasons I haven't reciprocated playdates (God I hate that term) not least of all because I was suffering from depression and just didn't feel I could *cope* with having any of the children's friends over, supervising them and my other two children. Thankfully I'm pretty good friends with most of the children's friends' mothers so they understand why I haven't felt able to do it.'

(FAQ)

'My son probably goes on more playdates than having friends around here. Little matter of me working full-time whereas most of his friends' mums don't. We do try to take them out on trips instead – took one to the panto, to a soft play and for a meal for example, another to local science museum. Their mums know our circumstances are different, so I'd hope don't expect end of school invitations from us.'

(LunarSea)

'I rarely had kids over. I don't like them that much.'

(custardo)

Other reasons for not having playdates: Working from home parent, shambolic house, small difficult baby, ancient dependent grandparents . . .

Schadenfreude corner: other people's awful playdates to enjoy

We have edited out the ones involving nudity and bloodshed. Here are the best of the rest:

'I have got my son's friend coming tomorrow and am filled with dread. He soils himself (he's going on for eleven) and we have to smell him for two hours. He does it every time – deliberately. Bet no one has a worse kid than that round for a playdate.'

(nametaken)

'A few weeks ago we had someone in my daughter's class round for tea – the parents had just moved into the area and were friends of friends. For the half-hour the mum stayed this little girl was an angel. As soon as her mum left, she farted on my leg. She then refused to eat tea ("I only eat pasta with pesto on it") and when it came to pudding (an ice cream), she took her bowl and tried to go upstairs. When I told her that in our house, we all eat at the table, she stood at the top of the stairs and announced, "MY, you're a bossyboots aren't you!" Needless to say I stood there till she came down. When I bent down to clean under the table after tea while they were playing in the lounge, she jumped on my back and tried to give me a wedgie by yanking my knickers really hard. The minute her mum knocked on the door, she reformed back into sweetness and pie. Absolutely unbelievable. Needless to say, I'm not inviting her back again!'

(playdatefromhell)

'My twin daughters (five-and a half) had two schoolfriends round for tea yesterday. They were only here for two hours and during that time the four of them managed to get every single toy, game, bead, piece of Lego, etc. etc. out and smother their bedroom floor and the lounge floor with it all. I've no problem with normal mess but this was ridiculous. They didn't even seem to play with anything, just go from one thing to another. Then when I was on the phone I discovered that they had emptied their wardrobes of ALL their clothes, put them into suitcases and were having a pretend "holiday" in the garden with it all. It took me over 2 hours to get the house straight again. Surely this isn't normal. My two blamed the friends, the friends blamed my two.'

(Sandyballs)

Sub-rule: Serve pizza

The following somewhat depressing advice is for anyone who doesn't feel like Jamie Oliverishly educating other people's children's palates. We are not discouraging you from embarking on such a project, but we are saying that if you start a crusade to turn all your neighbourhood children into lovely omnivorous French-style children, you will probably lose.

Also a word about consultation. Obviously it is important to establish whether a child has any allergies or intolerances or special dietary requirements. Beyond that, anything a parent says to you about her child's eating habits is approximately 50 per cent likely to be correct. Except "He eats anything", which is a lie 98 per cent of the time.

Here is what tends to happen at playdate mealtime:

'My daughter had a friend here for lunch. I had put a sandwich and some cucumber on her plate.

"I don't like cucumber," says friend.

"OK," says I, "what about cherry tomatoes?"

"I don't like cherry tomatoes."

"What about apple?"

"I don't like apple."

"What do you like then, what can I get you?"

Silence . . . I had some vegetable soup and she asked if she could have some. Yes of course I said, put some in bowl for her. She poked around it.

"What's the yellow stuff?"

"Sweetcorn."

"What's those lumps?"

"Potato."

She put some in her mouth then spat it out again . . . and declared she didn't want it. Grrr.'

(emkana)

So we say to you: 'Italian' food, she is your playdate friend. Pizza and pasta are the two substances eaten by the two largest subsets of British children (with sausages and chips in third and fourth place respectively and hummus improving its performance year on year). Pasta is particularly versatile. You can virtuously make a sauce (or reasonably virtuously open a jar). Then for the tomato/meat/pesto-hating child you can simply dress the pasta with cheese. And the child who hates sauce and cheese can have bloody naked pasta. Remember as you serve up a plate of white or dun-coloured food: the child is there for one evening, you are not responsible for educating or nourishing it.

'I sit them down on a little table in the playroom and leave them to it. If they don't eat it I just take it away. I'm not their mum.'

(Cappuccino)

A tale of three pizzas or: evolutionary stages of a minimalist approach to playdate food

Stage One: Homemade dough with homemade sauce and bits for children to decorate pizza with: children tap suspiciously at chewy and large crust and eat topping off.

'We made pizza one day with their friends, kneading the dough, fresh sauce and did all the toppings. Pulled them out of the oven to hear squeals of delight and they started tucking in when a voice pops up saying, "I don't like pizza!" Grrrr. Luckily had a bit of leftover pasta to serve up quickly but no more, no more, no more . . .'

(pollypots2)

Stage Two: Readymade pizza bases for children to decorate: children enjoy arranging foodstuffs into face. Then eat topping off cardboardy circles. Or not, if they have made sweetcorn hair and don't like sweetcorn.

Stage Three: Those frozen fellers in flavour 'margarita'; only. And no fancy margaritas with sundried tomato or tomato *pieces* or mascarpone or some-such. And watch out for green bits. The colours on the pizza should be red and yellow only. If you have bought wisely, these pizzas will be consumed in their entirety . . .

Main event which is not pizza or pasta

Some children will eat some of the following some of the time:
- Meat or vegetarian sausages
- Breaded chicken bits, nuggets or 'goujons'
- Fish fingers
- Meatballs

Other children will consume nothing in your house apart from crisps, their own fingernails and snot.

We cannot be held responsible if you stray further from pasta and pizza and serve, say, chops. But if you were feeling puckish, you could experiment with organ meats . . .

Vegetables

The easiest thing is to chop up, say, three or four salad vegetables and arrange them in separate bowls. Do not mix them. Do not sully them with salad dressing (although you may offer this alongside, to disbelieving and disgusted looks). You can pretend apple is a vegetable for these purposes. If you want to cook the vegetables, your safest bets are: carrots, peas, broccoli and sweetcorn. If you wish to provide a potato, we recommend mash, chips, or small new potatoes.

Sandwiches

Remember that one filling at a time saves misery. Cheese. Ham. Tuna. Jam. Crisps. A chocolate bar. Vegetables or fruit on the side.

Other

Have lots of unchallenging fruit on hand (= apples). And yoghurts. And ice lollies in summer. Have whatever you want by way of puddings.

And finally

Beware of offering any dish which is at all complex to prepare and which occurs in different formulations:

'Me to daughter's eleven-year-old friend: Do you like spaghetti bolognaise?
    Friend: Yes, I love it.
    <<Later.>>
    Me: Umm, is there something wrong with your dinner?
    <<Whilst watching child poke at dinner.>>
    Friend: Oh, I don't like onions.
    Me: Doesn't your mother put onions in spag bol?
    Friend: Umm, I think so, but I can't see them like I can see your ones.
    <<Continues picking at meal.>>
    <<Me looking askance.>>
    Daughter: Oh X doesn't like tomatoes.
    Me: Huh? I thought you liked spag bol?
    Friend: Oh I do, it's just that I don't like the big bits of tomatoes. I only like it when it's smooth.'

                                                        (*twelveyeargap*)

Chase other people's children away in public places

This is one of the fundamental tenets of rational/idle parenting. It has a very important corollary which is that you mustn't chase them away if their presence is facilitating you sitting on a park bench and reading a paper whilst they keep your children entertained. No, the children you must chase away are the lost chickens who hang at your side needily asking questions about the meaning of life and trying to get you to teach them to play cricket. Some of these children will cling to you even when your own children have wandered off to get away from your new small best friend. They are often inordinately bossy and chatty children. And generally less easy to like than your own children, who may be intrinsically no less irritating, but at least blur your judgment with some shared history and the fact they express your own genes.

'I am a magnet to small unruly boys that have just been told off (by me). They follow me around for the rest of the day, probably seeking more discipline.'

(coldtits)

'I get the ones who explain everything like Magnus Pyke. I'm married to someone like that, I don't want to hear it on the beach too.'

(cyb)

'The thing I find with these child magnet situations is that the stray child usually comes and hangs around for long enough for everyone around to presume s/he's yours and then s/he will go and do something totally "unasseptable" (swear, thump passing random child, steal another child's ball etc.) and you're left, with everyone's eyes on you, wondering what to say or do. Or if they're potty-training age they'll fill their kecks with a stinking poo and continue hanging around.'

(NorbertDenStressangle)

Prevention, as always, is better than cure, so:

- Avoid doing wildly attractive activities in public places. A family of six digging an enormous trench on a beach will stir the heart of any random passing child, who will then be yours for the rest of the holiday.
- Do not be a vocally jolly *playing* parent, splashing and diving and organising games of water polo. Children are fun-seeking missiles; do not make yourself a target unless you enjoy being the parent who disappears under a mob of small children like Dorothy when she is attacked by the flying monkeys in *The Wizard of Oz*.
- If necessary, you can ignite a game or sporting activity, but then retreat quickly, before a passing child decides you are integral to the fun.
- Spot the parents who are looking to attach their child to your family – they will be reading *Heat* and sipping a latte (or maybe that's just us). Give them and their offspring a wide berth.
- On holiday, find some sweet and obliging teenager for all the small children to bond with. A teenager who will let his/her hair be styled or lead rowdy games of hide-and-seek is very heaven for a small child.

What this mostly boils down to is that you need to encourage independent play. Don't organise a game of beach volleyball and then be surprised when your family trebles in size for the rest of the day. It is lovely for children to find one another and muck about outdoors together; you just do not want to be the surrogate parent for all of them.

'Actually, particularly on the beach I think adult involvement should be limited to providing sunscreen, drinks and food and breaking up MAJOR fights. Children should play in semi-feral groups without adult interference – that's what beaches are for.'

(*seeker*)

'This is what camping was invented for. The kids set some game up in the middle and the adults can sit round drinking.'

(*LeninGrad*)

In cases of very persistent hangers-on, some parents suggest drastic solutions:

'Here's your line: (stare into distance) "Kiddo, I think someone's calling you, over there," (point). As kiddo looks away, grab all your children and run.'

(*MrsMargate*)

But if all this is too harsh, have some pity. The mother on the lounger with the latte may be mortified at the fact that her child has joined your picnic. It is not easy being the parent whose child is always looking for some better craic:

'As someone who has an only child I constantly try to field her away, BUT she is, of course, drawn like a magnet to groups of children (whether with an adult or not) as otherwise she either has no one to play with, or just me. She spends a lot of time playing just with me, I cannot force her to play just with me, and ignore the fascinating group having lots of fun right next to us.

And when it comes to swimming pools etc., I am always ready to get in there and willing to play, but she is six, and may not want me – she wants to play with your kids.'

(*kickassangel*)

If you are that parent, try to observe some boundaries. Make it clear to the parent your child has adopted that you are there to take the child away if needs be and that you are appreciative of the entertainment. Retrieve your child at mealtimes. Toilet him or her yourself. Animate yourself into some loud playful parenting of your own to lure your child back. And possibly some others. Who will then imprint on you . . .

Don't hire a limousine for children's parties

'Do as little as you can get away with, for as long as you can get away with.'
(*TutTutter*)

For some of us, there is a strange masochistic cycle with children's birthday parties and a yearly blunting of the memory which is a bit like that muzziness of recall you get round childbirth. In the run-up to the party, you find yourself getting quite excited about the Power Rangers cake you have promised to make and the decorations and the party-bag crap. Then there is a maelstrom of cleaning and food preparation and some frenzied small-hours manipulation of crumbling slabs of cake which look nothing at all like a Power Ranger however many cocktail sticks protrude hazardously from the body armour. Followed by two or three hours of madness and mess and then you at the end of it contemplating that mess and vowing that you will never have such a party again . . .

On trying to make a pirate ship cake:

'Well, I know many of you have been waiting breathlessly to hear all about this.
Course of events:

8.30 p.m., kids in bed, make two round cakes.

9.30 p.m.: two cakes sawn in half and stuck together with icing and stood upright, growing unease, stick three skewers through to be on safe side.

10.30 p.m.: cake covered in icing, Playmobil pirate in place, plus treasure chest full of silver balls, SS son's name piped on side. Congratulate self and take break before attempting pirate ghosts.

11.30 p.m.: back to kitchen, cake has fallen to pieces along fault lines, Playmobil pirate peering from rubble.

2.30 a.m.: finish round cake decorated as above – very fat round pirate ship

WARNING: if making Disney pirate ship cake, make with very dry cake stuck together with glue!'

(GhostofNatt)

So this rule is not about raining on your parade if you actually love to organise enormous parties; it's about guiding you once again towards an enlightened minimalism if you don't love it.
Here are:

Some parties not to have

- Supersoaker party in your garden. Unless you live at Balmoral or that place where the Pedlars people live. And have servants with armfuls of toasty dry clothes.
- Paintball party. Under any circumstances ever.
- Party where you take more than two children to Legoland/other theme park. Unless you are a Rothschild. The price will be beyond rubies.
- Bouncy castle party with large number of small children. It is a health and safety horror unless you supervise in sergeant-major type way and make yourself hoarse with shouting.
- Swimming: unless you want other parents to see you in your costume. Just think about it, is all we are saying. You might not care.
- Mass sleepovers. Nothing will drive you closer to infanticide.
- Fancy dress unless it's clearly OPTIONAL.

And here are:

A range of rational parties

For toddlers (under three)

Think about having the party in the morning – it gets it over with and hopefully avoids most folks' naps. Also you can, if you want, just make it a toddler/parent get together kaffeeklatsch type thing with a bit o' cake. Very small toddlers really are happy with some family and/or a friend or two and some balloons. Or a picnic or a trip to the zoo. Only have a party for a gazillion children and the entire extended family if you would enjoy it and your toddler would at least not mind it. Under-threes really are too small for competitive games but they like some toys and music and maybe some very low key games like they do at playgroup – sleeping bunnies for instance. And balloons of course. And a bubble machine or just an adult with a tub of bubble mixture is a good photo-opportunity enhancer.

In the summertime you can retire to your garden if you have one and set up a paddling pool or small toddler bouncy castle (the £20-ish kind).

'I've been to three types of children's (two/three/four) birthday parties:
  a) type 1; hall is hired for two hours with bouncy castle. In order to fit in bouncy castle, musical statues, pass parcel and tea whole thing is planned like a military operation. At end there is a sit-down tea where (I kid you not) parents stand behind their children like posh nannies did in the olden days. Much futile urging to eat some sandwiches before the jelly and crisps. Children leave rather wound up.
  b) type 2: same basic set-up but at a home so you get the added stress of making sure that no one makes too much mess.
  c) type 3: host has room for adults and clears out a safe place with toys for children. Sandwiches/booze etc. laid out in the kitchen. No organised games but adults (at various stages of drunkenness) take turns to make sure children are having fun. Cake with candles in brought out at some point.'
  (witchandchips)

About three to about five

Again, don't feel you have to invite more than a handful of children unless you really want to. Here you can begin to introduce some of the trad games like pass-the-parcel, musical chairs, pin the tail on the (insert appropriate item for your party theme), musical bumps but be prepared for wailing and gnashing of teeth. A little bit of organising is possibly required but you don't need to go mad.

'I am a party organiser/entertainer and think the best parties have some structured activity or entertainment and some "freeform stuff". Games for four-year-olds need to be pretty simple, without "winners" featuring too heavily.

Arts/crafts e.g. making own party hats, decorating own cakes etc. are a good way to fill time.

If you don't have helpers, then why not have an entertainer and enjoy being part of the party yourself (this is what mums say most to me – and strangely it is mums who seem to do all the work)?'

(RubyRioja)

Here is a game you may not be familiar with but which might be fun if you have no shame about the contents of your underwear drawer.

'Basically you get your teddy (bigger the better – he has to wear pants). You find four pairs of different coloured pants. (We have had boxers, y-fronts, g-strings. Whatever. As long as they are different colours.) You colour a corresponding pair of pants on to four separate pieces of paper. You stick a pant picture in each corner of the room (it doesn't have to be a big room – it's not a race, just a boogie and a guess). Teddy and pants (plus teddy helper) go outside room. Music plays. Kids boogie. Music stops. Teddy helper sticks head round door. "What colour pants do you think Teddy is wearing?" Kids guess by going to corresponding pant picture. Teddy comes in wearing . . . (say) PINK SPOTTY PANTS!!! Yay! All the kids in the pink spotty corner get a sticker/Haribo/a point (number of which won corresponds to a prize at the end)/a big cheer/etc. Teddy goes out of room and repeat. A lot. It is amazing how thrilling they will find guessing the pant colours. Honestly. No one can resist a teddy dressed in pants. (Although it will descend into mayhem eventually when everyone wants a turn at being teddy pant picker. At that point you leave them to it and go and pour a large glass of something medicinal . . .)'

(merrylegs)

Six and up

You can begin to substitute outings for traditional parties if you want to (you may already have been making use of soft play facilities). Many cinemas will do cheap children's films on Saturday or Sunday morning, which can be a good basis for a party which then goes on to fast food/your house for some lunch. Start very modest on the outings if you don't want to end up in the sort of arms race which ends up with paintball.

Making-and-doing parties can also be good and cost-effective.

'We had an "arty party" for my daughter's last birthday – a pot of clay, some paints, decorate your own T-shirt (I bought £1 T-shirts from a supermarket and a packet of fabric pens!) and various other ideas (there are load of art sites on the net). They had a ball.'

(*Joolyjoolyjoo*)

If you look on the internet or in pound shops or for bargains in art shops, you can find all sorts of craft possibilities – candle-making, that shrinky plastic stuff you cook in the oven, felt handbags and cheap photo frames you can decorate, jewellery, china-painting . . . If you are doing games and/or outdoor things, you can always have a craft activity as well – just some things to cut and paste and draw for the very junior end of the market, for older ones a project like paper plates to make into masks or shields (if you have a knight or viking theme, say).

You could also (and we are not necessarily encouraging this, mind) have a cooking party or a cooking element to your party. Some things that work:

- For the very young, just decorating a cake or cookie with icing pens or tubes, sugar flowers etc.
- For bigger children – making pizzas or maybe spaghetti and meatballs, something uncontroversial. Chocolate truffles. Chocolate-dipped fruit /other sweets.
- Assemble your own sundaes. Give child a bowl with some virgin ice cream in. Lay out sprinkles, cream, chocolate sauce, fruit, marshmallows, whatever.

You do need to be ruthlessly organised, have a largish kitchen and some other adult helpers for such a party. And probably something else to do for some of the time (decorating aprons, decorating a tablecloth, watching a DVD).

Some games for this age group (and they will probably still like pass-the-parcel and those musical games):

- Apple-bobbing
- Sweets in flour (have to extract sweets from flour with mouth – avoid game during e.g. flu epidemic)
- Consequences (for children who are basically literate only)
- Team quizzes

- 'Drawing in the dark – each person gets pencil and paper. Turn off lights, then instruct them to draw a scene (e.g. a castle with a princess, a pony, some fairies, trees etc.). Then turn on the lights and laugh at everyone's pictures!'

  (MumintheMirror)

- Chocolate game: you throw a six and then get to put on hat, scarf, gloves etc. then try to eat a big bar of chocolate with a knife and fork, meanwhile the dice is going around the circle and as soon as someone else gets a six they have a go. Hours of greedy fun.

- 'We had pass the bean bag (no wrapping – yay!) and when the music stopped the child picked a forfeit out of a pot. These were things like:

  Tell a joke.

  Do an impression of a chicken, lion, dinosaur, monkey etc.

  Say something in another language.

  Do an impression of your teacher.

  Choose a friend and do a dance round the circle.

  Name five animals beginning with p.

  Name five things you eat which are red.

  Went down well with twenty girls aged eight–ten.'

  (liitlefish)

More for eight- to ten-ish-year-olds

The more sophisticated games are usually still going strong as are the more sophisticated craft-and-cooking activities.

Getting outside can be a very good thing if the weather permits:

'Tug-o-war is a great party game for testosterone frenzies (and girls). You will need a large (e.g. marine grade) rope – hardware store? It can go on for ages as they organise themselves into teams; then you can have an adult (or three!) against all the kids etc. We always have one and it is always hugely popular.'

(spinspinsugar)

'If you have a garden, get the following:

Garden canes

Old sheets/blankets

Clothes pegs

String
Rope
Masking tape
Bin bags
Hammers
Tent pegs
Scissors

Set the children a challenge e.g. must make a shelter big enough for at least three people to get in. Must use at least four different pieces of equipment. Cook a barbecue outside while they are happily playing. Let them eat their food in the dens! Warn parents in advance that the children will be outside the whole time and to dress them accordingly.'

(littlefish)

Ten-ish years

Outings like cinema, bowling, lasertag etc. may dominate in this group. But 'cooler' art projects may also be popular as part of a hanging out with pizzas and a DVD type of do:

'Fabric pens and T-shirts or pillow cases – they all sign, decorate etc. each other's, especially the birthday girl's. Also, your going home present is done.'

(grumpypants)

And they will still like some flagrant silliness:

'You could have an eating doughnut game, I used to love that when I was ten! You get some sugared ring doughnuts – mini ones would be good too – then loop them on to a long piece of string and then they have to eat them without using their hands.'

(Baileysismyfriend)

Some girls (or indeed metrosexual boys) will enjoy a 'pamper party'. You can have manicures, pedicures, facemasks, a beauty bar with nail varnish and hair doodahs. And hair straighteners if you are brave.

You can also have singing and karaoke-type games if you have a Wii/ Xbox etc. (or just make up your own with some backing music).

Delivery pizza is often a thrill, or the add your own topping and put in oven option, followed by a sundae bar. Fondue is fun for children who are not too boisterous and you can create a home cinema-type experience by serving bags of popcorn to DVD watchers.

Having said all of this, there is a good chance your children will tell you in detail exactly what kind of party they want from about age four, rendering most of the above otiose. Except perhaps as an indication of What to Ban.

Outdoors in a public space

If you have somehow been blackmailed into inviting a very large number of children and it is spring/summer and you are devil-may-care about the weather, you could consider having a party in a park or on a green. Make sure you select somewhere not full of syringes and old condoms or next door to the house of a child you didn't invite. Depending on the age of children you can do a range of running-about-type games like hide-and-seek or an obstacle course or races. You could have a treasure hunt or scavenger hunt, a piñata hung from a tree, some simple facepainting, a bubble machine . . . Older children might like to have a game of football. The easiest way to provide food might be to use those cardboard lunch boxes and just prepack for each child, taking care the food is sufficiently anodyne as to offend no child (so crisps then).

'Many flavours of crisps. They don't want anything else. They don't want: lovingly made small sandwiches; cunning jelly boats made from oranges a la Annabel Karmel; meringues shaped like ghosts; cocktail sausages in finger rolls; fairy cakes etc. etc., they want crisps.'

(*Colinfirth*)

Appendix to rule: Do dole out party bags but keep them cheap

Men have died and worms have eaten them but not over party bags. This truly is not one to get exercised about. It is just a universal truth that modern children will tend to look puzzled and disappointed if there is no party bag, so really there is no point getting too crabby and self-righteous and saying, 'In my day we were happy if the pass-the-parcel had one sweetie right in the centre or even a lump of poo.' But you can without too much trouble produce something acceptable for, say, £1 per child. Here are some thoughts:

- Very minimalist party bag: piece of cake in napkin, balloon. Punch balloons are usually wildly popular.
- Slightly less minimalist: add small plastic toy/bottle of bubble mixture. And a sweet.

The truth is the internet is awash with small plastic toys for party bags available in cheap multipacks. Or go to a large and good pound shop. There are different schools of thought as to whether you should be adding to the mountain of gimcrackery, either globally or at the level of your neighbours' houses.

If you are not troubled about that, here are some ideas for:

Superior plastic tat

- Cheap glowsticks in their many forms: *loved* by children of all ages
- Whoopee cushions and other tricks available from pound shops like snapping gum, plastic poo and so forth
- Grow your own alien/frog/whatnot by adding water and waiting for item to grow/spring out of egg
- Small water guns
- Very bouncy balls
- Tennis balls
- Tattoos
- Inflatable guitars, microphones etc.
- Grabber guns
- Hair slides and bobbles
- Magic tricks
- Flashlights

At the more worthy end of the market

- Some frivolous socks with Peppa Pig, Power Rangers etc. from a multipack; seriously
- Crayons/pencils

- Tubs of glitter (parents will hate you)
- Felt tip or gel pens
- Tubs of playdoh
- Plasticine
- Small notebooks
- Packet of seeds, small plant pot
- Or a bulb with instructions
- Small paintboxes

If going down the worthy route, use decorated paper bags for eco-friendliness.

Incidentally, if you are wealthy and cannot be arsed, there are people on the internet who will ship you some ready made-up party bags. True thing.

Alternatives to party bags

Some party givers like a single item alternative to the party bag so that expenditure can be concentrated on one half-decent item rather than dissipated amongst numerous bits of frivolity. Some people recommend giving each child a cheap book (from multipacks available from suppliers on the internet – can work out at £1 or less per book) or a sticker book or magazine. Other folk think this idea is fun-deficient:

'Hmm I'd not do a book. I'd do predominantly sweets (the worse the better) with either a parachute man, or tattoos (I know but they love them). For my second son's sixth birthday party I did those wiggly straws for boys and bangles for girls from Toys R Us. Also a proper packet of sweets (think I got some boxes of skittles). My kids like books. They like parties.They like party bags. They don't like them mixing. A party bag BEST case scenario is sweets, with a football keyring (who has keys aged six?!) if you have to.'

(*PCCod*)

But even if you don't fancy the book idea (and many *parents* will look beamingly on the book), you can still try these party-bag alternatives:
- Large bowl of sweeties for children to help self from when leaving
- Sweets and marshmallows wrapped in coloured cellophane tied with a bit of ribbon

- Special decorated biscuit/gingerbread man wrapped in cellophane or tissue
- Lucky dip of presents from pound shop wrapped up and put into large bucket
- If there is a craft activity: the finished craft objet, possibly in a bag
- Small flowering plant
- Some highly desired object: pack of Top Trumps, gogos etc.
- Nice mugs or beakers with sweets or a small cake in, wrapped with tissue or cellophane, ribbon etc. to your taste.

Is there a statute of limitations on party bags? Many think you can start quietly ditching them around age eight or nine.

'I didn't do one for my son's year three party, so age eight, and they all stood about looking hopeful and I stared back at them with my arms crossed. One boy even asked for one. And then they went home. My son kept bringing some back during year three though, but I like to think I started their decline . . .'

(*ahundredtimes*)

And remember this: there is a reason for party bags and it is not just to make children vomit in the car on the way home. Nothing says 'this party is over, off you go' like a party bag. And that's got to be worth a pound of anyone's money.

Make them write thank you notes

(PARTY ETIQUETTE: THE RULES)

What not to do as a party guest

- Fail to RSVP: (especially if it's something like soft play where the hosts are paying per child). It is a great modern conundrum why, on average, 60 per cent of children's party attendees fail to RSVP. Particularly given the universal condemnation of the non-responders on chat threads. It is quite possible that 60 per cent of invitations are consumed by schoolbags, but that would not explain why 80 per cent of that 60 per cent turn up at the party anyway.

- Fail to RSVP and then turn up without explanation. Again this is more of a big deal if your host is paying per child than it would be at general riot in a village hall but it's a big deal nevertheless because if everyone does that then the poor hosts will be fretting that no one's coming, that their child will be irrevocably scarred and they'll be living off Twiglets for the foreseeable future.

- Arrive at the party with unannounced siblings. If your child is too young to attend the party unaccompanied (the watershed is somewhere around five – some four-year-olds are OK especially if it's a party with adults they know well already) and you have other children you cannot conveniently offload, speak to the host. If it's soft play or whatnot, offer to pay for siblings but graciously back down if they say no and perhaps bump up the value of the gift. If you are bringing a much bigger child, you must have a stern word in advance of the party. He is not allowed to win all the party games and hoover up everything that falls from the piñata.

- Fail to warn hosts in advance that your child has food allergies, intolerances or special dietary requirements. If your host sounds a bit wobbly about whether devising an alternative menu for your child will fit in with her preparations, think about offering to bring a bit of gluten-free cake or at least give her a steer as to what party foods your child can eat.
- Bring a child who is sickening to a party. Sickening with an illness, that is. Children with awful personalities are allowed to attend parties.
- Hang around at the party (parents of under-five-year-olds an exception here) unless you are a friend to the parents or helping out or they seem to want you there. A strange dad sitting in one's kitchen drinking tea and blinking can be a significant additional stressor to a party host.
- Fail to leave at kicking-out time. Unless the host is eagerly uncorking bottles of wine, the bestowing of a party bag or the commencement of dishwasher loading is likely to be a signal to leave.
- Rant about the quantity of sweets in the party bag, either at the party or in your neighbourhood thereafter. It's a party. If you want to edit the party bag once you get out of the door that is a matter for you.

What not to do as a party host

- Give the invitation to the child. If at all possible, you should try to get the invitation into the hands of an attendant adult. You will maximise your chances of an RSVP and, unlike most children, most adults will not gloat at other adults about the invitation, thus sowing sorrow in the breasts of non-invitees. At some schools you can discreetly put invitations into trays or bookbags which reduces gloating potential but ups the chances that no one literate will ever see the invitation. Here are some more ways to enhance the reply rate:
  - Include your telephone and mobile numbers and email address on the invitation. Some parents are just lazy or shy about picking up the phone and actually conversing with you.
  - Include a date by which you require responses in order to finalise numbers at the venues.

- A leetle more hardcore:

  'I love, LOVE, *LOVE* the idea of putting "RSVP or no party bag" on the invitation but I don't think I've got the nerve to do that!'

  (Snowstorm)

- 'The most effective strategy I've found is to create an invite, with a large tear-off strip to return saying: Yes, I can come to your party/ No, sorry, I can't come to your party. Love from . . .'

  (roisin)

- Telephone and hassle or beard in the street non-responders.

- Think that most people who haven't replied won't be coming and fail to cater for them. It is non-attenders who most assiduously RSVP; perhaps it is their politeness which makes them socially in demand.

- Invite all the children in the class bar three. You either have a party for the whole class (or possibly for all of one gender) – usually in nursery or reception when friendships may be a bit vague. Or you invite a subset which is no more than, say, two thirds. A party which excludes the two spitting unsocialised boys your daughter doesn't like is unkind. If everyone excludes only those two spitting boys, they are likely to continue spitting into adulthood.

- Invite half the children for a hysterical sleepover of a lifetime and the remainder to join in some other activity the day after with the drowsy but gloating sleepover children. This is divisive.

- Expect parents of very small children to bugger off. A mother of eight may be out of your front door before you have grasped the soft hand of her three-year-old but generally you need to allow parents of the under-fives to stick around.

- Expect parents of very small children not to have dependent siblings who will need some catering for. Not everyone can make arrangements for siblings – polite parents will give you fair warning so you can accommodate some additional children.

- Expect people to pay for stuff at a party – paintballs, say, or popcorn at the cinema. Have a party you can afford.

- Ban gifts. People do some desperate things to try to prevent more plastic crap coming through their front door. Mugging children seen approaching the venue with large, light, gift-wrapped boxes for example. But banning gifts or saying something wiffly in the invitation about gifts not being necessary is kind neither to the child nor to the parents of guests:

'Now I'm dictating for my eight-year-old daughter ... "If the child has to suffer the experience of not having presents in a party then they should definitely ring Childline."'

(Spidermama)

'When you go to a birthday party, you feel you should bring something. It feels awkward not to. Uncertainty about presents = awkwardness.'

(harpsichordcarrier)

'Why don't you accept the presents with good grace and then either a) sell them on eBay on behalf of a charity or b) donate them immediately to a local hospice, hospital or SN unit. I often phone and ask a parent if the child wants anything in particular and would be very happy to be told to give books or to donate to charity.'

(pagwatch)

- Have a gift list or request cash. This is just yucky.

'My son was invited to a party earlier this year – "Please do not bring presents, but X would really like one or two bigger items, such as a trampoline and a bouncy castle, so we would welcome donations towards these bigger items that all the family can use."

His school is full of competitive alpha mums at dawn, so I opted out of the £10 or £20 dilemma by refusing the invitation. I quite liked the mum beforehand, now I can't look at her in the same light – she seems v money-grabbing and materialistic to me.'

(milge)

- Request donations towards charitable gifts. You and your child can channel unwanted gifts towards charitable purposes after the party (see above).

'OK, kids lets all hold hands and close our eyes and imagine Chlamydia's birthday goat being given to the poor people.'

(Enid)

'And them eating it.'

(*TheHighwayCod*)

- Allow your children to fail to say thank you for gifts. Some folk think an oral thank you at the party is fine, especially if the gift has been lovingly torn open and effusively admired in front of the giver. Some folk are keen on personalised thank you notes, even in those circumstances, preferably with a good garnishing of glitter and maybe a photo of the happy recipient. We are sticking our necks out here, but would suggest that thank you notes are a good thing and making your child write them is a good habit to instil. They really don't have to involve large supplies of glue and glitter, though. No recipient is going to thank you for that.

Incidentally, on the open now or open later question, the answer generally speaking is:
- Large party and/or party not in your own home, open gifts later.
- Small party in own home: probably best to open gifts on the spot.

Don't let your kids do martial arts

'My opinion is that the only not negotiable extracurricular is swimming – the rest I can take or leave. Even that's a hassle.'

(*codswallop*)

This is not just about martial arts. It's about ponyriding and Brownies and ballet and cricket and recorder. Although it must be said that martial arts are a paradigm example of the inverted pyramid of increasing effort and expense that many extracurricular activities represent. Take taekwondo – you start with one afternoon a week and it seems like lovely exercise and the child is learning discipline or somesuch, some vaguely Eastern spiritually good for him amorphous kind of thing as per *Karate Kid*. You have a bit of a laugh, patting him on the head, and inappropriately calling him 'grasshopper' to annoy him.

And then they get hooked in by the exams and the belts. And the afternoons increase to two or three per week and competitions every weekend in far-flung parts of the nations to which you feel obliged to drag other offspring too. And then the money starts increasing as they need pricey sparring kits and the latest taekwondo high-tops. And you ponder whether they are actually growing more disciplined and spiritual or just better able to kick the crap out of each other. And you have cynical thoughts about what the point is anyway. Say they got black belts – are they really ever going to gain Olympic gold and feature on the conver of the taekwondo magazines you see lying around in the gym. Would you care? Do you want to watch them sparring on YouTube? If they were taekwondo champions of the whole world, would your parental heart be swelling up with pride?

Some rants about the spiralling costs of extracurricular activities

'I think this is really out of order. Firstly they have a club leotard – but they *choose* not to enforce it for normal lessons (nor do they warn newcomers that they might need one for other occasions) so the result is everyone has perfectly good leotards – but a complete mixture of colours and styles. One month before Christmas and their Christmas show (which is costing £10 per ticket to see) they announce that my older daughter's class all need club leotards (£25), plus a black long-sleeved T-shirt (my daughter hasn't got *anything* black so that'll be another fiver and, I expect, a painful shop as it's not the kind of thing you see much of) plus a mask of some sort that the club will make and charge us for (? let's guess £3). My younger daughter needs a new leotard too (another £25). So this whole thing is costing near enough £80. Plus an inordinate amount of practices and performances – it's basically taking up the whole of every weekend between now and Christmas. Not that we had anything else in mind . . .'

(*hatwoman*)

'My son got to brown belt in karate and something that started out with £2 once a week and a second-hand kit from a neighbour, ended up costing a small fortune in licences and grading fees and club fees. And his new karate kit cost me nearly £50!'

(*OrmIrian*)

So OK, this is not all about you. But it is somewhat about you if you are the person who has to take them to these activities and pay for them. And it's a bit about their siblings. If you're spending every weekend traipsing off to Bognor for a regional tournament, where does that leave his younger sister? And it's about you all having some unstructured time as a family. Your children need some boredom, some time to do chores and homework and learn to cook, to go to the library or muck about in a park.

'We have lovely weekends being all together and we do things like: my husband takes him out to play football; he has a friend round and they play yu gi oh cards; we watch a movie on our projector and have hot dogs and popcorn; we go to the cinema; we loll about a lot; he plays silly sweet games with his sister. Blimey, when we were kids we used to let ourselves into the house at 3.40 (latchkey kids we were called in the seventies!), make a mound of toast and mess about on our own until our mother got in from work at 5.30 p.m.'

(wickedwaterwitch)

So we say:

- Set rational limits to extracurricular activities – two per child is absolutely plenty, and possibly one for any child under the age of six.
- If a child starts something for which you have to pay in advance, you should make it clear to him that you expect him to carry on at least for the paid-for period. Other than that, don't force a child to carry on with ballet. If he doesn't enjoy it, what's the point?
- If they want to do instruments, they must practise. Either the child is interested in learning and the practising will bear some fruit or she is not really interested and the practising is not going to put her off. But if she really hates it, she should give it up.
- If they want to try new things, there are often week-long camps of one sort or another in school holidays. They can try out sailing or tennis or whatnot and see if it's important enough to become a regular gig.
- School clubs which take place before school or at lunchtime are another good, cheap way of trying things out which doesn't use up all their after-school time.

All children should have some exercise of a kind which suits them. Not competitive sports if they don't like those. They should all learn to ride a bike if that's a possibility and spend some time cycling. For children in urban areas with little outdoor space, you may find you need to sign up for some organised activities, especially in winter (swimming, trampolining . . .).

We are not saying your children won't possibly complain bitterly and at length if you don't let them sign up for every club and lesson available (some children; others will complain if you do sign them up for anything at all). But that's the distressing but inevitable thing about being a parent; it's like being the government – people have a right to resent you because you are in power and have no concomitant obligation to try to understand you.

Toddler life

IF IN DOUBT, GO OUT

There is an all-new kind of boredom that comes with parenthood, the boredom of frantically doing what looks like nothing much yet being prevented from doing anything which feels useful or enjoyable. This is your life with a baby/toddler – you scurry around the hamster wheel of little maintenance tasks without ever achieving anything tangible. Your brain and your limbs and stuff are all functioning but you can't really use them . . .

And that's just you. Your toddler is the same (your baby probably less so but some are restless little souls too). As some parents have observed, a toddler is just a dog with less fur. You must run him about a lot or he will be horrid. Older toddlers will sometimes wait hopefully by the door clutching their shoes. It is not just about exercise, it's about a change of scene for the both of you. And other company. Your house can seem quite spooky with just you and a toddler in it. The adult/toddler relationship needs the odd gust of fresh air to blow right through it. And your house needs you to be out of it so it can stop getting dirty and relax for a bit.

So go out. Only endorphins can save you. Go out every day. Go out even if there is a blizzard. Even if frogs are falling from the sky and locusts pattering on the rooftops. Even if your clothes are glued to your body with infant vomit and you have a twitching eye because being alone with your child has made you socially phobic. Especially if you have the twitching eye thing.

Have clothing suitable for all weathers. Make sure you have lots of cheap wellies in the right size and a rain cover for your buggy. Try to keep them near the front door. Have a raincoat with a hood for yourself so your hands are free.

'My children walked the dog with me every day from about one week old, regardless of the weather. They only stayed home if they were really ill. If you're dressed for the weather it's fine. We would have all gone mad if we were indoors all the time. And would have been bored senseless.'

(TheDuchessofCorposeBride)

If the weather is really really too awful, find an indoor place to run about in – a shopping mall, Ikea, soft play if you can bear it and you can get some exercise on the way. Go to a swimming pool.

'It's *good* for children to go out each day – healthy, fresh air, free entertainment (well, my two-year-old loves looking at stones, pigeons, garden walls lol), good exercise, encourages socialisation (visiting mummy's friends, saying "good morning" to neighbours), stimulating for their brain (learning route home, observing seasonal changes, learning how shopping works etc.), great starting point for talking about all sorts etc. etc.'

(EachPeachPearMum)

Of course it is possible to overdo anything and no doubt there is the odd parent who doesn't have the kid home long enough to ever read a book or bat some toys about. But we don't think it's a big risk:

'I love doing baking/crafty things but let's be frank. Half an hour is the limit of the kid's attention span, if you do something like that then you still have to fill up three or four or five hours before the next meal/nap. Out and about as much as you want to, I say.'

(justaboutagrownup)

NEAREST AND DEAREST

Help your partner
be competent to look after
your mutual children

OTHERWISE KNOWN AS: DIFFERENT IS
NOT NECESSARILY CRAP

Most of the advice/anecdotage in this book at least aspires to be unisex; this rule, however, is mostly a man/woman thing (or possibly a woman/woman thing if there are two mothers). But moving on . . . If you are the biological mother, you are pretty much forced to learn what to do with your baby. It emerged from your body. You may well be feeding it from your own body. You are there in hospital with it in the first instance. And you have to take at least a couple of weeks off work to get used to it; chances are you will take much more than that.

And you have all those hormones shouting at you to Be Careful, that what you have produced is terribly fragile. And it is *yours*. Not long ago when it was tucked away under your skin no one else could pick it up and let its head woogle around. Or drop it.

And him? He may be great, but he may not be. His handling may be fumbling at first; it may be worse. You may find yourself shrieking, 'For God's sake, she's alive!' as he plants his foot against the car seat to tighten the straps to sternum-crushing snugness. So there you are, positively electrified with health and safety concerns and presented with an impossibly vulnerable living thing requiring 24-hour-a-day care and you have to let someone else practise on it.

And yes, you do have to. Because the only way he will ever do his fair share is if he learns. The less time he spends with the baby the less competent he will be. We are not saying there is not a swathe of the human population which is chronically afflicted with poor judgment and inattentiveness. There is, but they are a minority and you probably knew whether the father of your children fell into that category before the baby was born. He probably hasn't changed radically in fundamentals since he crossed the bourne into fatherhood but he does need to acquire new skills.

'I can't agree that there is a widespread malady regarding men who display poor judgment. Some people do some of the time, in my opinion. Very few people exhibit poor judgment all of the time and I have no reason to believe men are any more prone to it than women.

I frankly find the whole business of infantilising men, writing them off as useless, incapabable, lacking in judgment etc., incredibly tiresome! *Men* are not incapable of looking after children in a responsible manner in my experience. All of the fathers that I know are fully involved in their children's lives – I genuinely can't think of any of them who are not capable of caring for their own children.'

(*soapbox*)

With the majority of the population of more or less trainable partners you need to resist micromanaging the things they do. You wouldn't have put your baby in those socks but they are OK socks. You would have brought him home sooner for his tea and he's a bit hungry and overtired, but maybe your partner's learned something for the next time. A few years down the line, you may even think some of the things he did instinctively were better than the ones you did. Probably it is oftentimes the combination of one overanxious/insanely controlling parent and one more relaxed/borderline feckless parent which enables children to grow up relatively physically and psychologically intact.

The Dad-type person needs to have a go at looking after your mutual baby all by himself (he will no doubt enjoy the fawning attention he gets in public for lone childcaring. Just don't let him go on about it):

'My partner rarely looked after our son alone for a long time. Not because he wasn't capable, just because he didn't need to. I didn't work and hardly ever went out. When we were together, we were ALL together as a family. It just never came up. But it came with a massive downside. He never learnt our son's routine, didn't bond with him like I did, didn't understand the hard work I put in every day because all the little things I had to do for our son never even entered his mind. It also meant he had no confidence in his ability as a parent and it scared me a bit. What if I got hit by a bus tomorrow and DP had to be a single dad? He wouldn't have a clue, not because he didn't want to, just because he had never had the opportunity. We argued about it once and he snapped at me "Well you never LET me do anything, sometimes I don't feel like he's my baby!" and that really upset me. I just did everything, without thinking to involve my partner.

So, I went back to work last summer, and my partner is at uni so he gets the school holidays off. He had my son all summer, he saw him twice as much as I did, and I forced myself to take a step back and let them get on with it. Their relationship changed so much. They are so close now. My partner knows just what to do. I can leave without giving instructions and I feel that we are equal.'

(*littlepurpleprincess*)

As children get older, the balance is likely to be between the parent who does more childcare and the parent who does less. And even in families where both parents work full-time there is often one parent who has ultimate responsibility for the administration of the children. Try to make sure there is a balance of duties which does not make one of you angry and miserable. Don't be the skivvy whilst he gets to be the funster. If he is taking the toddler out to the park, he can pack the bag with nappies, wipes, spare clothes, snacks. You will like him more if he is helping properly. He will like you more if you like him more. It helps to remember that whilst people do learn tasks and become more competent, adult personalities do not tend to change much, so try to have a division of labour which is both fair and plays to your respective strengths.

Differences in *style*, particularly relating to issues like discipline, may emerge as children get older. These are hard, because this stuff seems very important and you are often sure you are right. Also, the more challenging the child the more likely that there will be clashes of parenting style.

'We just had this out last night . . . it's a tricky one. I feel like my husband just uses terrible cliches that his parents used and uses an aggressive, threatening tone with her (though he would never hit her) and doesn't have any idea that parenting styles have moved on since the seventies, that you use positive reinforcement and try to ignore bad behaviour, especially if it's clearly aimed to wind you up. And that she's only 2 and you have to make allowances sometimes.'

(*mrsbabookaloo*)

Here are some things to think about. If you are really unable to agree, it may help to try some reading material. One of you may be pootling along just doing basically what your own parents did, appropriate or not. It can help to look at techniques. Provided you don't expect the books to make him do exactly what you do:

'If my husband told me to read a parenting book, I'd probably throw it at him. We've all got different personalities and the ways we approach challenges are bound to be different but that doesn't make them wrong.'

(*gingerninja*)

Keep talking about issues which arise – one of you may be persuaded by the other's viewpoint. Or you may decide you can carry on doing things a bit differently in this instance. Or one of you may have to shoutily overrule the other person. Try not to do that last thing in front of your children too much.

You should accept that some level of good cop/bad cop is OK and that your ways of dealing may be complementary. Quite often there is a shoutier person and a softer person. Or a lazier person. Children need to know people are different and have different ideas as long as you are not behaving so radically inconsistently that you are confusing them.

If one of you is doing the bulk of the childcare and spends more time with the children, it is generally reasonable for that person's views to carry more weight on how to deal with particular issues which arise. 'Look, he gets irrational and tantrummy when he is this tired. You need to stop trying to reason with him about the packet of pom bears and distract him.' But it is also important to recognise that actually having another adult's view is useful too. We all need to have some humility. There are of course limits – if a partner is truly dangerously incompetent or abusive, you probably have to bin him. For your sake and your children's.

In practice . . .

'My wife and I have slightly different parenting styles. I'm more strict and my wife less so, although not at absurdly different ends of the spectrum. Cue conversations (for example) with child making noise upstairs along these lines:

Me: "Let's try to give her five minutes and then just go in, reassure her and then leave again."

Wife: "It's been five minutes already."

Me (checking watch): "No, it's been thirty-eight seconds."

Wife: "Your stupid watch is wrong. Listen to the poor child screaming . . . she's getting really upset because of you. She'll never settle now."

Me: "She's whimpering, not howling. And if we go in now we'll spend the rest of our lives going in every night whenever she so much as farts."

Wife: "No we won't. And she'll make herself sick in a minute. Just let me go in quickly and make sure she's OK."

Me: "Of course she's OK. We only saw her fifty-three seconds ago. What do you think has happened to her in a locked room several feet away in less than a minute?"

Wife: "Stop being a twat."

We usually resolve this situation for example by me trying to wrestle my wife back downstairs whilst she tries to claw her way up the stairs during which we have an angry (but hushed) conversation along very similar lines to the one above. At some point the child stops crying, we get a large glass of wine each and agree that we'll try to leave her for a bit longer the next evening. It seems to work for us and, hey, our daughter sleeps through perfectly now!'

(*cestlavie*)

'My husband is way more relaxed and often thinking about other things and not noticing what needs to be done or what time it is. Fortunately he knows he has to and wants to do his share, and doesn't appear bothered about the way I ask him to do things, which varies according to how stressed I am. Even though he has had the children to himself plenty of times, I still end up directing a bit while he is around otherwise they would all decide to go exploring a ditch half a mile from the house just before it gets dark!

But he does bring plenty of other things to raising the children that I don't. Like taking the children exploring ditches for example! I have learnt stuff from the way he is with the children and he has learnt a bit from me but we are never going to do things in exactly the same way, but where's the harm in that?'

(*othersideofthechannel*)

Do argue in front of the children but do reconcile publicly

'I would prefer it if my children didn't argue in front of me, actually, considering the headache I get . . .'

(*TinyGang*)

This is all very difficult. Even in quite decent relationships, people have disagreements. And some people tend to have vigorous, shouty, unpleasant-to-listen-to disagreements. Which they may thoroughly enjoy in some cases. Or they may at least enjoy an agreeable erotic interlude after the disagreement.

But then you have a baby or two and it seems ugly to be shouting at their other parent that he's a despicable lazy twunt. Even if you know the twunt in question lets the abuse roll over him whilst contentedly maintaining his despicably lazy ways. And it seems positively Dickensian and awful when your four-year-old turns his big eyes on you and says, 'Please don't be mean to Daddy.' But does this mean you just have to put up variously with the other parent's derelictions in the catbox clearance department, his unreasonable critique of your driving, his mealy-mouthed repetition of your in-laws' demands re Christmas? No, it doesn't.

Now you could try to have all your disagreements with spouse or partner once your children were tucked up in bed. But the results of this experiment would probably be:

- Children hearing arguing in the night and fearing that parents were heading towards relationship breakdown, possibly writing misery memoirs in due course about the aforesaid.
- Children being utterly unable to deal with conflict as adults, having never seen it/seen it be resolved.

'I would not want to hide a part of my personality from my children though – they need to know who I am and that, whatever bad points I have and things I do wrong, I still love them all and still love their father too. That's stability. If my husband and I pretend things are sweetness and light the whole time and then one time we mess up and row in front of them by mistake, how on earth would they ever cope with that?'

(LindenLass)

- (A variant on the above) children growing up with an unreal view of relationships:

'My mum and dad never argued and I really thought they must have the perfect relationship when I was growing up. I gradually realised that in fact they do not communicate at all beyond small talk. There is also a lot of suppressed anger and passive aggression. The result of this was that I had no idea how to handle negative emotion.'

(alwaysmoving)

We suspect that most parents who store up tension and go about in an atmosphere of repressed anger until the children are not there are not fooling their kids or doing anyone any good:

'Children pick up on atmosphere. So if you are both seething but have to wait to have the row until they are in bed, your kids aren't going to be in happy ignorance of the emotions around them – they will realise something is wrong. Better to have a row (within limits) and make up than leave them on tenterhooks all the time, IMO.'

(edam)

But we also think there is a distinction to be made between quotidian rows and the ugly everyday eruption of rancour in a relationship which is or should be in its terminal stages. No one, apart from the parties and possibly their professional advisers, should be exposed to the latter.

Ordinary rows

Most people in most relationships have disagreements and those disagreements sometimes become heated. If the people in the relationship do not hate each other the rest of the time, an element of disagreement is something that children generally can cope with. With children who are old enough to understand, you can explain that ordinary rows are not desperately serious and do not mean the parental relationship is breaking down:

'I have said to our daughter (five) that occasionally people disagree just like when she and her friends argue and fall out in the playground about what game to play etc. I tell her that after we have argued we always talk and sort it out and say sorry if necessary and become friends again, just like she does with her friends in the playground.'

(oneplusone)

'I think that disagreements between parents can actually be a healthy thing. Only if any quarrels are resolved. If there is an issue which cannot be resolved then this should wait until the children are in bed, or out, as the case may be. If children do not see minor disagreements being resolved in a "safe" situation, then they will not be able to learn how best to reach amicable agreements with their peers. A really important part of disagreeing is an ability to debate issues, if this is not learned in the home, then many children would find it difficult to do so in the school environment. Children need to learn that others have differing opinions to themselves and it is OK to have your own opinion.'

(grannie)

A very large part of what children learn about intimate relationships they learn from the everyday dealings between their parents. So a relationship you previously inhabited privately like a smelly but tolerable old sock is now set up on a kind of plinth in front of the small audience of your offspring (to mangle some metaphors). So we would also venture to say that it is important to not make it seem that one parent is being victimised, which can happen if a parent always bites her lip in the face of ill temper or unreasonableness. It is probably especially important for girls to see their mothers sticking up for themselves:

'If I feel my husband is being unpleasant I stick up for myself big time, and I hope my daughters pick up on this, so they will learn to stick up for themselves in a similar situation.'

(*ReneRusso*)

If children are upset by ordinary parental arguments, you need to reassure them in a way which doesn't ignore their feelings. Discuss how they felt and why they felt it but explain why the argument was not ultimately that serious.

Notwithstanding all of the above, if you and your spouse/partner are especially sweary or your arguments descend to personal abuse, you should probably work on this. It's often not a marvellous way for you to be inter se (although it works fine for some people) and it's not fantastic modelling for your children. If you can find a more rational mode of dealing with disagreement, it will be better for all of you. And there must be no flouncing off, no threats to leave or wild talk about how it's all over when you know it isn't.

And what they really need to see is how you resolve conflict – you may disagree, one of you may behave selfishly or hurt the other's feelings but you can resolve your differences. The person or persons who have behaved badly can apologise. The underlying relationships are not so delicate they can't survive all of this. You can all survive anger.

'The three Rs of arguing: **R**ein it in immediately your child is aware of it. Demonstrate that **R**esolution can be achieved and show **R**emorse.'

(*suzywong*)

More serious relationship problems

If there are serious problems in your relationship, you do need to find a way of dealing with these away from your children (and not by shouting in the living room whilst they hold their hands over their ears in the bedroom). Endless personal sniping in front of children or constant rows which rake over issues between you which are essentially unresolved are obviously going to be upsetting. Take them outside.

'Arguing in front of children is about showing an example of how to behave, not giving detailed ins-and-outs of your relationship and problems.'

(*MarlaSinger*)

Never ever drag your children into the argument:

'The other thing that I found very difficult about my parents' rows were them making comments to me and sis (e.g. "Look how childish your father is being, he's so pathetic," etc.) and trying to draw us into it and make us take sides. (For example: "Don't you agree with me?", "Surely it's just basic to do xyz you must agree with that?") That was horrendous.'

(*TheArmadillo*)

Don't sulk with your spouse/partner around your children. It is better to clear the air with a suitably constructed actual disagreement sans abuse and hysteria if at all possible.

Don't complain about your spouse/partner to your children.

'Another thing my mum does is wait until my dad leaves the room then moans about him to me. She didn't do that when I was little but I think it had started by my teenage years. I always hated it and as a result tend to tell my husband what I think right away, in front of kids or not! I've had some horrified looks from my mum when this has happened . . .'

(*alwaysmoving*)

Sometimes being someone's parent makes you look at the little bogs of unreasonableness and neglected thickets of ancient resentments in your relationship and sort them out. Because what was tolerable when it only affected you and your spouse or partner isn't so good when it is affecting your children. For some of us, helping other people grow up means having to grow up a bit ourselves.

Be kind to
your in-laws

This has probably already made your hackles rise if you think your in-laws are not very kind to you. And yes, it's a two-way street. But it's a relationship you are going to have to live with, pretty intimately, for a long time, so it's worth thinking about what *you* can do to make it as good/tolerable as possible. What follows assumes that your spouse/partner was not raised by actual psychopaths. In the latter case, please refer to Rule 101: *You don't have to put up with being dismembered at Christmas.*

Why in-law relationships often go wrong

In families, we put up with the idiosyncrasies of our own parents and they put up with ours. And/or depending on the parties involved, we can all tell each other to f*** off when appropriate. But in-laws are people who are thrust into intimate contact and Christmas with us and with whom we probably don't have a history of either tolerance or plain speaking. Which can be fine until grandchildren arrive and your mother-in-law thinks she should be in the delivery room to greet them. Whereas you think you don't want anyone who hasn't seen your bits already and is not a medical professional peering up the birth canal at this sensitive time . . .

Remember it's still love even if you don't like the way it looks

Try this thought experiment. Imagine yourself forward thirty years. Your child is having a baby. This may well bring back memories for you of those early days with your own babies (assuming you liked or think you liked that period when they were snuffling and invertebrate and had hair you wanted to sniff, rather than recalling the whole experience with horror).

You might find yourself purchasing six dozen tiny sleepsuits, a pram, a zoo-full of stuffed animals, the entire series of Baby Isaac Newton DVDs. You might find yourself telephoning your daughter-in-law to find out whether she is eating soft cheese/smoked salmon/wine gums during pregnancy. You might start clipping articles out of the *Daily Mail* and popping them into an envelope to your daughter-in-law on a daily basis. You might parcel up some fetching brown polyester babywear your own son wore in the seventies and then expect to receive studio portraits of your new grandson modelling the same.

Or you might be passionately waiting for the birth but frightened to trouble your daughter-in-law, who is a bit prickly and doesn't share your politics and hides bits of your speciality homemade chicken pie in her napkin when she comes for lunch. Without realising that she is grumbling on an internet forum about how you are showing no interest in your forthcoming grandchild.

Or you might wurble on about how the baby looks just like your beloved son apart from that crinkled ear thing which he gets from you and his obvious intelligence which probably come from your Great-Uncle Timmy until she shrieks, 'I am not just an incubator!' and runs sobbing from the room.

It may be ugly, it may be irritating, but it is all actually a kind of love and excitement. If you can see it that way, it will make it easier to tolerate. And there is a good chance that, after an initial period of private wailing and gnashing of teeth, things will settle down.

'Life is too short to be so precious as to reject unwanted gifts. Of course we can all hurt our mothers-in-laws' feelings if we choose, but then we don't really have a right to complain when we don't have a good relationship with them long-term. Little acts of kindness and unkindness are what make up overall long-term relationships and it might be an idea to bear that in mind when dealing with as fraught and sensitive a relationship as that between a mother-in-law and a daughter-in-law.'

(*Caligula*)

Allow for cultural and historic differences in childrearing practice

Your in-laws, like your own parents, probably grew up in an age when people smoked in the car whilst the baby travelled on the parcel shelf. So don't get too exercised if they tell you to crumble a rusk in his bottle if he's not sleeping through the night at three weeks or that he shouldn't be sleeping in your bed under any circumstances or that it's good for his lungs to have a cry at the end of the garden for an hour or two. Find a tactful but firm way of batting off advice that is stupid or dangerous. And a firm way of stopping them attempting anything silly.

Remember how much power you have and use it wisely

It can be very easy, especially when you are a postnatal loon, to see every bit of outmoded parenting advice proffered by your mother-in-law as a scathing criticism, to get uptight over the fact that she has bought a cot for your newborn when it was desperately important to you to select your own, to think that the fact she is camped in your spare room/the B&B down the street means she is going to be in your living room/head every day forever. But you need to relax. The truth is you are in control of your own child at least until it gets to be in control of itself.

And you need to communicate. Your in-laws don't know whether you would welcome lots of help or find it overbearing. Whether you are desperate for someone to take your baby for a walk so you can sleep for an hour or will feel like they are interfering with the bonding process. They don't know whether you want them to be making you cups of tea or can't bear the thought of them rummaging in your grubby kitchen. For paternal grandparents, the daughter-in-law is likely to be the gatekeeper to the grandchildren and some grandparents may find themselves offending her continuously without really knowing why.

'I would say that as a paternal grandparent you are not always seen as being as important as the maternal grandparents and this isn't entirely fair. It is understandable, as I recall wanting my own mother around when my babies were small, and not my mother-in-law. Before my son was born, I worried terribly about how interfering my mother-in-law would be. And after he was born I found myself getting uptight about visits etc.

Then I learned to let go a bit and let my mother-in-law "in" if you like. Now we have a great relationship. So the advice I would give to mothers-in-law is: give your daughter-in-law time. Always respect her wishes. Don't butt in. And daughters-in-law – don't be so quick to judge your mother-in-law. Sometimes they're just human/enthusiastic/interested.'

(Shodan)

Some boundaries are rational and some are ridiculous

Paternal grandparents should not be treated as second-class grandparents. However, there are some fair distinctions to be made. It is reasonable for a new mother to want her own mother but not her mother-in-law at the birth/in the aftermath of the birth/assisting her with a very new baby. The issue here is not about anyone's rights in relation to the baby but about your needs during a period when your body and life are undergoing momentous change. If your husband/partner cannot see that, try asking him whether he would want your mother holding his hand whilst he has a colonoscopy. Aha.

There are some things none of the grandparents get to do. These include:
- Naming the baby
- Deciding when the baby gets weaned
- Deciding where the child goes to school
- Deciding what haircut the child should have

But there is also a whole wealth of small stuff that first-time parents in particular get exercised about that you should try to get over:

'Someone I know was outraged recently because when her mother-in-law was babysitting, she had used the wrong terminology for potty-training (something like the mother-in-law had said, "Go plop-plop" instead of "number two"). She said she "had a quiet word" with her mother-in-law as her mother-in-law was leaving. I bet that was a lovely thank you for a day spent dealing with poo free of charge.'

(SnotBaby)

Your childcarer is not your friend

At least not at the beginning. And even further down the line he or she is not a friend in any normal way, because money is involved and issues of control and all your sensitivities about your children. It is an uneasy cross between the intimacy of a family relationship and the distance of a business arrangement.

And most people who get childcare haven't had an employee before. Or had the kind of professional relationship you have with a childminder. And a childcarer provides very unusual services – not just attending to the physical needs of the child but also to her emotional needs. In a sense you are purchasing love and that is of course a delicate and difficult transaction. You want your children to feel affection for the childcarer and vice versa. But giving your child into someone else's care, especially the first time, can make you feel, variously, paranoid about whether you have made the right decision and your child will be happy and safe, slightly envious about the childcarer's place in the affections of your child and often tearfully grateful when you appear to have found a good one. All of which is not necessarily conducive to a professional relationship unless you are a person naturally born to command.

There are major differences in terms of how the relationships are structured depending on the various types of childcarer. With a childminder, you have little input into how she runs the show and you need to question her closely and look at her references and an Ofsted report to make sure she is going to suit you and your child. In terms of charges, overtime and holiday arrangements, she is likely to set the terms and you will have to accept them or look elsewhere. With nannies, you can offer terms which suit you, but you may have to negotiate a bit to secure the nanny you decide you want. With au pairs, well, you just have to have very modest expectations.

Establishing a professional relationship at the beginning

The problem is that many of us are so grateful to find someone apparently nice and not insane to look after our children, someone who clasps them to her bosom and extrudes a tear or two as she entertains us with albums depicting her past charges enjoying her lovely homemade birthday cakes, that we fail to get businesslike at the appropriate moment. Which is before the relationship begins, nay before the deal is done by which the relationship will start. Instead we sit staring at the paragon like not very bright dogs, beagles maybe, gazing at owners who have just walked in wearing a suit made out of steak. And babbling. And trying to grapple her to us with bonds of steel.

But much unhappiness is caused by a failure to make expectations very clear from the outset. You really need to deal up front with the following:

- Duties and responsibilities, in particular (for nannies) what housework comes with the role – cleaning up after the child's activities, doing children's laundry, cooking etc.
- Hours of work, overtime arrangements, holiday entitlement/arrangements, what happens if child/childcarer is sick, notice requirements. These things should be contained in a proper written contract between you and the nanny or childminder.
- Disciplinary methods (for children). You need to know you and your nanny are ad idem before she turns up with her spanking stick.
- How problems of performance will be dealt with (nanny or au pair).
- Children's food and activities. What they should and shouldn't eat and what you would expect them to be doing with their time (nannies and au pairs; but you should ascertain from a childminder what the food and activities on offer are and whether they meet your standards. If any).
- Your children's idiosyncrasies and how these are best handled.
- Expectations about computer and mobile use (nannies and au pairs).
- Expectations about her meeting her friends/old charges (nannies and au pairs).

With a nanny, it is sensible to have a probationary period with weekly reviews during that period and, if possible, a lead-in period before you go back to work. If there are things that your nanny is doing which you really don't like, you need to act quickly and tactfully:

'Always intervene if it's wrong, but in a positive way. You're brilliant at so-and-so and they were so pleased with the meal you cooked. Thanks for that. By the way we don't want to make eating too much of an issue so if the food isn't eaten let's not comment on it please or just encourage pleasantly.'

(*Judy1234*)

'When our latest nanny started I stuck a list to the fridge of key things which were important such as key duties to be performed each day but there is no reason why yours couldn't include a "reminder" of how to discipline, what to do if your child doesn't want to eat etc.'

(*Whoosh*)

Expenses

Your childminder should tell you up front what additional expenses there are – meals and activities such as soft play which need to be paid for. Some childminders will just go to cheap/free stuff and there will not be any additional charges.

With a nanny, you can run a kitty or pay her expenses in arrears but either way you should make it clear what the budget is and that you expect her to ask you if she wants to do something especially pricey. Otherwise you may end up miserably broke and resentful:

'I give an advance on expenses each month. She is free to do as she chooses with it. And I do all the grocery shopping so I can keep a lid on the budget and not buy the expensive kiddie junk food that I so hate. I buy wholesome ingredients and she is expected to cook them (which she does).'

(*Eleusis*)

'We run a kitty system in our house – keep a jar in the kitchen topped up with cash, nanny enters expenditure in the book, asks for more if necessary – it's more in the holidays, but she uses it if she needs petrol for the car, we run out of milk, she takes our son out somewhere after nursery, that sort of thing.'

(*jura*)

Having trust

Well, trust is like love, you can't force it to happen but you can nurture it when it puts up a green shoot and allow it to be fed by positive things the childcarer does. Many of us who have made both good and duff choices have found that the bad eggs became apparent pretty quickly.

'For any childcare situation, you need to trust your care provider. This applies for nurseries, preschools, childminders, nannies, babysitters, etc. If you don't trust your childcare provider . . . it's time to change provider.

You can never be sure what is happening when you can't see. Thus trust is vital. Many providers have an "open door" policy, whereby as a parent you can collect your child early, thus see how things are when you are not "expected". However, practicalities can get in the way, as childminders are not at home all the time – they take/collect children from school/preschool, they go on outings. So if you do turn up unexpected, and CM is not at home, then don't be alarmed – the children may be having a great time at the park.

With babies – childcare providers do daily diaries that help you get a feel for how your baby has been that day.

Childcare providers know that first-timers are anxious about leaving their precious bundle of joy, so don't feel that you can't ask them things part-way through the day. However, try to avoid constantly worrying and calling up every ten–fifteen minutes, as then both you and your CM are on tenterhooks all day.'

(nannynick)

Once basic trust is established, you have to allow for some differences in how your childcarer does some day-to-day stuff and not micromanage him. He has to be allowed to cope with the many choices and incidents and minor emergencies which arise without you breathing down his neck. You will drive both childcarer and yourself mad if you are planning every snack and nappy change.

You must respect your childcarer

This is his/her job. You must not be that awful wheedly sort of employer who pretends to be your nanny's friend and then asks her to ped egg your feet.

- Don't have insane expectations, e.g. thinking your nanny will be doing weekly themed craft activities with your two-year-old and performing non-stop flashcard flashing.
- If you have a young or inexperienced nanny, treat her like a trainee. You may need to draw up a schedule of activities or at least suggestions for activities. And sit down and have catch-ups about how it's all going.
- Don't expect endless babysitting and overtime. Give as much notice as possible and don't try to get extra babysitting in a sly way:

'My employers are beginning to think that they can ask me to babysit whenever they want, without any notice. Babysitting is not in my hours at all but I will generally do it if it is pre-arranged. I go away every Friday night and come back on Monday morning, even though I'm fully live-in, this is because I spend the weekend with my partner. On Friday night just before I was leaving my bosses asked if I had any plans for Saturday night (in a conversational friendly manner). I said that my partner and I weren't going anywhere in particular but were just going to chill out. She then asked if I could babysit on the Saturday night. I was so pissed off that she was trying to act like my friend, by just enquiring what I was doing for the weekend and then asking me to babysit. I said that I couldn't as I wanted to spend time with my partner. She wasn't pleased to say the least. I pointed out that if she had asked me in advance then I probably would have said yes. I don't think some people realise that just because you're live-in, it doesn't mean that you are a live-in slave!'

(*lilybeto*)

- Be realistic about your finish times – don't say that you will be back at 6:30 p.m. if the reality is that it is usually 7 p.m. If you are going to be late, telephone and apologise and try to make it up to your nanny/childminder by coming home early one day.
- Remember that her finishing time is when she leaves (nanny) or you take your child away, not when you arrive home/at her home. If you want some time to chat, get there before her finishing time.
- Always pay on time and in full. Review her salary at agreed intervals (nanny).
- Be sympathetic about genuine illness rather than just saying, 'Aaah, aaah, what am I going to do?'
- Show appreciation especially for extra effort made:

'We have just given our nanny a bonus on the successful completion of her probationary period. We also let her go early when we can and also gave her an extra, paid day off after she had done something brill.'

(rubyslippers)

- You should deal compassionately with personal problems but also be clear about what you as a needer of childcare can cope with. If she is off every week because of boyfriend issues, you may have to make it clear that the relationship won't last unless she gets over herself.
- You should deal professionally with any performance or health issues – by having proper meetings and warnings if needs be.
- Don't let your nanny be imposed on by every other parent in the neighbourhood:

'Think you must be *very* careful about the slippery slope of offering for a neighbour's children to come to your house and be watched by your nanny. It is amazing to me how many times I am called by mums of my daughter's school mates to ask if my nanny could "pick up little Isabel at school and take her with you to Tumbletots as you're going anyway", or would my nanny mind if little Anna came over after school as mum has an appointment and can't find a sitter. These mums would never dream of imposing on me, but somehow it's different with someone who is being paid to look after a child – there very much seems to be an attitude of "what's one more anyway, and besides little Sam isn't much trouble . . ." I want to be helpful (and so does my nanny), but we're both very careful about what we volunteer for as we don't want it to become a regular/expected thing. After all, I'm paying for the nanny's time and my nanny contracted to work for a single-child family.'

(Earlybird)

Have rational expectations of au pairs

An au pair is not only not your friend, she is more like an older child who helps out. They are not there to provide full-time or sole-charge childcare. Expect her to stand around eating chocolate bars and weeping and then you may be pleasantly surprised. Don't get one unless you are prepared to look after her:

'Assume the au pair knows nothing – you will have to teach her from scratch. She probably won't have a clue – I have had to tell mine not to leave the children alone in the bath, I have had to show her how to cook sausages, I have had to show her how to do everything I assume people know how to do. But when I was eighteen I was very similar!

Write a very detailed list of duties (mine takes the form of a timetable) – assume that she won't do anything unless it is in the list – you will probably be pleasantly surprised.

Remember that often the au pair is not more than a child and might be away from home for the first time. Mine is nineteen and I feel that I have to be responsible for her too. I don't mind this, but if you do, maybe you should go for someone older.'

(*Pollybloodyanna*)

Moving on

As we have said above, the bad eggs usually out themselves pretty quickly. If she is unkind/inappropriate with your child in the early days when you are around to witness it, it is not going to get any better. If she is shouty, she is probably going to stay shouty. There is a distinction to be made between someone who is basically fine and who just needs a bit of direction and someone who is fundamentally lazy/unkind/mad or whatever. Most people really can tell quite quickly which kind they have.

'Usually in anyone's first week at work they at least make a little extra effort. I had a nightmare nanny too once for a week and I really did want to kill her. My daughter at eighteen months was calling her name from the bottom of the stairs, saying, "hi" and was completely ignored. One very minor example of her behaviour.'

(*Whoosh*)

It is better to act quickly, with all the attendant disruption and expense, than to carry on with a scary childcarer.

Children coping with a change

Parents tend to angst more than children when there is a change of childcarer – even a long-term and beloved one. Explain to the children why the change is happening, if at all possible. As long as they are happy with the new carer, they probably won't pine. Many children enjoy contact with an old carer by ways of emails or letters or visits. And as with all relationships, one happy experience tends to set you and the children up to enjoy the next one:

'If you can persuade your current nanny to write a briefing note for your new nanny, that can be extremely helpful. Our last nanny wrote a thirty-page A–Z about us, the children and the job. Its detail betrayed such a depth of love for and intimacy with the girls that I sobbed whilst reading it on the 7.18 a.m. to Waterloo.'

(*Issymum*)

Do not covet thy neighbour's grandparents

(AKA GRANDPARENTS ARE NOT OBLIGED TO BABYSIT/PROVIDE CHILDCARE)

Like all types of envy, grandparent envy is corrosive and unproductive (we are speaking here of the grandparents of your children, not your own grandparents). It is very easy to look at your friend's mother-in-law who provides regular childcare, stimulating conversation and delicious home-made bread and feel disconsolate about driving your children 200 miles in their finest clothes to be paraded before the offensive fossils who happen to have brought forth your husband from their unthinkable loins.

But, really, you must make the best of the grandparental relationships which you have, both for your own sanity and for the sake of the relationships between your children and their grandparents. And it helps not to have any particular expectations about what grandparents should be like or do.

In particular, grandparents are not obliged to provide regular childcare for grandchildren. Some do, sometimes many days a week, sometimes a day or afternoon and generally speaking those who benefit from these arrangements, be they parents or children, are very fortunate. But there are many many cogent reasons why grandparents might not offer to do any regular childcare:
- They are too old and clapped out.
- They are busy with their own work, hobbies, other grandchildren or dependants:

'My work is not more important than her work, or her life.'

(*pukkapatch*)

'To me, my parents' chance of finally doing things they have dreamt of before they get too frail is as precious as my own career; I would not dream of asking them to sacrifice their dream to mine. After all, I have more years left to fulfil mine. And I can't forget that they were always ready to sacrifice their dreams to my needs when I was little – I want them to have them now before it is too late.'

(cory)

- They don't want to look after babies or small children in any kind of intensive way.
- That's not the kind of relationship they want with their grandchildren. A regular carer is a very different person from a doler out of sweets/slightly-age-inappropriate DVDs:

'Grandchildren are there to be enjoyed. Once it becomes a case of providing regular childcare so a parent can work, I think the relationship changes, even if just in a subtle way. It can be a lovely relationship, but it shouldn't be about feeling an obligation to provide regular care.'

(inthegutter)

- They just don't want to.

'I think it's a shock that people don't vocalise.
   Grandparents don't automatically like your children – just by virtue of you having them."

(custardo)

'When I think of my own mother, who had no microwave, no electric washing machine or tumble dryer, no car, no ready meals, no weekly cleaner. It was hard, hard work. She does now help out with my lot, but I would never expect her to commit to doing a regular childcare JOB. She's worked hard all her life. Now she's better off and has a nice life. Good for her! She's my mother, not my employee or servant.'

(Ozymandius)

Remember also, that it is easy to get all hoity-toity about the fact that you are quite sure that you will in the future provide any childcare necessary for your delightful future grandchildren. YOU MAY NOT FEEL LIKE IT.

The positive side of not having grandparents who provide regular child-care is that you don't get into the wearing intergenerational wrangles about sugar and television and other trivia (and a lot of it truly is trivia, you just can't see it at the time). And so actually all of the relationships can be more relaxed. And some grandparents who are not all that mad for babies and toddlers may turn out to be stimulating company for older children or a great support for your children as teenagers.

Some grandparents don't want to perform or feel capable of even some ad hoc babysitting. Again that's fair enough. Try to make sure that you are not frightening them off by wincing every time they hold the baby or offer the toddler a Mars bar. Rather than resenting them, see whether opening channels of communication might help. Probably the worst that can happen is that they give you the knockback, but at least you don't go to your grave thinking you missed out on some great babysitting opportunities.

'Why not ask them if they'll babysit? Out loud, I mean, rather than by text. Are they nervous perhaps? I know my MIL was scared of my daughter when she was smaller. Unless you ask, you won't know . . .'

(*beckybrastraps*)

'Have you ever sat down and had a long chat with your parents? I ask this, as it took a row to clear the air between PIL and us. They spent lots of money on our daughter but that wasn't what I wanted. I wanted them to call and see how she was. Play with her in my house. I think if you tried to talk to your parents you could understand what is going on. Perhaps it is because they don't see her often they find it hard to be attached to her? Are they used to being around babies a lot? I know that my husband's gran hadn't been around children for thirty years until we had our daughter! And therefore found it very hard to know how to react!'

(*fireflyfairy2*)

Having bent over backwards to be fair to grandparents, we feel entitled to say that some people are objectively a bit crap as grandparents. Their interest in their grandchildren may be minimal or sporadic; they may show favouritism towards certain grandchildren and so forth unto the whole spectrum of family dysfunction. This stuff can be painful where it seems to recapitulate old family patterns – if you felt like your sister was your parents' favourite child, the fact that they spend more time with her children than yours can make you feel like an underloved child again. But, putting all those feelings to one side, on the whole if there are any decent interactions between grandparents and grandchildren, you should foster them.

'Some grandparents' attention may seem lacklustre but they do seem to make an effort at times and I think it is one of those times when we put our children's needs in front of our own. Unless there is good reason to suspect that the child will be treated badly then she should enjoy the experience of her grandparents wishing to be with her when it is offered.'

(*pagwatch*)

Let grandparents who babysit do it their way (within reason)

On the whole it is a great kindness for anyone to look after your children free of charge. And hopefully, it is a source of pleasure for the grandparents too. But it can also be a source of anxiety for the parents and an occasion for affront to the grandparents. It is easy to try to micromanage the situation especially if you are postnatally full of very firm ideas about how babies should be handled. But you need to gain some humility. The fact that there are grandchildren means that you and your partner survived to adulthood. The grandparental childcare skills may need some polishing; there may be areas of difference between you and them. But allowing for some fringes of real incompetence, ignorance or insanity, the bulk of grandparents can be trusted to do a bit of babysitting.

Cut grandparents who do a bit of occasional sitting some slack

Grandparents will not have read all the same parenting guff as you have. They will have brought their own children up at the height of the synthetic food boom or in its immediate aftermath (unless you and they reproduced as teenagers). Even if your children eat nothing but organic broccoli-flavoured ricecakes at home, some sugary crap abroad won't kill them or even ruin their diets. And actually some grandparental spoiling is part of the grandparent deal.

We suggest that you shut your eyes to differences in technique which are not actively dangerous. It is worth having a fight about a failure to use a car seat. Or an attempt to administer chocolate buttons to a newborn. Or the forcefeeding of foods a child is known to be allergic to.

It is not worth fighting about too much CBeebies or a toddler having a choc ice.

Of course, there are some total mads out there – mothers-in-law who sneak out of the house unannounced to take the newborn for a walk by themselves or who want to take a six-month-old for two weeks in the Algarve sans parents. Some firm handling is appropriate in these situations.

But for vaguely normal grandparents, have some sense. Don't give them five closely typed A4 pages of directions when you leave them for two hours with a sleeping baby. Give them some idea of what foods the baby or child likes and dislikes and certainly flag up allergies but don't get on your high horse about people disrespecting your rights as a parent if they go off piste a bit.

'Me, I think respect has to go both ways. YOU are not the holy Madonna because you have produced a child, and if you are getting free loving childcare, you had better stop acting like an iron-curtain dictator.'

(*aloha*)

As one Mumsnetter said in response to a lament about a grandmother feeding a toddler Weetabix:

'Whatever happened to the idea that "it takes a village to raise a child"? That there are other people who love and cherish a child? That other people have wisdom on offer? I do understand that if something definite is decreed it should perhaps be respected, but why be so untrusting of the common sense of a woman who successfully raised the man you fell in love with? We are so determined, these days, to programme everything in our children's lives, rather than letting them experience life as it crops up.'

(*Blu*)

If you are fortunate enough to have regular grandparental childcare but you are struggling to agree about matters such as nutrition (which almost always seems to be the real battleground), some grandparents are suckers for a little flattery:

'You could try thanking her and saying, "I really appreciate you helping me try to give them a healthy diet, it's SO easy to give in to temptation and give them cakes and sweets, I always struggle to get them to eat apples, do you think you could have a go for me?" I always find that a little implying that they are soooo much more experienced than me goes a long way.'

(empie)

Some grandparents would look on such efforts with a very gall eye indeed, and carry on as they were before. If you really cannot bear it, you will have to make other arrangements:

'If you don't like the childcare, employ a professional.'

(newgirl)

Remember that if someone is looking after your child for whole days at a time, she has to be allowed to use her initiative and rely on her instincts. When a child is crying, whatever you have written down in your ring-binder of rules and guidance may not work – you cannot programme the whole relationship.

'We are lucky with grandparents. My mum comes up every few weeks, and my in-laws come up every other month, and both sets take the kids out and spoil them and give us a break (and we turn a blind eye to the junk they eat and the plastic tat they feel the need to buy them and so forth).

I think grandparents do pretty much have a (moral) right to a relationship with their grandchildren and I've always wanted them to have this without me sticking my nose in all the time. Some parents I know will basically not let their kids see grandparents without them there, they will not allow the relationship to develop between them – and we are not talking about cases of suspected abuse or anything, we are talking about fear of imbibing a Fruit Shoot or being spoken to a bit grumpily.

My kids love being with their grandparents and the grandparents love the kids.'

(fillyjonk)

SCHOOL GATES

Choose the best school for your child, not the 'best school' (primary variety)

Before we had children we swore we were never going to be those people talking in cheery voices thinned with anxiety about which school their children were going to go to and the merits and demerits of every type of schooling within a 100-mile radius. We were not going to be those people and we laughed those people to scorn. In retrospect, this was not wholly unlike when we were teenagers and we were never going to be those people who worried about their mortgages and didn't think it was quite funny to abduct traffic cones. In thirty years' time we will probably be cussing out extended breastfeeders on buses.

Those of us who struggle with choice tend to struggle even more angstily with choices we make for our children. And with a sometimes paralysing sense, often fostered by other parents and their choices and their *opinions* about their choices, that an early misstep might be disastrous, that if we don't get it right from nursery school, our children may endure a lifetime of penury and disappointment.

So there is an element of getting over yourself which needs to be brought to bear, a sense that life is never going to be predictable but that mistakes are generally remediable and that a choice of school is neither the overwhelmingly important decision it can feel like nor the end of the story. That your involvement in your children's education requires a prolonged attentiveness and maybe ultimately some flexibility and the odd change of course, that it is likely to include some patches of difficulty, some wrong turnings.

It is easy to say choose the 'right' school for your child but what is that anyway? Particularly for four-year-olds, whose long-term talents and interests may still be wholly concealed behind an enthusiasm for chocolate and the Waybuloos. And how do you assess the schools available to you?

Assuming you have any realistic choices anyway. Here are some rules of thumb from those who have chosen and in some cases chosen again.

Location, location, location

If there are schools within walking distance from your home, there is much to be said for making use of them. Children who all live near to a school have an easier time visiting one another and congregating in local public places. They are more likely to be able to share childcare – whether that is in the form of a local childminder, after-school club or some mutual parental assisting. There is likely to be more of a sense of community and a local newsagent who at least tolerates them all because they buy the *Beano* there. Even big cities like London fragment into little villages clustered around schools.

Visit candidate schools, observe carefully and ask the right questions

How does the school feel? Different elements contribute to this. Some parents and their offspring prefer a smaller, homelier school. Or a larger school might feel lively and offer facilities which are important to you.

Do the children seem happy and well-behaved? Sometimes you are given a tour by some older children – what are they like?

'Gut feeling means a lot in my book. I'd say: atmosphere of building when you go in; pictures and displays on walls; children look ordered when moving around corridors (try to watch at least one "move-around" while you're there, e.g. beginning of school, breaktime, lunchtime, etc.); how children react to visitors; lack of litter; attitude of person showing you round. Also try to talk to a few pupils.'

(*Moomin*)

Some parents suggest you can test the academic credentials of the school:

'With respect to academic standards in the school, a good benchmark is to ask to look at the English/literacy books of a year three class. By that age the vast majority of the class should be able to produce a reasonable length piece of writing, with sensible spelling, legible handwriting and acceptable punctuation. Joined-up writing gets extra brownie points, but is not essential. If large numbers can't do this, then standards are likely to be low. There might be a legitimate reason for this, but it bears consideration. And watch out for the sleight of hand with which teachers will manage to pass you the exercise books of the class genius – ask to see the whole pile and have a good riffle. The standard of marking will also tell you something about the school – it should be reasonably regular (i.e. not pages of unmarked, half-completed work) and should include constructive suggestions for improvement as well as cheery little stickers saying "Brilliant!"

(*frogs*)

Some people even recommend hanging around the school gates at arrival and departure times to get a feel for the children's demeanour and behaviour. You may think this is a useful activity or you may think it is weird.

Look at the extras

In both the state and independent sectors, there will be big variations in what the school offers by way of art, music, sport, drama and other activities and what school clubs are available. Also there are variations in terms of the amount of out-of-school-hours childcare that may be provided on the premises. Some schools will have breakfast clubs and after-school clubs on site which will take a child from 8 a.m. to 6 p.m. At other schools your child will have to go from school to other premises for out-of-hours care.

'Good after-school care = priceless.'

(*Marina*)

Scrutinise the headteacher

The quality of the headteacher matters on both a macro and a micro level. An energetic head can revitalise a school:

'When we moved to our neighbourhood, our son was four months old and there was no way he would have gone to our closest school. Now four-and-a-half years later, the school has had a new head for almost three years, replaced

70 per cent of staff and is fab and our son is very happy there (reception class). In the last three years they have started an art club (classroom dedicated and refitted to art), a drama club (external link with Shakespeare's Globe and refitted theatre in school), football club (local football team come in to coach), Drench club, revamped playground (ongoing with wildlife garden) etc. There is a great social life, sense of social responsibility and the kids are learning well.'

(*Twiglett*)

But you also need to think about whether the head is someone you would feel able to talk to if your child had a problem at school or if you were concerned about a teacher. Does the head welcome involvement by parents or has she banned PTAs? A headteacher who greets children by name whilst you are there is giving some evidence of a healthy involvement with the kids. Remember when you meet teachers and management that some eccentricity amongst the school staff is probably inevitable and no bad thing; education would be dull without the odd maverick/outright loon.

Be analytical about Ofsted reports, test results and league tables

Ofsted inspections are carried out by trained and experienced inspectors but they are carried out over a limited period of time and use, necessarily, a limited evidence base. They are useful but they do not tell you everything there is to know about a school:

'Having watched Ofsted at work and seen how a school can prepare for, manipulate and "fiddle" their inspection I pay little attention to Ofsted reports unless they are negative.'

(*Twinsetandpearls*)

Some parents simply use the Ofsted reports to weed out the seriously dodgy but treat the positive endorsements with some caution.

Also, behind the rankings 'outstanding', 'good', 'satisfactory', 'inadequate' there is a wealth of detail that may be important to you, so look at the whole report, not just the scores. And there is an ongoing history. A school with historically unenthusiastic Ofsted reports may be the recipient of a dynamic new head and may turn out to be improving dramatically.

Remember the older an Ofsted report is, the more you need to view it with a critical eye; much can change over a few years, particularly if there has been a change of leadership.

SATs are the National Curriculum-based tests administered to children in the state sector in years two, six and nine and the results of which are used to rank schools. They are at best a crude tool for analysing school performance, because they do not tell you anything about how well the school has served its actual community (some members of which may, for example, start off with no or little English, or which may include a high proportion of children with educational difficulties).

'Don't be fooled by results! My eldest went to a primary which concentrated so much on the achievers that those with lesser ability or learning difficulties fell by the wayside. In five years, she was never diagnosed as having ADD requiring special attention. Educational assessments put her above average but her results suggest a very low-achieving child. Meanwhile, those children who were high achievers were pushed with extra tuition to improve the school's statistics. The result? Everyone wants to go there because it is a high-achieving school. The schools which recognise that children may be either above or below the average and adjust their teaching accordingly would get my vote! Results (from SATS) are only there to improve the school's image and not to help an individual to achieve his or her potential. Look beyond the statistics and quiz the head to see what really makes them tick! There is more to life than exam results.'

(*Chelz*)

Equally, you do not want an academically able child to feel bored and frustrated and SATs results can provide at least some evidence that bright children are able to thrive.

Be cautious about other people's opinions

By which we mean pick these opinions up and give them a good kicking, interrogate the motives and prejudices of those expressing them, scrutinise their sources. People who have not chosen to send their child to a particular school are not necessarily objective. Nor are people who have. They often feel a need to justify their own choice by exaggerating the merits of their chosen school. The opinions of people who just live in the neighbourhood and Have Views are probably not worth the time you expend on listening to them.

It can be useful to talk to parents of older children at the school – whereas everyone may love the play-based early years unit, there may be dissatisfaction further up the school.

And don't overestimate how sensible crowds of people can be; as well as the recently discovered and much lauded wisdom of crowds, there is also the historically better documented idiocy of crowds:

'It's funny to watch the way local schools come in and out of fashion. New headmaster at one of the village schools? Suddenly it's all the buzz at playgroup about getting in there. Our junior school across town went into special measures six years ago; suddenly our close-by primary was almost over-subscribed for reception intake. Many people still drive past the across-town school to bring their children to our local school. Then eighteen months ago the infant school across town (next to the junior school with former problems) got an Outstanding Ofsted; mega stampede back by local parents to get into that infants, even though it means their children feeding into the junior school with previously awful reputation. Now people who live 200m from close-by school brave morning traffic every day to drive their children to across-town infants school.'

(*Can'tSupinate*)

Demographic

Well, this is a difficult one and here you need to really examine your own prejudices and try to assemble some actual evidence. If you are concerned about your child being in a very small ethnic or cultural minority in the school you are considering, are your fears realistic? Can you talk to some parents at the school about whether there are in practice divisions along cultural lines? If the school is near what everyone is telling you is a rough housing estate, does that actually mean that the school has problems with behaviour? Your ideal school might be a melting pot of race, culture and class but in the real world you need to assess what your child's experience is likely to be in the schools actually available.

And remember, there's always home education . . .

Secondary school

DON'T WORRY IF IT LOOKS LIKE
A PRISON, THEY ALL DO

This is likely to be a harder choice than primary school (if you have an actual choice – in the state sector you may officially express a 'preference', which means you can and will get the knockback from some or all of your 'choices'). Because, whereas primary schools are mostly adorable at least in parts, secondary schools are mostly not. They are other people's teenagers revolving en masse in an institutional vastness. And they provoke whole new phyla of angst. Should you have moved to the suburbs? Will your child need body armour? Will she be able to do three modern languages? Or any? Why does the only decent school you can find have a catchment area of three centimetres past the school gates? Why does all of this make you feel older than a very old tortoise on an island in the Galapagos?

Change can be hard. But try to remember that your children do not have glass skins. Adaptation, coping with change, is part of what you are supposed to be teaching them. They will get used to a new school and make new friends. Your job is to make sure that you find the most accept-able school reasonably available to you.

What constitutes an acceptable school? This is a pretty pithy summary:

'Happy and disciplined pupils, in a school that celebrates achievement and takes care of its environment and community.'

(*SqueakyPop*)

Behaviour is hugely important because children can't learn and teachers can't teach if behaviour is very poor.

The things you thought about when applying for primary school are still relevant, but with some modifications:

Location – check out the journey

It is probably less crucial to be very near school, particularly if the secondary your child will attend draws from a fairly wide geographical area and so friends travel to visit one another anyway. But do consider whether there is a safe and sensible way for your child to get herself to and from school. Even if she needs or wants to stay late on some occasions. Will so much time be spent on transport that homework, extracurricular activities and rest will be compromised?

Ofsted/league tables – do look behind the figures

At this stage you do want to feel that the school will enable your child to achieve the best exam results she is capable of. If your child has a particular leaning, it is worth looking particularly at the results in those subject areas. Also consider the 'value added scores' – these are scores which show how well the school has done, given the level of attainment of the pupils when they arrived and various contextual factors such as gender, special educational needs, family circumstances. A score of over 1000 is an above-average score. But look behind those figures as well – a school with a decent value added score may be doing OK by a very low-achieving intake but might not be the place for your very academically able child.

Size matters a bit

When visiting schools, small can seem cosier but a large school may offer more options in terms of curriculum, extracurricular activities and resources and potential friends. Having said that, very large schools of, say, 2000 pupils can be somewhat impersonal.

'The best advice I've been give so far: don't just try to imagine your eleven-year-old child there; imagine him/her there at sixteen. Stops you choosing small and cuddly but possibly stifling school instead of larger, perhaps more scary – initially – school with scope for kids to spread their wings a bit.'

(*Porpoise*)

Go to open days and evenings

'You will need to visit several schools to get a feeling for them – start with one you are less interested in.'

(clerkKent)

Open evenings tend to be a depressing scrum during which you may find yourself mostly preoccupied by the fact that schools often look very different from what we are used to from the old times. Also when you are being herded rapidly past displays of history texts and demonstrations of teens working out the calorific value of Wotsits over Bunsen burners, it can be difficult to ask the questions you want to ask.

'An hour or so looking around with a gormless child doesn't seem much to base the decision on.'

(pyjamaqueen)

So treat the open evening as a preliminary recce. Schools will usually let you come and look around on a school day and your primary school may be happy for your child to take some time off to visit with you. See what snooping about you can manage.

Don't shy away from a thorough interrogation

Be aware that the lovely teenagers who show you round are likely to have been hand-picked for the job. And de-hoodied, if necessary, for the occasion. Do grill them as much as possible:

'If you're being shown around by a pupil, ask them what the best and worst thing about the school is.'

(KTeePee)

'Things to ask the pupil showing you round: What happens if you're late? Do you say good morning to the teacher when s/he comes in? (So does the lesson start right away or is there 10 mins of the teacher trying to calm everyone down?) What really happens if you don't give in your homework?

What happens if someone says the F word in class? (The reaction of the child can be very informative!) I like to try to find out if "everyone" gets detention from time to time or if it's very rare – gives an idea of the way the discipline is handled.'

(amicissima)

Some parents find soaking up the atmosphere and looking at the children tells them a lot. Others insist that the key to the whole thing is to look at the loos. Maddeningly, they are not specific about what it is you might find in the loos which will somehow illuminate the whole issue but perhaps it will be obvious when you get in there.

Some specific things you should look for and ask about:
- Are there displays of pupils' work?
- Do they have lots of positive things up, like reading competitions, Duke of Edinburgh stuff, evidence that the kids raise money for local charities/get involved in the local community?
- Do the sixth form act as 'buddies' or mentors for the younger kids?
- Do the teachers talk to your kids or just to you when you visit?
- How many staff left at the end of the previous year?
- How is the pastoral care organised, do children usually have a form tutor or head of year for the five years of school prior to A level?
- How much feedback is given to parents in their child's first term in year seven? Do they contact you to let you know how things are going, for example?
- How many parent-teacher meetings are there per year?
- Do they have a review evening?
- How much progress do they expect a child to make over the Key Stage 3 period?
- Does the school have a virtual learning environment, i.e. does the school website allow the children to access lesson plans, homework etc. on the computer from home? This is a boon for children who miss lessons and forget homework.
- How much responsibility are children given in relation to running the school?
- What do pupil/teacher interactions look like?
- Try to observe pupils between classes and see what their behaviour is like. Does bad behaviour get challenged effectively by teachers?

- Do the pupils at the top of the school look like human beings you would want your children to resemble?
- Can pupils study the options they want, within reason?
- And, perhaps most importantly, does it seems a good fit for your child?:

'A school could be utterly fantastic for a sporty child, with loads of teams and great facilities, but if your child is totally *unsporty*, would it be the best place for them? Or music, or drama or whatever.'

(*Blandmum*)

Don't fret if there's no sixth form

Many secondary schools have no sixth form. This can be a frightening prospect – another change, another choice. Most people agree there are advantages and disadvantages and that the absence of a sixth form is not a disaster:

'I do think schools benefit from having a sixth form attached as they provide academic role models and tend to recruit highly qualified subject specialists.'

(*IonlyreadtheDailyMailincafes*)

'While broadly speaking I agree that a school with a sixth form is more likely to attract specialist teachers, on the other hand you could argue that an 11–16 school will give 100 per cent focus to GCSE, because there is no A level to take their eye off the ball. If it's a good school, with good results, then your child has every chance of getting a strong set of GCSE results. She may have her own opinions about where she wants to go next anyway. In my experience many young people welcome a change at that point anyway. Some are more suited to college, and others to a traditional school-based sixth form.'

(*violethill*)

'I loved sixth form college. It was a great experience – very different to how school had been, and a real stepping stone between school and university. We were treated as adults and were happy that there were no little kids getting in the way. We could wear our own clothes and called teachers by their first names, etc. Another great thing about it was that it gave us all a chance for a new start, to shake off any negative associations we'd had at school. I was seen as a bit of a geek at school, but somehow miraculously became one of the cool crowd at sixth form. I did a fair bit of "coasting and partying", but also got very good A level results.'

(*BotBot*)

In the end it's your decision, not theirs

Ultimately the choice of secondary school should be your decision but it's a decision it's wise to make only after hearing and judiciously considering representations from your child. Remember, though, many of his reasons may seem or actually be frivolous:

'My ten-year-old boy was easily swayed by the fact they were cooking (and letting the visitors taste) pizza at the one school . . . perhaps not the *most* important factor in our thinking.'

(*cat64*)

You can usefully involve your child in research from about the start of year five – thinking about what different schools there are and what they offer, looking at websites etc. A thoughtful child is likely to make some perceptive observations about schools but may not be able to assess how important different factors are, particularly how important it is (or is not) to go to the same school as your primary school friends. Ideally you will both agree on a school, but if you cannot, you get the casting vote:

'I definitely didn't let my children decide which school they should go to. They both go to a selective grammar school and the first one particularly didn't want to go there. We had a lot of discussion about what was "best" for her, but she really wasn't having any of it and wanted to go with her friends to the local comprehensive . . . It wasn't easy when she first started at secondary because she wasn't keen on going and we had tears, etc. However, I am glad that I stuck to my guns and got her into the grammar school – it was the best thing for her and she really is thriving there. I don't know what I would have said if she hadn't been happy, but I think children are quite resilient and change at age eleven isn't all bad.'

(*figroll*)

'I looked around all the schools that *I* liked in year five (without my DC). I narrowed it down to three schools that I was happy for them to go to and took them with me in year six when I went to look again. Son I preferred my first choice (selective boys, lots of sport). Daughter I preferred my second choice (liberal but top comprehensive). They both went to my first choice. I can see further into the future than they can and I knew which schools suited *them* better than they did. Both are doing incredibly well and are completely happy. They are still at the age when I need to look out for them.'

(*MarsLady*)

If a child is unhappy about your choice, talk to her about how she can maintain old friendships if she wishes to, whilst having the opportunity to make lots of new ones:

'I wouldn't actually base my decision on where my child's friends might go. In my experience (and two of my children have started secondary school in the last two years), many of these ties loosen very quickly. I'll admit it is nice for the children to have some friendly faces around in the initial days, but really they do make new friends very quickly."

(*portonovo*)

Some types of state schools: a small glossary

Some categories you will come across – such as community schools and foundation schools – refer to the way the school is run and who manages its budget. The important things to know as a parent are what the school does and how it selects its pupils. Here is a whistlestop tour of the main flavours:

- Comprehensive schools: accept pupils across the ability range. Admissions usually based on a limited range of factors such as distance from school and presence of a sibling in the school.
- Academies: independently managed, mixed-ability schools set up as partnerships between central and local government and sponsors from industry, faith or voluntary groups. Admissions policy likely to be similar to comprehensive schools.

- City technology colleges: found in cities. Mixed ability with an emphasis on science, technology and work-related skills. Admissions policy likely to be similar to comprehensive schools.
- Community and foundation special schools: special schools which cater for children with specific special educational needs. These may include physical disabilities or learning difficulties. Admissions criteria will obviously include presence of the relevant special need.
- Faith schools: may have a faith-based element in curriculum and selection procedures. May select on the basis of ability.
- Grammar schools: select all or most of their pupils based on academic ability. Some areas have no grammar schools at all.

Most state secondary schools now have specialisms (e.g. sports, arts, maths and IT) because they get extra funding for doing so. What this means in practice varies – it may mean that children have to do a GCSE in a relevant subject, it may mean the school has good resources in that area, but it may not. Some choose a proportion of the children based on aptitude for the specialist area.

Get organised then feed and leave: starting school

This is often an emotional, nay maudlin, time for both parent and child, although for some full-time childcaring parents it is also the dawning of an exciting era of uninterrupted free time. Now if you are down the lachrymose end of the spectrum, you could spend a lot of time singing that Abba song about time slipping through your fingers and feverishly planning another baby. Or you could, we would firmly suggest, focus on the practical and reserve any howling for a few private moments on the eve of the great day. Even for those who have been at full-time nursery school, there is something epochal about starting big school and there are some basic dos and don'ts you need to know.

Before they start

What to buy

Clothingwise, obviously much will depend on whether there is a uniform or not. Re outer and underwear, many of us will continue to be caught out yearly by every predictable change in the weather. But if you want to not be that disorganised person trying to buy gloves at the newsagent on the way into school or putting socks on your child's hands, here is your basic all-weather wardrobe:

- A sun hat for any hot days which persist into September.
- A manageable warm coat, i.e. one he can do up himself, ideally.
- Ditto a waterproof coat.
- Warm hat, spare warm hat.
- Warm gloves and reserve warm gloves.
- Wellies to walk to school on wet days.

- Durable and comfortable shoes that he can put on himself – think about Velcro here.
- Trainers may well be needed for PE.
- Many more identical socks than seems rational.

If there is a uniform, you will want many more shirts than skirts, pinnies, trousers, jumpers or sweatshirts.

If you are doing packed lunch, you need an appropriate lunchbox, i.e. one the child likes. They all tend to fall apart/stink by the end of the school year.

If you are an organisational genius/OCD sufferer, here are some further thoughts:

'This year and every year you will need a red T-shirt (Comic Relief Day), a Christmas play costume, a Book Week costume, you will need to send in food for Harvest Festival so keep something half decent in the back of the cupboard in a few weeks' time so at midnight when you remember you have to send something in you will have it!!, you will need to send in bottles for bottle tombola at Christmas and Summer Fair, goodies for Christmas Hamper Raffle, goodies for Summer Raffle, get a CRB (police) check done if you want to go on school trips and these can take a couple of months to come back so get a form from the office now. I think that's it for now!!'

(*Kbear*)

You need to get organised

Put nametags or write names using one of those special pens in every piece of clothing which might conceivably come off at school. Somewhere there is a gap in the space–time continuum into which year on year millions of garments are gracefully dancing from the hands of schoolchildren onwards to some great black hole of smelly fleeces and spanking new winter coats and mouldering swimming kit. Or something like that. It is like the movement of the tides in its inexorability but you can make some tiny efforts to stem the flow. And writing names in clothes is a start.

'I am the epitome of "Can't be arsed to do this again" laziness. I ironed our surname in all of my son's reception uniform and have been biroing them in ever since.'

(*SoupDragon*)

Do some training in getting into and out of clothes for children who are not skilled in this area. Coats and shoes are obvious ones. But they may also need to get into and out of PE kit. If the school uniform includes shirts with buttons, consider this:

'If it's a cheap shirt, then I know lots of people make a little snick into the top few button holes (not big enough so that the button is constantly undone, but easier for little hands). Sew a little stitch into the end of the snick so it doesn't get bigger and he should be OK (and then show him how he only has to undo the top few to get it off).'

(*foxinsocks*)

Here are a few more organisational points to think about. Firstly, toileting: now is the time to master the art of wiping one's own bottom if one has been laggardly in that department heretofore. And you may also need to ensure that your child knows to ask to go to the loo.

'My son can't wipe his bum either – but has informed me won't be using the toilet at school!'

(*Merlin*)

'From experience, be prepared for skiddy underpants. My son eventually sorted his body clock so he pooed before school and when he got home.'

(*SoupDragon*)

Another thing to think about is bag recognition. For a child who does not recognise his own name, a schoolbag can be differentiated from all the other schoolbags with unreadable hieroglyphs on a special sticker or badge or keyring.

If packed lunches are to be eaten, the comestibles need to be accessible. Can the child open the box itself and then any packets it may contain? Can he remove the lid of the yoghurt, if yoghurt is provided, without the contents ejaculating all over his shirt? Can he insert the straw into the drink box or open the water bottle?

Some children might need help with socialising.

'The one thing that my daughter needed pointing out was how to cope with playtimes. Despite being a very sociable child used to having lots of friends on tap she hasn't quite worked out that sometimes she needed to ask someone to play with her or to ask if she could join in a game rather than to watch and wait!'

(*keyworthkid*)

And finally, do something to celebrate. But not anything that involves you clutching at the child and saying, 'My baby, my baby.'

Once they start: What to expect and what to do

You have to expect some surprises. The child who has been desperate to go to big school may not make the easy transition you expect. Remember to talk the child through what will happen in advance – so if there is a staged process, explain how long he will be staying on each day. Explain about staying for lunch.

To help yourself you could entertain the idea of instituting some kind of wall-planner or calendar for reminding you of what day is PE kit day etc. etc. It may not be your kind of thing but it can make your life much smoother.

You will find that exhaustion and taciturnity on the part of the school starter are extremely common. Here is the conversation:

'"So how was school?"
"Umfff."
"What did you do?"
"Nothing."
"Well, who did you play with?"
"Can't remember."
"So did you have a nice day?"
(Child exits, screaming. Parent falls to lamenting damaged career, tattered social life and fallen breasts.)

So: DO NOT SPEAK TO THEM
LEAVE THEM TO STEW IN OWN JUICE.'

(twinsetandpearls)

'This applies to me as well. I need to be left with coffee, chocolate and the PC for at least an hour after work until I feel nice enough to speak to anyone.'

(cornsilk)

If you are really desperate to extract information from your child for some reason, you may have to use indirection to find direction out. You could try supplying manifestly false information which goads the child into issuing a correction, e.g.:

'What did you have for lunch?'

'Can't remember.'

'So it was horseburgers and tangerine pie.'

'No! It was sausages and cake with custard!'

'Feed and leave' is often the best policy in the early weeks. Arrive to collect the child with suitable snack at the ready (i.e. held out in front of you in posture of person feeding a steak to lion), be that an egg and cress sandwich on wheatberry bread or a family-size pack of Haribo, and don't prod too much.

'Food on the way home – you will need to up the treat status of said food as the week goes on. In fact, on Friday just inject e-numbers and pour Fruit Shoots in their eyes. Tears, screaming and sleeping on sofa mandatory. All the above applies to children as well as parents.'

(FabioFlangeCat)

To minimise these symptoms, try injecting a larger, more protein-rich breakfast into your child.

You might find some bed-related issues popping up when your child starts school. A recurrence of night-time bedwetting is not uncommon. For a child who is still in night nappies, now is not the time to be working on getting dry.

Some children will sleep from approximately 4.30 p.m. until 7 a.m. the following day. A consummation devoutly to be wished for by many. Lying slightly about the time may be a way of achieving an earlier bedtime for a child who is inclined to stand on his rights despite exhaustion.

When it comes to extracurricular activities it is wise to defer consideration of any after-school clubs, lessons etc. at least until after Christmas and possibly until year one. And scale back your weekend gadding and educational entertainments. Let them sleep late on Saturday and allow for a good deal of pottering at home. In the early days, consider allowing unlimited television watching or other relaxation of choice:

'Take the TV remote to school so you can switch it on from outside the house, *then* ruffle about your handbag for your keys, while your darlings release each other's throats momentarily and stare at the TV through the window (you may have to rearrange furniture or move house to achieve this). Feed, pyjama, brush teeth and if necessary bathe the children in front of the TV.'

(*FabioFlangeCat*)

Starting school takes its toll on children in other ways too. By Halloween, the new reception starters will be so ravaged by every passing bug that they will look like the undead and can be sent trick-or-treating with perhaps just a winding sheet as a costume. This is regardless of whether you have been feeding them on organic milk and pulses gathered by virgins from the slopes of sacred mountains or simply stuffing them with Monster Munch. But buy plenty of oranges anyway.

Consider reinstating the buggy for school pickups if you don't drive to school. Ignore appalled looks from ignorant persons.

Don't forget to expect worms and nits. Treat worms and nits for the good of your child and the school community.

It's important not to believe everything your child tells you when he comes home from school:

'I'm a teaching assistant in reception class. One parent came in to complain because her daughter had told her that she wasn't given any snack even though I was giving her toast, fruit and milk every snack time! Little kids lie!!'

(*memoo*)

Finally, try befriending some highly organised parent who will have at her fingertips information such as when school trips are occurring and what you are supposed to be doing about the school fair.

Emotional stuff – don't panic, they'll get over it

What can be really devastating to parental equilibrium is the child who is not just tired and grumpy but who turns the commencement of school into a tragedy in three acts, stage littered in corpses at close and boring but laudable minor character pawing over the remains:

'My daughter had her first reception day today . . . and boy oh boy do I have *my* come-uppance from all my blithe assertions she'd be fine, more than ready, life and soul by the end of the day, etc. etc. etc. She has, I think, had some nice bits but she's also done a bit of crying – during the day as well as on her return – and she's informed me tonight through her tears that (a) the best bit was coming home (b) she wishes she didn't have to go tomorrow (c) she misses her sister.'

(motherinferior)

Also worrying is the child who says that school was fine, but they won't be going again, thank you. It may not have occurred to some children, particularly eldest or only children, that school is a twelve–fourteen-year stretch. After a day or perhaps a week, they are happy to pack it in.

There are various ways of supporting this Romantic poet style of reception starter, for example carefully couched and calibrated bribery:

'Something along the lines of "Gosh you are a big girl, and you're doing so well. I expect you'll be tired and hungry after your busy day tomorrow, so you can choose what kind of biscuit/sweets/crisps you'd like me to bring when I pick you up. So if you feel sad during the day you can remember that and it will cheer you up."'

(frogs)

Other bribes in this vein might be special TV privileges or some other treat which differentiates the school-starter from a younger sibling still cosily ensconced in the nest.

'Ask your daughter what she would like to do when you pick her up from school. My daughter wanted a picnic for all her Barbies on her first day at school. So I arranged them all on the living room floor and made tiny little sandwiches and put out baby bowls of crisps etc. This greeted her on her return from school and she loved it.'

(tamum)

Ditto flattery about how big and impressive they are to be starting school. But not flattery which denies their feelings about actually being little and sad. So lard the flattery with empathy:

'My tack would be to emphasise how normal and understandable it is that she feels like this – and that it's OK to have sad bits at school as well as happy bits (but "big up" the happy bits, Joyce Grenfell stylee). My son was very like this and I told him that I had been just the same at school (I was) and that a lot of people were feeling the same as he was, even if some of them hid it better. Explain that *everyone* feels overwhelmed by school at first – make it funny, maybe use her teacher as an example: "Even Mrs X would have been a bit sad and wobbly sometimes at school . . . and look she ended up liking it so much she never left!"'

(marthamoo)

You also need to stress that it will get easier. Remember how little sense of perspective small children have (i.e. none). Telling stories about your own school experiences (the ones with happy endings) can be really helpful.

For the more sensitive child, i.e. the child who is not simply exhausted and grumpy, 'feed and leave' (see above) is the wrong approach. You need to allow time for lots of chatting about feelings. And don't forget that finding a friend is often a turning point for a child adjusting to school. Talk to your child about how other children are likely to be feeling shy too and how he might approach another child. Feed him some lines if needs be. Once there is a potential friend on the horizon, consider having that child over for a playdate so as to grapple him or her to your child with hoops of steel.

Here are some more suggestions to make things a little easier:

'Give her something special of yours to hold in her pocket as a secret message from Mummy? (Er not the family heirloom jewellery, obviously.)'

(aloha)

'My little tip is to sit them down and tell them to close their eyes and concentrate really hard. Then bend down and put your arms gently around them and slowly – really slowly – hug them tight. Then tell them to close their eyes again and talk them through what you did, then get them to talk through what you did and finally get them to close their eyes and talk through your hug in their head.

I told them that every time they were sad, they now had one of Mummy's bestest ever hugs ready to use, right in their own head. All they had to do was close their eyes and concentrate and Mummy would be right there giving them a big hug! It does seem to work – but needs reinforcing a lot – I would go through the process every night and morning for the first week and then every night and then maybe every week!'

(*soapbox*)

If your child is really struggling, mention it to the teacher so he can keep an eye on the situation. And remember that the child who weeps and clings at drop-off is often quickly settled once you have left. Emotions run high in four-year-olds but they often pass quickly and are forgotten.

'IME a crying, clingy child NEEDS the dump and run approach (if the dumping is dumping with a staff member of course). This is week three and today we got a last-minute whimper from my daughter, whereas last week she started wailing at 8.10 a.m. and school doesn't even start till 9.10 a.m. . . . and still within two minutes of my leaving she was happily running around and playing . . . it is my presence that makes her upset.'

(*Twiglett*)

Remember that it will pass. It truly will – the child who finds it difficult to adjust is often the child who loves school ultimately.

Et enfin, do they need to be reading when they start primary school?

No.

You are not six

DON'T WORRY ABOUT OTHER PARENTS
AT THE SCHOOL GATES

There is a fairly stark divide amongst chatters on chat threads about what goes on at the school gates.

Some people are firmly of the view that, at the school attended by their children:

    a) There is a group of alpha mums who look down on others sartorially and will run you over in their 4x4s if you are scruffy and/or fat; and

    b) Other parents are gathering in cliques excluding others and gossiping about them on the basis of some of the following – scruffiness, well-groomedness, working-out-of-the-house-ness, staying-at-home-ness, youthfulness, agedness, difference-from-them-ness . . .

Other people say that they have never seen any such things. Here are some typical representatives of the two extremes:

'Keep yourself to yourself. These types hate not knowing what you are doing as they are nosey for the sake of having a good bitch about you later. If they talk to you, best to give one-word answers and no juicy details as they thrive on your downfalls or bitch about your achievements.'

(Goober)

Versus:

'I've never understood this. Threads like this make me think women are a bit mad. I think this is all in your head. Either that or there is a whole world of bitchiness which has passed me by completely.'

(morningpaper)

'I can honestly say that in about four years of taking my daughter to playgroup and school, nobody has been mean to me. Or given me dirty looks or made snide remarks.

Not

one

person.'

(*Oliveoil*)

And something in between to think about:

'Someone once told me "Don't compare your insides to everyone else's outsides". I am aware I'm on a bit of a roll with the trite homilies today, but this stands me in good stead when I feel vulnerable. For what it's worth, I think there are genuine unfriendly cliques, but I also think some of us can be paranoid (me included).'

(*Jamieandhismagictorch*)

At first we were inclined to believe that this was one of those parallel universe things that crop up from time to time (viz the Universe Where People are always Looking at You Funny and The Universe Where No One is Looking at You Funny) – with some parents trapped unwittingly in Mean Girl Universe and others ending up somewhere more convivial on the space–*High School Musical* continuum. And then we realised the truth was, as usual, much mushier than that.

So, having studied the evidence in some depth, here is our Universal Theory of What Goes on at the School Gates:

- Many people feel a bit insecure at the school gates. They are confronted by groups of adults they do not know, many of whom seem to know each other. The experience can tap into bad memories of feeling shy and/or excluded at school with an underlay of anxiety on behalf of your children and a top note of fear of sudden small talk deficit – the moment when you and another adult just stare at one another in horrified silence. Even if you are now a mega successful international brain-surgery-performing and novel-writing concert pianist and ex-supermodel, you can suddenly have a great inverted epiphany of loserishness.

- There will be groups of parents who have pre-existing friendships or acquaintanceships because of having older kids or because of other contacts in the community. Little groups huddling together are often a mixture of sociability and insecurity rather than conspiratorial cells of persons plotting to overthrow your self-esteem.
- A friendship group is not by definition an evil clique and those within the group may well be very happy to make new friends/acquaintances. Probably there are also some evil cliques as well.
- Parents who are unable to do many drop-offs and pick-ups because of the hours they work may not themselves form many social ties at the school gates. Some of them will make a big effort to do so because they want to. Others won't.

'Getting to know the other parents is also difficult if you don't do the school run but I'm afraid I've taken the slightly anti-social route of deciding it doesn't matter if I know them or not – I have difficulty keeping up with the friends I already have and am not really looking for any more. My children will make friends where they want to now – independently of my being friends with their friends' mothers.'

(*Mrs Wobble*)

- Some parents who have older children and/or busy lives are probably not looking to make any very intense new friendships. They are not big meanies and if they don't want to hang out with you it's not personal:

'There comes a point, two or three children in, where you have a group of mummy friends, your kids have their own friends, your younger children are equipped with siblings of the older children's friends, and your main aim is getting the children through primary school with your sanity intact. Making the effort to invite new little friends with complicated eating habits and over-anxious mummies does tend to get sidelined.'

(*frogs*)

- Friendships take time to develop, at the school gates as in life.
- People who look 'unfriendly' are probably not thinking about you or dissing you. They may well be away in their own heads wondering

how they are going to get through a difficult meeting, how many WeightWatchers points there are in a Mr Whippy, how they are going to cope with their aggressive four-year-old.

'Some mornings if my daughters have been fighting I would stab the Pope, god help any friendly mums in the vicinity. I have FCUK OFF WORLD writ large on my forehead.'

(*Oliveoil*)

- A group of people not making eye contact is often just a group of shy people wishing someone else would make the first move. 'Standoffish' and 'shy' are visually impossible to distinguish from one another. And it is misogynist nonsense peddled by a tabloid newspaper which shall remain nameless to suggest that women in groups are generally looking to exclude and bitch up other women.
- Being well-groomed and attractively dressed does not = being a snotty person who despises others who are not so well-presented. Being scruffy and speckled with breakfast does not = being an uninteresting drudge.
- At almost all schools there will be some parents with whom you can form at least functional acquaintanceships.
- There are no doubt some judgmental snobbish folk at some schools and the odd sociopath. That's life.

So what we say is this:

- If you don't feel like trying to make friends with other parents, that is totally fine. But don't assume you have nothing in common with them from the get-go. You are all just a bunch of people who happen to have reproduced:

'What I find completely baffling is that people think that they are the only interesting person with a child at their school! What are all the others, Stepford wives?!

At my son's school parents are high-flying career people, ex-high-flying career people, SAHMs, musicians, cleaners, a bus driver, a fire fighter, an artist, a vicar, shelf stackers in Tesco, a driving instructor, carers, a town planner . . .

and a hundred other life stories that I don't know. How can there not be inter-esting and congenial people in that lot, and why is it wrong to make friends with them and chat to them in the playground?'

(seeker)

- Forming a social network with other parents at your child's school can be useful for you and for them. It facilitates their social arrangements and may help with emergency childcare. So think about whether the effort might be worth it, even if it doesn't come easily to you.
- If you are feeling paranoid, do some DIY behavioural therapy on yourself:

'It is pretty unlikely that you have happened to join a class where every single mum is unpleasant.

So you need to be much more rational about what is happening. Most people go where they feel welcome and cling to people that make them feel included.'

(pagwatch)

- Remember that most people are just muddling along. Don't read too much into social encounters. Parents of small children often conduct radically interrupted conversations which sometimes never get back on track. It is a distracted and distracting state and social interactions suffer.
- If you want to make acquaintanceships/friendships, try just smiling and saying hello to all relevant persons in the first instance. Try chatting to someone standing on her own – sometimes this will go wrong. Sometimes it won't. Persevere.
- If you literally just want someone to pass a few words with whilst you wait, dads are often easy meat. Especially if you throw some football or current affairs into the conversation.

If you want to pick up some mates at school and it's not happening, here are some thoughts:

- If you have the time, do some hearty joining-in. Join the PTA or become a class representative or even a parent governor. You may find you are suddenly the Queen of the Playground and really it was all a bit of an error.

- If you are feeling shy, try chatting to small children. They are mostly easy to talk to (although they sometimes just race off on their scooters) but you can usually segue eventually into a conversation with their parents. Blethering to small children makes you look friendly and harmless.
- If you are trying to set up dates for your children or yourself, you may have to be a bit bold and specific. 'Would little Indigo like to come to tea some time?' is quite likely to get a fairly wiffly response. Whereas 'Would Indigo like to come for tea on x date or y date? Could I have your phone and fax numbers?' may actually result in an actual arrangement.
- 'A super-shy mum in our year had the bright idea of setting up after school at the local playground every Wednesday when the weather was good. No one is excluded, bring snacks, stay for five mins or fifty. No one's house gets trashed, no limit on group size, doesn't matter whether you can't make it at the last minute. Works really well and might suit those who don't want to find new "best friends" but don't want to feel totally excluded from your child's schoolfriends.''

(bobdog)

'My son is in reception and about a month ago there was a note in all the book-bags from a mum who said she felt she hadn't got to meet any other mums yet and did we all fancy a drink one evening. Almost everyone went and we moved along a seat each course so got to chat with mums we didn't know very well. It was a really good evening.'

(myredcardigan)

And from the surrealist school of social manipulation:

'If you think other parents are talking about you, start wearing outlandish wigs or dressing every day in a different costume to pick up your son.

It'll give you both a giggle and them something to really talk about. It could be though that you are just feeling a little sensitive at the moment but nothing that wouldn't be cured by picking your son up dressed as a hotdog.'

(Ronaldinhio)

Most of all, don't get any of this out of proportion. Maybe you won't pick up any big mates at your kids' school. It's not a big deal. By secondary school, your presence anywhere in the catchment area of the school will be verboten.

But if in the meantime you can approach the whole thing in a buoyant but pragmatic way with a modicum of hopefulness, you might get some nice surprises:

'My mother died last week, and my schoolgate-mother friends have had a whip-round to buy me some flowers, phoned me every day, offered me free childcare at the drop of a hat, squashed me to their bosoms and generally been bloody lovely. I guess they have offered me the same sort of support that co-workers would have offered me had I been in paid work. I'm extremely grateful to them and very touched.'

(policywonk)

'They don't turn into pimps and hos because of sex ed.' (custardo)

SO JUST BUY A BOOK, YOU SQUEAMISH BUGGER

'My mum used to run the Sunday school jumble sales and donations used to sit in our utility room until the sale – aged about eleven, I found a book called *The Happy Hooker* in amongst the tea cosies and *Reader's Digests*. My views on sex were mainly influenced by this book for a long time – I thought everyone fantasised about horses, put beads up their bums and did the thing with Jello.'

(*CornishKK*)

It's not that it was necessarily that damaging for some of us to get most of our ideas about sex from *Clan of the Cave Bear* and *The Happy Hooker*. Although the information to be derived from bonkbusters can be a bit specialist. And maybe if one were less strangled by one's own inherited embarrassment, a discussion about the function of tampons (making heavy use of the word 'linings') would not lead to one's seven-year-old son summing up brightly: 'So you put that in your mouth, then?'

No, some of us are woefully squeamish and apt to look at our children with a wild surmise and equivocate and hem and haw when hard questions are asked about matters sexual. And it won't do. Ideally we would all be wholesome and earthy and matter-of-fact. And our children would be wholesome and earthy and matter-of-fact and no more disgusted than is right and proper for an eight-year-old. But if we can't be as wholesome and earthy and matter-of-fact as that naturally, we can make intelligent use of literature.

Sex is natural, sex is good . . . But it still sounds
pretty gross to the under-tens

'My daughter is nine and had her first sex ed lesson last week. She was most unimpressed. She spoke to my mum and said, "I had sex at school today Grandma." My mum replied, "Oh yes – was it your first time?" Daughter answered in a disgusted voice, "Yes and it will be my last. I don't know why on earth anyone would want to do that." My mum was most amused.'

(*dustystar*)

'When I got pregnant with my second daughter, my first daughter was eight. She was horrified when we told her, and said, "At school if your mum is having a baby, everyone teases you!" "???????" says I. "Yes," she says, "they go: 'Aaah! Your mum and dad have sexed!'"'

(*frogs*)

There will of course be discussions of sex and relationships at appropriate points in the school curriculum but you may get questions or they may hear crap in the playground well before sex ed occurs. And many parents would rather do at least part of the job themselves. You may also think it's better for them not to be walking around with the usual misinformation. That misinformation can persist for years and only surface later or it may cause immediate, if comic, anxiety:

'They need the information, otherwise all sorts of misunderstandings can arise. My son knew that a sperm and an egg were required to make a baby. Out of nowhere he asked me when he would start making sperm. He was very anxious. Turned out he thought sperm would just burst forth from his penis and impregnate any passing females. So yes, he learned the mechanics of it all at five . . .'

(*TheFallenMadonna*)

'When I was a child we were never told about erections – I could NOT for the life of me work out how a boy's penis could be dangled into my vagina. Did I have to do a headstand? Did he?'

(*fluffles*)

Some children are curious and ask lots of questions very young and it is sensible to give them accurate answers couched in language they can understand. If they think you are holding back on information, they may sense the subject is taboo and may not feel comfortable to come to you with serious questions later. And curious under-fives often find basic reproductive facts, once they have elicited them, no more interesting than any other new piece of information about the world, like how diggers work or how earthworms breathe.

Other children don't ask or say much but you can get a sense of when their peers are beginning to discuss the subject and this may be the time to provide a little information from a reputable source (you). And worries that they will immediately try to apply the knowledge are usually ill-founded. The fact that eight/nine/ten-year-olds have accurate information about some reproductive mechanics isn't likely of itself to make them think, 'Oh, I must go and try that.' It is much more likely they will think, 'How weird, why would anyone do that?'

And you really don't want them thinking sex is something shameful they can't talk to you about at some future stage when they might actually be thinking about doing it and in need of some decent information on sexual health and contraception and the like. Ideally the channels of communication will have been open from an early stage. But if they aren't, and if you are a bit constipated about it all, do a little research yourself.

There are many books available for different ages and stages on the subject of puberty/sex/relationships. Read them yourself and get over the twee cartoon penises and the talk of special cuddles. Find a book you can bear and chat to your child about the book as a starting point, then hand it over (assuming the child is literate) and indicate your availability for the answering of questions. Try to do a bit of preparation so you are ready to give age-appropriate answers to the questions they ask. A five-year-old who asks how the baby gets into the mummy's tummy does not need chapter and verse on techniques for stimulating female arousal.

'Tell as much of the truth as he seems interested in. Go into whatever detail he seems to want or need to know. I recently had to disabuse my son of the notion that men make babies by peeing into women. I'd rather he knew the truth than thought that.'

(cory)

With children approaching puberty, you really do need to be frank and unembarrassed about practical stuff they need to know. You want your daughter to be able to talk to you about the practicalities of towels and tampons and coping with period pains. And if all your children, male or female, have been au fait with the notion of periods from a reasonably early age, it will be less of a shock for the girls when it happens to them. And maybe the boys won't go screaming round the room when they encounter a menstruating girlfriend. And both sexes need to know what to do about spots and body odour and the other evils of adolescence.

School sex education

'They are not going to be taught about blow jobs, anal sex and the Kama Sutra in year six, contrary to what some parents seem to think.'

(*sidge*)

Some parents very understandably worry about school sex education and whether it will be inappropriate for their own children. If you are concerned, have a talk with your child's teacher and a look at the resources that are going to be used.

'I'm a school nurse and we support the Sex and Relationships Education programme delivered by teachers in many schools. Please credit the teachers with some intelligence – the material to be delivered to five- and six-year-olds will not be the same as the material they deliver to ten- and eleven-year-olds. Generally the content for years five and six is based around puberty, how babies are made, how they are born and a small amount about how babies are prevented. They are taught about feelings, relationships and respect. Reception SRE is based around our bodies, how they work, knowing what bits are called what (with proper names as well as names they might use) and about feeling safe and happy. I have done group work with year fives who think they wee out of their vaginas, as they have never been told otherwise.'

(*sidge*)

Ideally you will then be able to answer questions and clear up misapprehensions which occur. And they will occur:

'My nine-year-old son attended the sex education lesson at school. I warned my husband that questions might arise. Sooooo . . . they are in the car on the way to mini-rugby and my son asks from the back seat: "Dad, is it really true you have to put your willy inside the girl then?" (Cue long long long pause while Daddy struggles to watch the road and find an answer . . .) "Yes," he says. Even longer long long long pause, and then a very worried little voice pipes up "So how do you ask her for it back, then?"'

(*SalVolatile*)

Why it's good to talk

'My five-year-old knows the whole lot – sex, babies, childbirth, placenta/cord, pubic hair/breasts/voice changes/male and female hormones etc. He's a very curious and analytical child who wouldn't take kindly to being fobbed off with euphemistic claptrap. He was four when he started firing questions at me about it (we were in the veg section in Sainsbury's at the time and my second son was having a tantrum). I don't think he's "lost his innocence" or "grown up too quickly" or any such twaddle. Nobody who met him would think so either, he's *completely* innocent. Perhaps that's because, although he knows the nuts and bolts of human reproduction he *doesn't* know about all the shame and stigma and general silly hysteria that surrounds these issues in the minds of so many adults.'

(*Greensleeves*)

'Told my daughters (twelve and thirteen) that I'd be palming them off on someone else for Sunday night so my husband and I can have a nice evening together.
    Younger daughter: "I hope you'll use a condom if you are having some bed action."
    Me: "Being infertile I don't need condoms, also I'm too tired for that sort of thing."
    Elder daughter: "You still need a condom to stop you getting STIs."
    Me: "Where would either Dad or me get an STI from?"
    Elder daughter: "Well, chlamydia and AIDS don't have symptoms so you might have had them for ages."
    Younger daughter: "You better get some just in case."
    Shall I write to the school and congratulate them?'

(*EccentricaGallumbits*)

Bribe and corrupt them to get them through exams

Lots of the things that helped us through exams as teenagers are frowned on in modern times – by which we mean cash payments determined by grades, knee-trembling quantities of caffeine, the use of brandy miniatures to promote sleep and cigarettes to aid concentration and punctuate the learning process. But you may well have a child who won't revise. Or a child who is so anxious he can't sleep. Or a child who is so foul-tempered you are tempted to let him go ahead with his plan to fail his GCSEs, get a job and move out . . . So here are some more wholesome ways of getting through.

Sleep

Be a sleep enforcer. Don't let them stay up all night revising. Throw some science at them about how badly their brains will work if they have had no sleep.

Make them finish revising at least a good half-hour before bedtime and do something relaxing – reading, TV, hot bath. If they are anxious, try soothing hot drinks and lavender oil in the bath. Or try some of the techniques for relieving stress. Teach them some simple relaxation techniques like visualisation and controlled breathing. A bit of yoga can help, and make sure they are adequately exercised generally.

'My son has been having panic attacks about his SATs. Was so bad I went to the GP for advice. In the end we were helped enormously by a book for kids (I think it is one of a series of mental health things for kids) called *What to Do When You Worry Too Much*. Not specifically about exams but it worked BRILLIANTLY and instantly . . . It used cognitive behavioural therapy techniques but adapted for children up to about aged twelve. Basic idea was Worry Time (fifteen mins a day to worry and no more, but you do it regularly), a Worry Box (in your head to put worries in rest of time), visualising a Worry Bully (which you learn to talk back to and "flick" off your shoulder etc.) and then either exercise or relaxation to help with symptoms. Finally "changing the channel" to find your happy place etc. (distraction, remembering a happy memory).'

(*DavidHameron*)

Helping a very worried child to get the exams into perspective will help with the immediate stress and also give her skills which will help her deal with other stresses as she gets older:

'If you have a child who is likely to get stressed, try to keep calm yourself about the whole business, and point out that while it's convenient to get a good set of qualifications first time round, the world will not stop turning if they don't, and their life will not be ruined. (It's more convincing if you start taking this tack *before* exam time, so they don't think you're just trying to make them feel better when it's all getting stressful.)'

(*AMumInScotland*)

Food

Make sure they eat – regular meals and healthy snacks and some comfort food as well. And lots of water to aid concentration.

Exercise

A decent amount of exercise every day – of a sort that tires them out physically and which provides pleasure and distraction.

Pampering

In some instances, this may feel like cuddling a bobcat, but really it is worth it and there is a perverse and growing satisfaction in being terribly nice to someone who is grumpy and foul (if they are being grumpy and foul). Reduce chores and administer appropriate treats.

Preparation

Help them to assemble everything they need the night before, especially what they are going to wear and everything they need to take:

'The most practical thing I have found is to know in advance which exam is when and make sure that you have everything they need (pens, maths instruments, calculator, colouring pencils, etc.) specifically for each exam ready the night before. And don't assume they will bring it home afterwards – lost his calculator between Maths 1 and Maths 2, so we were lucky we had a spare.'

(maryz)

Teach them revision techniques

Now maybe their teachers will do all this, but if they don't:
- Help them devise a revision schedule well in advance. Work out what needs to be done and how much time there is. Build in breaks and treats and mix up subjects to make it more interesting (so don't e.g. have a whole revision day of physics). It is very satisfying for the child to be able to tick off tasks as they are completed and having a plan will help her feel in control.
- Try to help them figure out what sort of breaks work best – fifteen minutes every hour or an hour on/an hour off or some other system tailored to their concentration span.
- Get them to discuss what they are revising with you – talking about it helps it sink in.

'Teach them some revision techniques – flash cards, making notes, drawing flow charts and diagrams. Teach them how to turn diagrams and pictures into words, and words into diagrams. Teach them how to test if their revision has worked – you test them Q&A, they speak for two minutes on a topic, write as much as you can in two minutes, reproduce a diagram.

But mostly, good revision is about using your strengths. If you are a visual learner then flash cards and mind maps will work best. Auditory learner – have a discussion. Kinaesthetic – act out, move counters ...'

(Womblesaround)

- Some other classic techniques involve active engagement with the material rather than just reading textbooks or notes. Try condensing notes:

'Assemble all the notes on one topic then condense them down to four sides of A4 by reading through the original notes and prioritising the most important arguments, evidence etc. Then you do it again from those reduced notes, to one side of A4. This version needs to be a bit more organised – organised thematically, or in order of answering a dummy essay question. This bit is important because often remembering one part of an answer/argument will lead on to another, and if they have a good idea of the core structure of what they want to say, the detail will often follow. This full A4 sheet of notes should then be reduced again into a skeleton structure and then this can be reduced again to a filecard with key words on, for last-minute revision. This condensing process gives them things to "do" for different sessions, and focuses their understanding of the topic quite well.'

(*DavidHameron*)

- Fewer more efficiently used hours are better than endless hours of vapid timewasting so devise realistic timetables.
- Revision guides are useful for some children and can help you as the parent to know what they are supposed to be learning.

Teach them exam techniques

Again, you may have to make up for deficiencies at school:
- Planning – if there are four essays to do in two hours, they need to budget time accordingly.
- They should read the question carefully before setting out to answer it.
- They should look at how many marks are allocated to each question and, again, budget time appropriately.
- Encourage children to do a little plan for essay questions. It is a few minutes well spent.
- If a child panics, he should know he can have a drink of water, put his head down for a minute and take some deep breaths. There is usually something he can write and if he can't, well, the world won't end.
- Get him to practise on old papers, maybe under timed conditions at home if he has difficulty with time budgeting issues.

- If he doesn't have to answer the questions in the order they appear on the paper, suggest that he may do better if he selects his best question to answer first.

Some hard facts for laid-back teenagers

If you have a teenager who is just plain old lazy you need to dispense the following knuckle-polishing advice. But don't even think of saying these things to a neurasthenic insomniac.

'This is gold-standard advice for teenagers. Your school may be too PC to tell you this but I'm not.

1. Revision is your job, not your parents' or your teachers'.

2. It is bloody dull and hard work. It was bloody hard work and dull for your parents and it will be for you. Suck it in and get on with it.

3. The worse you are at a subject the more effort you need to put into it. There are no short cuts. This is a fact. Live with it.

4. The more work you do, the better you will do in your exams. And potentially the easier the rest of your life will be.

Full stop, end of story.'

(*durrobvious*)

Reward the effort not the result

Well maybe in our day, people did get £x for an A and £y for a B but your children may survive the whole exam process with their self-esteem in better shape if the rewards are directed at the effort they have made rather than the results they achieve. Maybe this is how they award bankers' bonuses.

Talk to them and let them keep talking

Beyond the exams themselves, they need to know that you are there supporting them, whatever the outcome:

'When I was writing essays and taking exams (some years ago now!) and getting very stressed about it, my mum used to just let me talk about what I had learned. I'd start by saying, "I don't know anything, I'm going to fail," and she would gently ask questions about the subject I was revising, acting all interested, and I would tell her what I *did* know, until I realised that I actually knew quite a lot. It helped me to get things organised in my head and also made me feel very secure and loved at those difficult times.'

(greenbananas)

POSTSCRIPT

Just because you're a parent the world doesn't owe you a parking space

Yes, your life is harder since you had a child. You do not travel lightly. You are physically and mentally encumbered and tasks like shopping are far more onerous than they ever used to be. But it's easy to become a little bit self-pitying about your condition. And that self-pity can take some unfortunate forms – you can begin to feel entitled to special consideration and indignant when you don't receive it, as exemplified by the regular and enormous clouds of rage generated on talkboards about misuse of the parking spaces provided for the use of parents and children.

'Last summer I was sooo annoyed when a woman in a 4x4 with no kids parked in the last mother & baby space in our Tescos. I pulled up behind her, blocking her into the space and asked her politely if she knew it was a parent and child space. Her response was that she had a dog in the back and this was the only space in the car park that was in the shade! (Wtf she was doing bringing her dog to Tescos I'll never know.)

Anyway I left my car blocking her in, took my two kids into Tescos and told the customer services, who made an announcement over the tannoy informing "the driver of vehicle registration XXX XXXX that they were parent and child spaces, not woman and dog spaces and could she come and move her car"!! She came and moved it and I had the space!! Tee hee.'

(anon)

What it amounts to is this: it is convenient to be able to park nearer to a supermarket if you have babies and toddlers and it is nice to have the extra door room that parent-and-child parking spaces tend to come with so you can comfortably remove an infant car seat. When you have a toddler who seems determined to break from your grasp and throw himself under car wheels it can even feel necessary. But it is not a fundamental human right. It is a 'trivial luxury' and that is all.

So do not allow yourself even to notice the row of two-seater convertibles parked in parent-and-child parking spaces. It is just not worth the expenditure of anger and distress. Do not examine elderly people emerging from cars in parent-and-child spaces in order to ascertain whether their level of frailness justifies their desire to be right next to the supermarket whilst you drag your children in the rain from the far end of the car park. You are better than that. And no human child will dissolve in the rain. Although if you happen to have given birth to a litter of sugar mice you might want to worry.

'Do you know?? I think there must be something wrong with me . . . I have four kids, aged between three months and eight years but if I can't get a P&C space I just use another space. Yes . . . you know *all* those other spaces that fill the car park. The ones without little pictures on the floor. I use one of those. Shocking, really.'

(*Lady TophamHatt*)

And what is true about parking spaces is true more generally. Don't get aggravated because the world in general is not paying any attention to how difficult your life is with your baby/child. The only person you hurt with your outrage is yourself.

This gnashing of teeth and rending of hair about parking spaces and other amenities as often as not involves a conflict with an older person, which is why we say, in more general terms:

Help the aged

Or at least try to understand them. There are many occasions when something ghastly happens between an old person and a hassled mother of a baby, clutch of toddlers, boisterous older child. Possibly an old woman on a bus has called you a dirty hoo-er for public breastfeeding. Or several older people have grumbled openly about how you shouldn't be on the bus with your buggy, you should be *walking*. Even if nothing is said, the mouth pursing and tutting and uninhibited glaring that can go on in a café where your toddler is being only ordinarily noisy and messy can make lunch seem like slow death.

None of this is in the least bit pleasant. And it may reduce you to near-Tourettic levels of cursing and snarling as you walk in the rain with your buggy and your convulsing toddler.

Some thoughts that just might help you get through this period: for a start, remember that some very frail elderly people are just frightened by small children. They are afraid they will be bumped or knocked over. That is why they glare at them and beat them off with their sticks.

Many older people have forgotten what it is like to be struggling with pregnancy/babies/toddlers. There are also often cultural differences between generations particularly when differences of class, region or culture become involved as well. Some people speculate that perhaps strangers just did beard one another rudely all the time in the olden days (say 1960). Without time travel it is hard to confirm or deny this hypothesis.

It's worth reminding yourself that some very elderly people have themselves become disinhibited in the way that small children are, so they don't repress their reflections about you and your child and your doings. Extreme old age can be what Philip Larkin called an 'inverted childhood'. So just as you hope other people will tolerate your not-yet-civilised child, try yourself to tolerate those who may be losing their grasp on civility.

Some old people are, like a proportion of everyone else, just plain nasty. And a proportion of them are lovely, and everything in between.

'Bigots grow old. As do lentil weavers. As do you. Trite but true.'
(*SerendipitousHarlot*)

There are predictable flashpoints for intergenerational misunderstanding and misery. Buses in particular are a scene of pretty much permanent turf war between buggies and old people's trolleys. Department store cafés in the middle of the day are other such places, as is anywhere with an 'OAPs' special'. Old people and those who care for very small children have to share a space which has been vacated by the rest of the population, which is at work or school and the two camps often regard one another with mutual apprehension.

'I have often argued for Boudicca-type scythes on buggy wheels. Of course that might lead to blade proliferation when the old ladies put them on their shopping trolleys too.'

(*OrmIrian*)

Some general guidelines:

- Don't respond to sub-verbal aggression such as tutting and evil looks. It's just not worth your while to get into a confrontation you can avoid. Rise above it.
- If someone says something rude to you, a snappy rejoinder is fine, but don't stoop to insults. You are better than that. Here is an example:

    Old person to breastfeeding mum: 'That's disgusting, that is.' Breastfeeding mum: Not '*%$&* off, you old $%&*£' but 'No, it's not, it's perfectly natural and none of your business.'

- Remember: wheelchairs and old people do trump prams and parents in terms of seats and spaces on buses.
- Age is not all anyone is – don't become wary of old people on buses in general. They are all individuals. Just as mothers of rowdy toddlers are all individuals, some of whom will be considerate and careful, some of whom will not.
- Try to have some empathy, not so easy we know when you are struggling with small children and lack of sleep, but try:

'I think it's a collective terror – we're all going to be there one day so we go into denial. I think there is nothing more tragic than being old, losing many of your friends and family, seeing the world you know slipping away and then being chastised by younger people for simply being old, slow, doddery or bad-tempered. A little empathy and tolerance is needed.'

(*OrmIrian*)

A mature society should be able to cope with children being children and sometimes being noisy and running wild and crying. It should also be tolerant of older people who have become fearful or disinhibited. And you should have some regard for the fact that anyone can have a bad day.

And you know, one day when the constricting carapace of early parenthood falls away, you are going to look back at yourself huffing and puffing about parking spaces and angsting about old people being mean to you on the bus. And you are going to feel a bit of a plonker.

INDEX

MUMSNET

Created in 2000 by two mothers, Justine Roberts and Carrie Longton, Mumsnet is widely regarded as the UK's leading online parenting community. It has 2.5 million monthly visitors, and its members are loyal, active and passionate about the site. Fans of Mumsnet include India Knight, Sarah Brown, Dr Tanya Brown and Prime Minister David Cameron.